UFO

UFO investigations from 1892 to the present day

Investigations Manual

First published in November 2013

A catalogue record for this book is available from the British Library

ISBN 978 0 85733 400 8

Library of Congress control no. 2013944258

Published by Haynes Publishing,
Sparkford, Yeovil,
Somerset BA22 7JJ, UK.
Tel: 01963 442030 Fax: 01963 440001
Int. tel: +44 1963 442030 Int. fax: +44 1963 440001
E-mail: sales@haynes.co.uk
Website: www.haynes.co.uk

Haynes North America Inc.
861 Lawrence Drive, Newbury Park,
California 91320, USA

Printed in the USA by Odcombe Press LP,
1299 Bridgestone Parkway, La Vergne, TN 37086

Acknowledgements

The following people have helped greatly, either directly or indirectly, in the creation of this book: Tim Printy, Kevin Goodman, Paul Devereux, Peter Rogerson, John Rimmer, Robert Rickard, John Harney, Kevin McClure, Jenny Randles, Nick Pope, Hilary Evans, Peter Brookesmith, Andy Roberts, David Clarke, Granville Oldroyd, John Spencer, Thomas Bullard, Roger Sandell, Mark Pilkington, Nigel Wright, Malcolm Robinson, Philip Mantle, Christopher French, Martin Kottmeyer and Nigel Mortimer.

Less directly, the works of Charles Fort, John Fuller, John Keel, Jerome Clark, Charles Bowen, Gordon Creighton, Budd Hopkins, John Mack, David Jacobs, Whitley Strieber, Jacques Vallée, Isaac Koi, Kevin Randle, Timothy Good, Brett Holman and Darren Ashmore, have all been very helpful and thought-provoking.

Special thanks to Janet Bord of the Fortean Picture Library for supplying so many images that grace these pages.

001.942

Contents

Introduction   **6**

Chapter 1   The Great UFO Wave: 1892 to 1947   **10**

Chapter 2   Official UFO Investigations   **24**

Chapter 3   Waves, flaps, hot spots, polls and patterns   **42**

Chapter 4   Classifying and identifying UFOs   **60**

Chapter 5   Identifying Type I cases   **72**

Chapter 6   Physical evidence   **90**

Chapter 7   Close encounters of the third kind and retrievals   **108**

Chapter 8   Close encounters of the fourth kind: abductions   **124**

Chapter 9   Contactees and Space People   **138**

Chapter 10   The search for theories and explanations   **146**

Appendix 1   Producing a UFO investigation report   **156**

Appendix 2   UFO investigation kit essentials   **157**

Appendix 3   Skywatching   **157**

Appendix 4   Web references   **158**

Glossary   **160**

Index   **162**

Introduction

Ufology – the study of UFOs – is equally exciting, educational, exhilarating, enlightening, exasperating, exhausting and embarrassing. It is also a subject that embraces all sorts of wonderful theories and explanations, so it is essential that the data used to support these claims is as well investigated and researched as possible.

The term 'unidentified flying object', or UFO, was introduced in 1952 by the United States Air Force (USAF) in preference to the more sensational 'flying saucer' label, which did not encompass the wide spectrum of things seen in the sky. When the USAF-funded Condon Committee started investigating UFO reports in the late 1960s, it noted that: 'An unidentified flying object (UFO, pronounced OOFO) is defined as the stimulus for a report made by one or more individuals of something seen in the sky (or an object thought to be capable of flying but seen when landed on the earth) which the observer could not identify as having an ordinary natural origin.'

However, even the term UFO does not meet with the approval of ufology purists. For a start, what is initially unidentified can become identified after a few moments of observation, or in the light of more exhaustive research and investigation. This means that the term UFO is only a temporary label for most sightings before they become categorised as identified flying objects (IFOs).

Another bone of contention is the use of the word 'object', as this implies that a sighting is generated by a solid 'nuts and bolts' vehicle, or at least something physically tangible that creates the stimulus for the sighting.

What is ufology?

Ufology is the study of UFOs, and ufologists are the people who investigate UFO reports and anything related to them. It encompasses a very wide range of subjects – everything from astronomy, hypnosis, physics, history, literature and genetics, to theology, sociology, parapsychology, meteorology, geology, archaeology, astrobiology and psychology. Indeed, virtually any 'ology' can be useful in the analysis and study of UFO reports and theories. No single person can adequately cover all these specialities, and the role of the ufologist is often to collect all the available evidence which can then be submitted to suitable experts for more detailed examination. This is often

the case when photographic evidence, or ground traces recorded at the site of an alleged UFO landing, are collected. Hypnotic regression experts have often been employed to uncover alien abduction experiences, and experts have been used to X-ray abductees to look for evidence of alien implants inside an abductee's body.

For a thorough investigation of UFOs you really need to take a multi-disciplinary approach, and a range of experts is needed to obtain the full picture. This rarely happens, though the Condon Committee – funded by the United States Air Force – did have a team that included astronomers, psychologists, a chemist, a physicist, an electrical engineer and several consultants from other disciplines.

Amateur UFO groups, which began being formed in the 1950s, gather members with the aim of investigating reports in more detail. Their memberships include people with different levels of expertise and specialist knowledge, but are ad hoc compared to the range of experts specially selected to work on the Condon Committee. So in reality, even in the most scientifically orientated UFO groups, analysis and investigation can often be a low priority. Instead, much of a group's efforts are often exhausted in running regular meetings, organising speakers and publishing a newsletter or magazine.

The British UFO Research Association (BUFORA) has developed a few special projects using the expertise of its nationwide membership. One is its 'Vehicle Interference' project, which chronicles cases where UFOs are alleged to have caused cars and other vehicles to stop, and only restart when the UFO leaves the scene. BUFORA states that: 'We have research specialists in many overlapping fields of study from specific cases or UFO effects, spirituality, media influence, the wider paranormal and crop circles. BUFORA prides itself on investigating in a scientifically factual approach the research of the physics of the universe and how this affects time, travelling distances and other dimensions, chemistry and propulsion. Psychology and how cases can be influenced and affected by belief systems and wider agendas are explored.'

All these efforts are the tip of the iceberg, and are only as good as the time, effort, expertise and finances that individuals or groups can devote to a project. It is sobering to learn that in Britain the average murder investigation costs £1.5 million;

OPPOSITE: Like a scene from H. G. Wells' novel *The War of the Worlds* featuring the invasion of Martians, a UFO terrorised the neighbourhood of Quiney-Voisin airfield, France, with beams of light on 30 September 1954.

Mary Evans Picture Library

by contrast, amateur UFO investigators have nowhere near this budget to study the *entire range* of UFO phenomena, let alone to spend this amount on one investigation. Even if they did have such resources, you only have to look at the claims, counter-claims and evidence that are used and variously interpreted to acquit or convict a murder suspect. Like UFO cases, many criminal cases are never adequately solved, and fact, fiction, rumour and myth circulate and increasingly confuse matters as time passes (for example, the infamous Jack the Ripper serial murders in Victorian London, and – in terms of ufology – the Roswell 'crash' case, which has taken on a life of its own since 1947).

In this Internet era most UFO organisations have stopped publishing their own magazines and now run websites. Fortunately, however, many back issues of old, obscure and hard to find UFO publications have been made available on such sites or on dedicated archive sites. Local and national groups still exist despite the Internet, and a few conferences are held annually, or on a one-off basis, to provide an opportunity to discuss the latest issues surrounding the subject. In the virtual world you can keep in touch with the latest ufological activities through Facebook, Twitter and similar social media groups.

Considering the vast amount of UFO information available, an amateur ufologist can either be a generalist who tries to collect all the pieces of the UFO jigsaw in order to achieve an all-embracing view of the subject, or, alternatively, a specialist who concentrates on just one or two particular areas. At its simplest, you can collect and investigate cases in your local area, or you can concentrate on specific types of cases, like close encounters, UFO photographs, car stoppages or abductions.

Within the loosely scientific realms of ufology there are two major types of ufologist: the field investigators who go out and interview witnesses and visit sighting locations, and the armchair ufologists who analyse UFO data and comment on cases. Armchair ufologists are generally frowned upon, and tend to be regarded as aloof and more sceptical than investigators who have taken the trouble to get out amongst the UFO spotters. However, the same person can, of course, take on both roles, and both approaches are equally valuable.

Another type of ufologist is the 'virtual ufologist' or 'digital ufologist'. These are much like armchair ufologists, except that they rely on the Internet for all the information they use to study the subject.

US ufologist Jerome Clark terms ufologists who are overtly sceptical 'pelicanists'. This tag derives from the famous 1947 Kenneth Arnold sighting being explained as having been caused by

a flock of pelicans, much to the disgust of those who regard the Arnold UFO case as being both significant and extraordinary.

Outside of the realms of ufology are numerous groups and cults that believe UFOs are operated by god-like or supernatural beings that take an interest in protecting humanity. Members of such UFO religions are generally known as cultists.

As might be expected with a controversial subject like ufology, there are many divisions between groups and individuals. Disputes mainly arise over the validity of different cases and the importance of one theory over others. There is a spectrum that runs from believers to outright sceptical debunkers. There are also groups that are more interested in crop circles, who are known as cereologists. Other groups are more interested in Ancient Astronaut theories, and look to such structures as Stonehenge and the Pyramids to obtain evidence that aliens visited us in the past and guided our early history and religions.

The past few years have seen a significant worldwide rise in the exopolitics movement, which accepts that UFOs exist and that human governments are in secret league with extraterrestrial civilisations. The movement's mission is to campaign for full disclosure of the details of such contacts, and the release of alleged alien technologies that could revolutionise our lives. Exopolitics encompasses ufology, SETI (the search for extra-terrestrial intelligence), psychology, ecology, anthropology and politics, and the term came into common use after the publication of Alfred Webre's e-book *Towards a Decade of Contact* in 2000.

Exopolitics obtains evidence of this suspected global conspiracy from UFO sighting reports, the testimony of whistleblowers who allege they have been involved in government cover-ups, documents gained from Freedom of Information Act (FOIA) requests, Ancient Astronaut evidence, reports of UFO crash cases, remote viewing and channelling. Overall, its supporters conclude that we are not alone in the Universe, and we never have been.

We all have our own prejudices and expectations regarding UFOs, but we can all work together to investigate UFO sightings and conduct research to the highest levels possible. This book provides the information that you will need to have a full understanding of the UFO phenomenon, and it will hopefully inspire at least some readers to carry out their own UFO investigations and research. For seasoned ufologists it provides a much-needed overview of the subject by utilising a variety of historical and theoretical perspectives.

Nigel Watson
July 2013

OPPOSITE: UFOs come in all shapes and sizes. When driving to Barmedman, New South Wales, Australia, Mrs Shirley Ryall and her brother, Bevan Adam, saw this UFO that even they admitted looked like it had escaped from a science fiction film or Jules Verne novel.

Mary Evans Picture Library

1

The great UFO waves: 1892 to 1947

Mysterious lights and objects have haunted our skies since the dawn of time. They were seen as the manifestations of gods, angels, devils, spirits of the dead, fairies, serpents, aerial armies and dragons. These extraordinary signs and wonders often indicated the coming of war, disaster, death and destruction, or they might herald changes for the greater good.

Since the 19th century, people began seeing what they thought were manned aerial vehicles flying in the sky. These phantom balloon, airship and aircraft sightings marked the transition from fears and superstitions about gods and spirits in the sky to today's technological 'nuts and bolts' UFOs.

The foundation of historical UFO research was created by Charles Hoy Fort (1874–1932), who spent much of his lifetime trawling through old newspaper archives and scientific publications for reports of out-of-the-ordinary events that challenged our orderly perception of the world. In his book *New Lands* (1923), he mused that 'between the jokers and the astronomers, I see small chance for our data. The chance is in the future. If, in April 1897 [during the US Airship Wave – see below], extra-mundane voyagers did visit this earth, likely enough they will visit again...'

Raymond Alfred Palmer (1910–77) was just one of the people inspired by Fort to search out more mysteries, and as the editor of *Amazing Stories* science fiction magazine he actively promoted the

idea that aliens are visiting our planet. Almost as a primer for the coming of flying saucers, Palmer wrote in the July 1946 edition of *Amazing Stories*: 'If you don't think space ships visit the earth regularly ... then the files of Charles Fort ... are something you should see. And if you think responsible parties in world governments are ignorant of the fact of space ships visiting earth, you just don't think the way we do.'

Besides seeding the idea of government conspiracy, his June 1947 edition of *Amazing Stories* carried UFO reports culled from the works of Fort and an article about mystery aircraft seen during the 1930s and 1940s. Amazingly, in the same month Palmer's dreams came true, when on 24 June 1947 Kenneth Arnold saw nine craft flying over Mount Rainier, Washington. They were coined 'flying saucers', and that nifty label opened the floodgates to a subject that still intrigues and puzzles us today.

Fort noted that airships and mystery aircraft are seen in what are called 'waves'. Suddenly, after one or two reports of a UFO-type sighting in the newspapers more people would report seeing them until you could get hundreds or thousands viewing them on a nightly basis. A wave might stay in one specific region or spread throughout a nation and beyond. Using Fort's books as a guide, ufologists rediscovered these waves of ancient UFO reports from dusty old newspaper archives and libraries. At first these reports were taken at face value as visitations of extraterrestrial spacecraft, but by the 1970s it had become clear that these reports were intimately connected with their wider social, media and political contexts.

ABOVE: Did a nuclear-powered spaceship crash over Tunguska in 1908?
Dezsö Sternoczky/SUFOI/ Fortean Picture Library

LEFT: Charles Fort, pioneer of 'damned' theories and facts.
Fortean Picture Library

1892
Russian Poland

This was probably the first large-scale historical UFO wave. Border tensions between Germany and Russia were escalating when hovering lights were seen over Sosnowice, Dombrova and Stremeszice on a nightly basis in March 1892. Not surprisingly, the German military was accused of sending steerable balloons on spying missions to the area. On at least two occasions these balloons were shot at when they were seen near military establishments. Like all the later phantom airship sightings, these balloons projected powerful searchlight beams on to the ground in the hours of darkness. Yet, at that time, searchlight equipment was extremely heavy and difficult for aircraft to carry, and night flying was extremely dangerous.

At least 100 similar sightings were made in Belarus, Finland, Bessarabia (Moldova), Warsaw and Russia during March and April.

BELOW: Newspaper illustration of 'The Great California Airship' seen in November 1896.
Fortean Picture Library

1896–97
USA

The idea of ships in the sky operated by technologically advanced foreigners or secretive home-grown inventors dominated the phantom airship scare that swept the USA from November 1896 to May 1897. The scare began shortly after a telegram from a New York inventor was widely reported in the press. The inventor claimed he had built an 'aerial torpedo boat', and that he was preparing to take a journey to California in it with a group of friends.

On 17 November 1896, at 6:00pm, hundreds of people on the sidewalks of Sacramento, California, saw an 'electric arc lamp propelled by some mysterious force' rising and falling in the sky as it sailed from the east to the southwest. Some witnesses said the huge object had an aluminium body and wings. Others heard voices and laughter

coming from it. This set the tone for further sightings
in the region of San Francisco and northern California,
and indicated that the New York inventor's boastful
story was true.

The vast majority of the sightings were of lights or
objects in the sky, but many people declared that they
met with the landed airship and spoke to its crew.
Judge Lawrence A. Byrne was surveying land on
McKinney bayou when he came across a landed
airship. It was manned by three men who spoke in
a foreign language and looked like 'Japs'. Seeing
his astonishment, they beckoned him to the craft
and showed him around. Apparently, it was built
of aluminium and they pumped gas into a tank to
raise it, and pumped it out to lower it.

Another encounter concerned W.H. Hopkins, who
described seeing a 'vessel' as he was walking through
hills east of Springfield, Missouri, 'about 6m [20ft] long
and 2.4m [8ft] in diameter. The craft was resting on
four legs and it had one vertical propeller at the stern
and horizontal propellers at the bow and stern, which
were all about 1.8m [6ft] in diameter'.

Next to the vessel, he saw a beautiful woman
plucking flowers and 'a man of noble proportions and
majestic countenance'. Both of them were naked.
Hopkins tried communicating with them through hand
gestures to ask where they came from. In response,
they pointed upwards and seemed to say the word
'Mars'. Inside the craft, he was shown revolving metal
balls that powered its propellers and lights. When
these balls starting revolving rapidly 'the vessel rose
as lightly as a bird and shot away like an arrow'.

At the end of March 1897, an airship crew even
tried to catch someone with their anchor. A farmer
called Robert Hibbard, who lived near Sioux City,

Milestones of flight

The Montgolfier brothers were the first to launch hot air
balloons capable of carrying people. On 21 November 1783
they sent two passengers aloft over the French countryside.
They travelled an impressive distance of 8km (5 miles).

Engine-powered, steerable balloons known as dirigibles or
airships were developed in the 19th century. Henri Giffard made
the first flight of a steam-driven airship over a distance of 24km
(15 miles) in 1852. In 1884, the electric-powered, 52m (170ft)
long *La France* airship was flown a distance of 8km (5 miles).

In July 1900, Count Ferdinand von Zeppelin began flying his
first huge Zeppelin airship from his base at Lake Constance
(Bodensee), Friedrichshafen (Manzell). His series of Zeppelin
craft were primarily intended for military purposes and
indicated that Germany was capable of attacking virtually
any target in Europe.

Lighter-than-air ships looked impressive but they were
fragile, hard to handle and vulnerable to strong winds. Heavier-
than-air craft, which have a fixed wing and an engine to propel
them through the air, took longer to perfect but proved to be the
best long-term means of navigating the skies.

The Wright brothers built the first heavier-than-air craft,
which successfully flew for 59 seconds on 17 December 1903.
Two years later they improved their design so much that it could
fly a distance of 39km (24 miles) before running out of fuel.

By 1906 similar aeroplanes were being produced in Europe,
and advanced to such a level that on 25 July 1909 the French
aviator Louis Blériot was able to successfully cross the English
Channel. Like the Zeppelins, aeroplanes were soon employed
for military purposes.

All these developments received worldwide publicity and
made pioneering aviators rich and famous. In this context, it is
not surprising that any light or object in the sky would be
interpreted as one of these newfangled aircraft.

LEFT: The
Montgolfier
brothers
launched their
hot air balloon,
with a sheep and
pigeons on board,
in front of the
royal family at
Versailles,
France, on 19
September 1783.
*Fortean Picture
Library*

The Air Ship As Photographed in Chicago.

—From the Chicago Times-Herald.

ABOVE: Picture of an airship built by a secret inventor represented by San Francisco attorney George D. Collins.

N. Watson

ABOVE: The airship is illustrated over Chicago in April 1897.

N. Watson

AND AFTERWARDS MR. COLLINS COULDN'T REMEMBER WHAT HE SAW.

RIGHT: A cartoon suggests that the 'Collins' airship is a pipe dream.

N. Watson

Iowa, had his clothing hooked by an airship's anchor. After being dragged along the ground for several metres he was able to grab a sapling to make his escape. The anchor flew away with a portion of his trousers as he fell to the ground. He was very lucky in the light of one Alexander Hamilton's observation of an airship containing six strange beings in the middle of April. He claimed it winched up and took away one of his three-year-old heifers. Ufologists were delighted to discover this gem, but subsequent research proves it was a hoax.

An equally suspect airship-with-an anchor story turns up in the *Daily Post* (Houston, Texas) of 28 April 1897:

'Merkel, Texas, April 26 – Some parties returning from church last night noticed a heavy object dragging along with a rope attached. They followed it until in crossing the railroad it caught on a rail. On looking up they saw what they supposed was the airship. It was not near enough to get an idea of the dimensions. A light could be seen protruding from several windows; one bright light in front, like the headlight of a locomotive. After some ten minutes, a man was seen descending the rope; he came near enough to be plainly seen. He wore a light-blue sailor suit, was small in size. He stopped when he discovered parties at the anchor and cut the rope below him and sailed off in a northeast direction. The anchor is now on exhibition at the blacksmith shop of Elliott and Miller and is attracting the attention of hundreds of people.'

Mars was also said to have been the home planet of an alien whose craft crashed into a windmill at Aurora, Texas, on 17 April 1897. The pilot and his craft were badly mangled, leaving tons of aluminium and silver wreckage. Papers containing indecipherable hieroglyphics were found on the body of the alien. In the 1960s, when the case was reinvestigated, it was discovered that there had never been a windmill at this location. In the 1970s several eyewitnesses to the crash were located at a nursing home, where they claimed that they never saw the airship crash and that the newspapers had made up their stories. This was almost certainly a hoax, yet this has not stopped UFO researchers from searching for the Martian's grave and fragments of his spaceship.

Newspapers fanned the flames of this wave, and there was an intense interest in the work of secret inventors. Yet many inventors working separately would need to have suddenly started testing their aircraft to have caused so many sightings. In addition, the various propulsion methods allegedly used by the craft and the differing descriptions of its appearance sound improbable and unfeasible for a man-made aircraft.

As many as 100,000 individual sightings were

made of a 'Great Airship' at this time, making it the biggest phantom airship wave on record. After spreading from California to the states of Nevada, Milwaukee and Nebraska, the 1897 wave faded away in mid-December, before being rekindled in January 1897 with sightings spreading to the east coast and cities like New York and Washington DC. Due to the work of pranksters and hoaxers and plain scepticism the wave finally fizzled out in May 1897.

Sociologist Robert E. Bartholomew, who has written extensively on this wave, notes that 'the sightings appear to have functioned as a reassuring symbol during a period of great uncertainty with rapid technological changes at the end of the twentieth century', and that they underlined 'man's dominance over the untamed and previously sacred skies.'

J. Allen Danelek agrees that misinterpretations and hoaxes produced many of the reports, but by considering all the technology available at that time, and studying the newspaper reports of the sightings, he makes a good case that some sightings could have been caused by a secret airship builder testing out their craft.

Whether there was a real airship or not, Americans certainly did not fear this new technology. Elsewhere in the world, however, the phantoms of the sky mainly brought fear and trepidation.

Stony Tunguska River, Siberia, Russia, 1908

A huge fiery object, flying over Russia from southeast to northwest, exploded over the Stony Tunguska River area at 7:17am local time (12:17am Greenwich Mean Time) on 30 June 1908.

The explosion was so great that it caused an atmospheric shockwave that circled the Earth twice. For the following two nights of July 1908 the night skies of Europe and Asia were unusually bright.

Local newspapers reported the incident but it wasn't until 1927 that an expedition led by Leonid Kulik, a geologist at the Mineralogical Museum of the Soviet Academy of Sciences, discovered the extent of the devastation it had wrought. The aerial explosion, which was at least 1,000 times more powerful than the atomic bomb dropped on Hiroshima in 1945, felled over 80 million trees.

Comets, asteroids, black holes, an anti-matter rock, natural gas escaping from the Earth's crust, ball lightning, the secret testing of a wireless transmitter of energy by inventor Nikola Tesla, and the crash of a nuclear-powered spaceship, are just some of the explanations that have been offered for this extraordinary event.

1908
Denmark

In June and July 1908, an object with lights and wings was seen throughout Denmark. It was thought that an aircraft launched from a British warship exercising in the North Sea was responsible for these sightings.

1909
United Kingdom

The phantom airships crossed the Atlantic and troubled Britain in 1909. The scare began in March, reached a peak in April, and dwindled away by the end of May. Sightings began along the East Coast, where fears of invasion from Germany were most acute, and then spread to most parts of Britain and as far away as Ireland. Everybody, everywhere, was a potential target for the night-flying craft, which probed the ground with its powerful searchlight.

A sighting of a powerful light associated with the sound of a high-powered engine, made in Peterborough at 5:15am on 23 March, sparked off

BELOW: Airship seen over Peterborough in the early hours of 23 March 1909. *Fortean Picture Library*

interest in what the press dubbed the 'scareship'. The witness was one Police Constable Kettle, who was regarded as a reliable person who could not have been mistaken. Perhaps in an attempt to calm public nerves, PC Kettle's sighting was later dismissed as a kite with a Chinese lantern attached to it. The noise of the alleged machine was explained as a motor running at a nearby Cooperative Bakery.

The spread of sightings throughout the country led to a special correspondent from the *Daily Express* newspaper to visit East Anglia, where he hoped to track down the base of the airship's operations. As he toured the countryside at night looking for strange lights or loud whirring noises he came across other motorists doing the same thing. Every village and town feared the night flier coming in from the North Sea.

Although the reporter saw nothing, Mr C.W. Allen gave him a very good account. He was motoring through Kelmarsh, Northamptonshire, on 5 May when, with two of his friends, he heard a loud sound like a car backfiring. He said:

'Then we heard distinctly from above our heads the "tock-tock-tock" of a swiftly-running motor engine, and we looked up. I was sitting on the front seat, next to the driver, and had a clear view of a dark shape looming up out of the night. It was an oblong airship, with lights in front and behind, flying swiftly through the air. It seemed some five or six hundred feet up, and must have been at least 100 feet long [30.4m]. The lights were not very bright, but we could distinctly see the torpedo shape and what appeared to be men on the platform below.'

At Clacton-on-Sea, Essex, on the night of 7 May, Mr Egerton S. Free saw a long, torpedo-shaped balloon displaying two bright lights. It travelled rapidly and disappeared in the direction of Frinton. The most exceptional part of his story is that on the next day he found a 0.9m (3ft) long rubber ball with a 1.5m (5ft) hollow bar running through it near his home. It had lettering 'Muller Fabrik Bremen' on its side and it was presumed to have fallen from the airship. This evidence was taken away by the Navy and a few weeks later they identified it as a 'reindeer buoy', such as were used for gunnery target practice. To add to the mystery 'foreign' strangers were seen lurking in the area, giving early signs of the presence of the mysterious Men in Black.

Another intriguing encounter occurred on the night of 18 May, which involved a Punch and Judy showman called Mr Lethbridge. He was crossing the top of Caerphilly Mountain, South Wales, when he saw two men jump into the carriage of an airship and fly away. The fur-coated men excitedly spoke a 'strange lingo' when they saw Lethbridge, and their craft burnt two bright lights as it zigzagged into the sky and went in the direction of Cardiff. When newspaper reporters visited the scene they found torn scraps of paper including a few news clippings referring to foreign spies and aerial

THE NEW PEGASUS.

AERONAUT (*clearing all the jumps in one*). "TALK ABOUT HORSEFLESH! GIVE ME ALUMINIUM AND GOLD-BEATER'S SKIN!"

THE MYSTERIOUS AIRSHIP.—The names of places where the craft is said to have been seen are printed in blacker type.

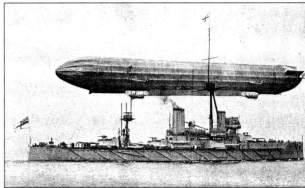

warfare, a strange valve cap, and a 16.4m (54ft) long gouge in the ground. Lethbridge was grilled by several sceptical reporters, who ended by conceding that he was 'an elderly man, of quiet demeanour, and did not strike one as given to romancing'.

1909
New Zealand

The German airship menace spread to New Zealand in July and August, when numerous mysterious lights in the sky were reported. Some boat-shaped objects were seen in daylight, and there was much speculation that the sightings were caused by airships being launched from the German cruiser *Seestern* or were produced by a home-grown inventor. In letters to the press there was even speculation that it came from Mars, but the vast majority of sightings were the product of misidentifications of stars and planets or caused by the work of hoaxers. In early August the strange lights were also seen over Australia for a couple of weeks.

1909–10
USA

The airship moved its base to the USA in December. Sightings were triggered by the claim of Wallace Elmer Tillinghast that he had flown his own invention from his base near Worcester, Massachusetts, to within a mile of the Statue of Liberty and back again. When this became public in mid-December, sightings of aerial objects soared. Thousands of people in Boston, Worcester and surrounding communities claimed to have seen this aircraft every night from 19 December to Christmas Eve. The majority saw a moving light, whilst some saw the body and wings of the craft. As usual, jokers capitalised on the craze by sending up toy balloons with lights attached to them. Venus was probably responsible for many sightings.

There were more sightings during January 1910 in Tennessee, Alabama and Arkansas. In the meantime, Tillinghast tried to get money to build an aircraft factory, and he even promised to put his machine on full public display. Neither of these things ever occurred.

TOP: Locations of airships seen over East Anglia in 1909 are marked in bold type here.
N. Watson

ABOVE: A German Zeppelin is shown nearly dwarfing a British dreadnought in *The Illustrated News*, 6 March 1909.
N. Watson

ABOVE LEFT: Airships are seen as a new replacement for horse transport in *Punch*, June 1909.
N. Watson

ABOVE: The skipper and crew of the *Othello* trawler saw a huge airship fly low over their vessel on 30 April 1913.

N. Watson

More sightings were made in the Orkney Islands and Scotland from the end of February until mid-March, though they were only reported in the local press. By that time the national media had moved on to other things.

One side effect of this wave was the hastened introduction of the Aerial Navigation Act, March 1, 1913, which prohibited unauthorised aircraft from flying over restricted areas of Britain.

1914
South Africa

A phantom aircraft was seen in many parts of South Africa just before and after the declaration of war with Germany. In Durban natives feared falling bombs, and in Pretoria on 31 August an unidentified aircraft was shot at. Most of the sightings were of lights, which were thought to be attached to an aircraft operating from German South-West Africa.

1912–13
United Kingdom

A strange buzzing sound and a dark object seen over Sheerness and the nearby Eastchurch Naval Flying School on 14 October 1912 triggered yet another airship scare. The event became public when the First Lord of the Admiralty, Winston Churchill, made a statement about it in the House of Commons on 27 November.

Churchill's objective was to make the British public fully aware of the growing danger of Germany's aerial superiority, and to gain more funding to defend the nation against such threats. His tactic was so successful that by the middle of January 1913 lights in the sky were seen every night in South Wales, and by February sightings had spread to the East Coast and Yorkshire.

Due to the greater range and durability of the German Zeppelins, and the greater acceptance of the German threat, the 1913 sightings were treated more seriously than the 1909 sightings. On 25 February it was alleged that Claude Grahame-White, a famous aviator and campaigner for protecting Britain against aerial attack, visited the Prime Minister in Downing Street. As a consequence of their conversation, Mr White left 'indefinitely' for the north, and it was assumed he was sent to investigate the airship sightings.

On 22 February Captain Lundie and his Second Officer, of the Grand Central Mail Steamer *City of Leeds*, observed an airship over Spurn Point, but they did not report it until March, when it created a lot of press publicity. Indeed, it aroused so much interest that on 3 March the Admiralty sent an official to Grimsby, who held a long interview with the two men.

1914–18
United Kingdom

Several waves of sightings were attributed to the activities of enemy aircraft during World War One, in Britain and beyond. Ironically, Grahame-White, who had been linked with the 1913 airship sightings, was the first person to carry out an air patrol in defence of London, on 5 September 1914. He was sent up to look for a Zeppelin that was reportedly in the area, but he saw no sign of it.

The day after the declaration of war, on 5 August 1914, a phantom aeroplane was heard flying near Carlisle, following the course of the River Eden. A couple of days later airships and aeroplanes became regular night-time visitors to the skies of Barrow-in-Furness, Lancashire (Cumbria). This was a sensitive area as it contained huge shipbuilding yards and iron works, and therefore was protected by the only anti-aircraft gun on the West Coast.

The wave of sightings quickly spread northwards to the Lake District, where Boy Scouts were enlisted to guard the water supplies in the area, and the Cumberland and Westmorland Yeomanry at Penrith were commanded to search for the phantom aviator. When these failed to find the aviator's base, Lieutenant B.C. Hucks was sent to search for it in a Bleriot XI aeroplane – painted white so that it would not be mistaken for the phantom flier. Hucks reached the area on 18 August and concentrated his search on Penrith, where there had been many sightings of aeroplanes and lights. Due to engine trouble Hucks had to leave on 20 August and he never returned.

At the end of August, Merseyside became the focus of phantom Zeppelin and aircraft sightings. Major de Wattevill at the Headquarters of Mersey Defences, Liverpool, was exasperated by them: 'The airship scares continue harmlessly. The Chief Constable of Lancashire is clean off his head over them. He has enlisted 20,000 special P.C.s for the war ... I am convinced Barrow is cracked on the subject.'

It was his view that the glare and smoke from the many iron foundries at Barrow were creating the 'airships'. This, however, did not stop the sightings. All the reports were gathered by the police and forwarded to Lieutenant Colonel W.S. Brancker of the Military Training department and Lieutenant Colonel Vernon Kell at Military Observation Department Five (MO5), which became MI5 in 1916.

The War Office determined that 89% of the sightings were satisfactorily explicable. What worried them most was that these sightings were becoming a nuisance, as munitions factories had to extinguish their lights every time there was an air raid. This loss in output and the congestion of communications with 'worthless stories' led to the distribution of Intelligence Circular No. 4 in March 1916, which pointed out that rumours about the possibility of air raids caused people to unduly hallucinate their presence: 'Reports and rumours thus repeated acquire precision and become magnified in circulation; they soon assume the form of definite statements that hostile airships have been actually seen in various localities.'

1914–16
Canada

Hostile enemy aircraft were frequently seen in the area of Niagara Falls from September 1914 to February 1916. During September 1914 an airship with red lights dropped a rocket near the Welland canal, which links Lake Erie with Lake Ontario. In the following months, guards at local military installations saw the lights of the craft, and one evening in July 1915 two men were seen to get out of an aircraft near Noyan Junction, Quebec. The men returned to the aircraft and flew away towards Montreal.

At Chateaugay an aircraft was seen to land and collect a German officer who had been living in the area. Over the winter of 1915 and 1916 lights were seen again at the Welland canal. At 5:00am on 5 February 1916 two aircraft flew near the Victoria railway bridge, Montreal, and later in the day a suspicious character lurking in the area was shot at. The major fear was that German aircraft were spying out the land to prepare for air raids on the country.

1916
USA

Sinister events also occurred in New Jersey and Pennsylvania during January and February 1916. Several du Pont gunpowder plants suffered explosions and mystery fires, followed by sightings of mystery lights or aircraft overhead.

On 2 March a Mr Porter saw a large aircraft land at Hines, 20 miles south of Superior. The crew got out of the aircraft and started repairing it. When he approached them, Porter was told to go away by one of the crew, who was 'undoubtedly German'. Shortly afterwards the aircraft flew towards Superior, and it was assumed it was on a mission to bomb a Du Pont plant in Wisconsin.

Another aircraft was seen to land on ice-covered Lake Vermillion, Minnesota, in April 1916. The two crew told the witness to go away, and 20 minutes later it flew away in the direction of Canada.

BELOW: Crowds gather to watch the dancing of the sun at Fatima in 1917.
Fortean Picture Library

Fatima, Portugal, 1917

The visions of three shepherd children at Cova da Iria (Cove of Irene), in the parish of Fatima, Portugal, from May to October 1917 culminated in the appearance of the 'sun' spinning and falling out of the sky, which was seen by thousands of people on 13 October 1917.

There is still plenty of speculation and controversy surrounding the regular visions of a radiant 'lady' floating above an oak tree and associated strange phenomena.

From the start, the sightings were regarded as encounters with the Virgin Mary, and they have been mainly interpreted in a religious context. In stark contrast, UFO researchers are of the opinion that if we strip away the religious beliefs and context of their sightings it was in reality a series of alien encounters.

1933–38
Scandinavia, Europe, USA, Australia

In Sweden and Norway a 'ghost flier' was seen from late 1933 and throughout 1934. A grey-coloured aircraft carrying a powerful searchlight was seen at close range, and on a few occasions it landed near the witnesses. It was suspected that these mystery aircraft were due to smugglers or secret German or Russian military exercises. The defence forces of Sweden and Norway both conducted searches and investigations without any success.

The aircraft was widely seen over Scandinavia at the end of 1936 and early 1937, and there was a sighting of one over Vienna, Austria, in February 1937. One explanation for many of these sightings is that the German Luftwaffe was conducting secret flights and training missions that 'strayed' over Scandinavia.

There were several incidents of aircraft flying over cities throughout the world that alarmed witnesses and governments. On 26 December 1933 an aircraft circled over New York City, and on 1 February a similar incident occurred over London, England. In July 1937 a mystery aircraft swooped over London again. Newspapers reported that on 16 July: 'Hundreds saw it at 12.15 passing over Trafalgar Square. The fuselage and the wings were plainly visible in the glare of street lights. It was still circling over the West End at 12.30, but soon afterwards disappeared northwards.'

The Royal Air Force (RAF) investigated this and other earlier sightings and determined that they were caused by their own aircraft and by a civilian aircraft on the 16th. On 29 July the following year a mystery aircraft flew low over Hobart, Australia, and it was speculated that it was of a foreign origin.

At this time, fixed-wing aeroplanes revived the same type of fears as the airships prior to World War One. Many of these 'ghost fliers' could have been daredevil stunt flights or propaganda stunts to highlight the dangers of aerial attack and lack of defences against them.

Another intriguing aspect of the mystery aircraft waves were claims that secret military aircraft had been stolen from aerodromes in France, Hungary, Poland, Holland and Czechoslovakia. The Germans were accused of these crimes.

1942
USA

A major war scare occurred in Los Angeles on the night of 24 February 1942. It was feared that Japanese aircraft were about to attack the area after unidentified targets were spotted off the coast. There was considerable tension as air raid sirens sounded and air raid wardens imposed a total blackout of the city in the early hours of 25 February.

Searchlights probed the sky, and at 3:16am the 37th Coast Artillery Brigade began blasting the sky with 12.8lb anti-aircraft shells. Some believe the UFO they were blasting at was a balloon carrying a red flare that was launched from Santa Monica at 3:06am. In the confusion of noise and smoke created by the bombardment, witnesses claimed seeing hundreds of

RIGHT: UFO photographed over Tientsien, Hopeh, China, in 1941.

Fortean Picture Library

enemy aircraft flying at speeds of up to 200mph (321.8kph) at very low and high altitudes. In all 1,440 rounds of ammunition were fired, with the result that three civilians were killed by this friendly fire and no aircraft was shot down, even though there were rumours that four had been blasted out of the sky. Afterwards there was considerable debate as to whether this was all due to war nerves or resulted from the belief that one or more aircraft had been launched from either a Japanese submarine or a secret land base.

1939–45
Europe and Japan

During World War Two there were persistent sightings of what were nicknamed 'foo fighters'. In December 1944 balls of fire and silvery spheres followed American aircraft over German territory. After 1944 they were seen over Japan, northern Europe and the Mediterranean. It was thought they were being used to confuse radar systems or as a psychological weapon.

One report claims that on the night of 14 October 1943 pilots of the 384th group, flying B-17 aircraft on a mission to Schweinfurt, Germany, saw clusters of silver-coloured discs. They were only three inches in diameter and an inch thick, and no damage was caused when the aircraft flew through them. Research by Andy Roberts in Britain has cast doubt on the validity of this case, which underlines the fact that original sources should be checked whenever possible, since 'facts' are easily copied from book to book and take on a life of their own.

USA 1944–45

From November 1944 to April 1945, the Japanese launched 9,000 bomb-laden Fugo balloons towards the USA. US intelligence listed six possible reasons for this campaign:

1. Bacteriological or chemical warfare, or both.
2. Transportation of incendiary and antipersonnel bombs.
3. Experiments for unknown purposes.
4. Psychological efforts to inspire terror and diversion of forces.
5. Transportation of agents.
6. Anti-aircraft devices.

Fortunately, only a fraction of these high-altitude balloons actually reached the USA, and they caused little damage and just a handful of fatalities.

The US government kept the balloon flights secret because they did not want the Japanese to get any feedback about the success rate of this operation, but when one of the balloons exploded after being found by a group of picnickers the government was forced to tell the public about them.

The cover-up of the recovery of these balloons, and the suppression of witness statements about weird things in the sky, established a precedent in the minds of the public that the US government would do the same thing with flying saucer evidence.

Equally, when V1 and V2 rockets rained down on Britain during World War Two the authorities suppressed this information to prevent a mass exodus from London and to prevent the Germans from knowing where they landed.

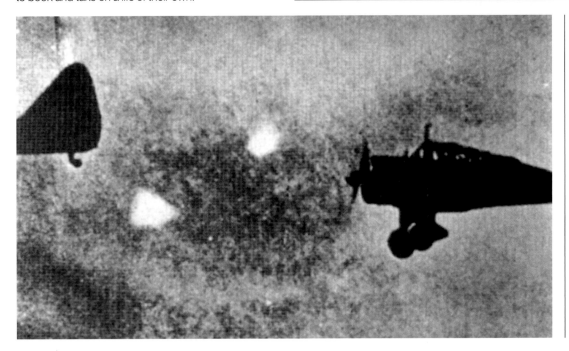

LEFT: Balls of light called 'foo fighters' sometimes followed aircraft during World War Two. They were regarded as either secret weapons or caused by ball lightning.
Fortean Picture Library

RIGHT: Karl-Gösta Bartoll investigates Lake Kölmjärv in Sweden after a report of a rocket-UFO crash there, 19 July 1946.
Clas Svahn/Fortean Picture Library

BELOW: 'Ghost rocket' at Lake Kölmjärv, Sweden, 1946. On 29 July men from the engineer corps started to build a raft to investigate the lake.
A machine for detecting metal was placed on the raft.
Clas Svahn/Fortean Picture Library

ABOVE: Ludvig Lindbäck, brother to principle witness Knut, at Lake Kölmjärv, site of the 19 July 1946 rocket-UFO crash in Sweden.

Clas Svahn/Fortean Picture Library

LEFT: 'Ghost rocket' at Lake Kölmjärv, Sweden, 1946. Between 20 July and 9 August more than 35,000 samples were taken from the bottom of the lake from two rafts. The electrical mining apparatus that was used at the start did not get any readings.

Clas Svahn/Fortean Picture Library

1946
Sweden

From May to October 1946 wingless, cigar-shaped 'ghost rockets' or 'ghost bombs' were seen that had a predilection for crashing into lakes. It was feared that the Soviet Union was testing German secret weapons that they had captured during World War Two. In Sweden a special committee was formed to investigate the affair, and the British and American authorities took an interest in the matter. There were hundreds of sightings but no convincing evidence was found to solve this mystery.

During this period odd fireballs and UFO-type objects were seen in France, Denmark, Norway, Finland, Greece, North Africa, Portugal, Spain and Italy.

The preceding incidents constitute the main waves of UFO sightings prior to 1947. However, as more newspaper archives are digitised it is becoming easier to search for ancient UFO reports, and to discover more potential waves in other countries and time periods.

The ambiguity and bizarre nature of these reports, combined with fears of foreign/alien invasion and the existence of foreign spies and secret inventors, allied with secret government investigations, exhibits many of the same features that are typical of ufology after 1947.

The comparison of historical aerial and related phenomena gives us the opportunity to seek out the mechanisms of such occurrences, and their impact and effect on individuals and society, and provides proof that UFOs are nothing new.

References

Aubeck, Chris and Vallée, Jacques. *Wonders in the Skies: Unexplained Aerial Objects from Antiquity to Modern Times* (Tarcher/Penguin Putnam, London, 2010).

Bartholomew, Robert E. 'The Airship Hysteria of 1896–97' *Skeptical Inquirer* vol 14 (Winter 1990), 171–81.

The Book of the Damned: A Hypertext Edition of Charles Hoy Fort's Book, edited and annotated by Mr X, at: www.resologist.net/damnei.htm.

Bullard, Thomas. *The Airship File* (privately published, Bloomington, Indiana, 1982).

— *The Airship File: Supplement No 1* (privately published, Bloomington, Indiana, 1983).

— *The Airship File: Supplement No 2* (privately published, Bloomington, Indiana, 1990).

Cohen, Daniel. *The Great Airship Mystery* (Dodd, Mead & Co, New York, 1981).

Danelek, J. Allen. *The Great Airship of 1897* (Adventures Unlimited Press, 2009).

Holman, Brett. 'Airminded' at airminded.org/.

— *The Scareship Age, 1892–1946* (e-book, 2011), at: airminded.org/publications/downloads/?did=2.

Magonia. A selection of articles published by Magonia is available at: magonia.haaan.com/tag/airships/.

Neeley, Robert G. *UFOs of 1896/1897: The Airship Wave* (Fund for UFO Research, Mount Rainier, USA, 1988).

— *The Airship Chronicle* (Fund for UFO Research, Mount Rainier, USA, 1988).

'Project 1947' website, at: www.project1947.com/.

Gross, Loren E. *The Mystery of the Ghost Rockets* (privately published, 1972).

— *Charles Fort, the Fortean Society and Unidentified Flying Objects* (privately published, 1976).

Roslund, Stefan/UFO-Sweden. *UFO flap in Tsarist Russia 1892*, at: www.ufo.se/english/articles/oldrussia.html.

The Tunguska Impact – 100 Years Later, at: science.nasa.gov/science-news/science-at-nasa/2008/30jun_tunguska/.

Watson, Nigel. 'Airships and Invaders: Background to a Social Panic' *Magonia* no 3 (Spring 1980).

— (ed). *The Scareship Mystery: A Survey of Phantom Airship Scares 1909–1918* (DOMRA, 2000).

2

Official UFO investigations

With the outbreak of World War One in August 1914, people throughout Britain started reporting sightings of mysterious lights and aircraft flying in the sky. The War Office diligently investigated and analysed the sightings to determine if they were caused by the activities of enemy aircraft, yet they could not find any solid evidence to support any of the claims. Indeed, they were not impressed with the evidence presented to them and found the reports from all quarters of the land to be a nuisance.

When flying saucers hit the headlines in June 1947, the number of UFO sightings and the theories surrounding their origins overwhelmed the United States. Several US government agencies secretly investigated the reports throughout the 1950s and 1960s, and these have since come into the public domain. Like the British War Office, the US studies were unable to explain all the sightings and never came up with a satisfactory answer to the UFO mystery. Rather than throwing light on the matter, many studies muddied the waters and caused greater confusion.

Official investigations were made into the ghost rockets seen over Scandinavia between 1946 and 1948 and Greece in September 1946. Most of the sightings were attributed to natural phenomena. Paul Santorinis, associate professor of Applied Physics at Athens University, who was on a secret committee to investigate the Greek sightings, thought that they were psychological weapons, launched by the Soviet Union. Others thought they were flares launched into the sky by Communist rebels.

US and British military officials were involved in analysing these reports, and British MI6 agents were even sent to the Soviet zone to get information about any secret rocket tests. Cynics thought they were the product of post-war tensions, and that the Swedish authorities might have encouraged the scare to promote unpopular defence expenditure. In 2012, in an attempt to find the underlying cause of this mystery, Clas Svahn, the head of UFO-Sweden, launched an expedition to a remote lake in northern Sweden in the hope of finding and recovering a ghost rocket.

The 'Flying Saucer era' truly began when Kenneth Arnold was flying his CallAir aeroplane over Mount Rainier, Washington, on 24 June 1947. As he was flying eastwards, he saw 'a chain of nine peculiar looking aircraft flying from north to south at approximately 9,500 foot elevation'. He calculated that they were travelling faster than 1,000mph (1,609kph) and he described them as flying 'like a saucer would if you skipped it across the water.' It was from this

ABOVE: Kenneth Arnold (1915–84) was an entrepreneur and inventor who ran a successful fire-fighting equipment business using his CallAir aircraft. He is shown here with his wife, Doris.

Fortean Picture Library

LEFT: An artist's impression of the nine 'flying saucers' seen by Kenneth Arnold over Mount Rainier, Washington, on 24 June 1947.

SUFOI/Fortean Picture Library

Arnold soon found himself out of his depth. It all began when six large doughnut-shaped objects were seen high above a salvage boat by Harold A. Dahl, his son and two crew members, as they sailed off Maury Island, Washington. The boat was damaged and their pet dog was killed by slag-like rock that rained down from the objects.

Samples of the rock were sent to Ray Palmer, who asked Arnold to interview the witnesses and write a report for one of his science fiction magazines. Palmer flew to Tacoma, Washington, at the end of July 1947, where he enlisted the help of Captain William Davidson and Lieutenant Frank M. Brown of Army A-2 Intelligence. They promptly interviewed Dahl and his employer Fred Crisman at the Winthrop Hotel, Tacoma.

The men were evasive and the rock samples were not very impressive. So, at 2:00am on 1 August, Davidson and Brown decided to return to their base at Hamilton Field, California. There was a tragic turn of events when their B-25 aircraft caught fire and crashed en route, killing both of them. Shortly afterwards an anonymous caller to a newspaper claimed it was shot down or sabotaged because it was carrying parts of a flying saucer.

Kenneth Arnold was nearly added to the list of fatalities. When he took off from Tacoma the engine of his aircraft failed and he had to make a crash landing. On checking his aircraft he found that the fuel valve had been switched off.

To add further mystery to the affair, Dahl claimed that on 22 June 1947, the morning after his UFO sighting, a mysterious stranger visited him. The man seemed to know everything about his sighting and warned him to keep quiet about it, otherwise there would be serious repercussions for him and his family. This can be regarded as one of the first reported instances of a Man in Black (MIB) encounter.

observation that the term 'flying saucers' originated, and it triggered literally thousands of people throughout the world to report seeing similar objects.

Not only did Kenneth Arnold initiate the whole flying saucer scare, he was also one of the first civilians to investigate a UFO incident. The Maury Island case has all the elements of a cheap detective novel, and

All the Dahl rock samples were 'stolen', as were photographs that had been taken of the UFOs. Not long afterwards Dahl's son disappeared for a week, and turned up in Lusk, Montana, with no recollection of how he had got there.

The Federal Bureau of Investigation (FBI) took an interest in this case due to the allegation of sabotage to the B-25, and they were interested in finding out more about the flying discs. On 6 August 1947, an FBI special agent was dispatched to Tacoma to conduct an investigation. The agent spoke to Crisman and Dahl, who were evasive and at a loss to explain how the rock fragments became connected with the story of flying discs. FBI documents indicate that the B-25 was not sabotaged, and the investigators suspected Crisman of promoting the case to get more money from Raymond Palmer.

Fred Crisman was certainly a shady character, as he had previously written for Palmer's *Amazing Stories*

LEFT: Two
photographs of a
UFO were taken by
Mrs Evelyn Trent on
her farm near
McMinnville, Oregon,
on 11 May 1950.
Fortean Picture Library

BELOW: Sceptics
think a model UFO
suspended from the
power lines was
photographed to
create the
McMinnville
pictures.
Fortean Picture Library

magazine. In the 1960s New Orleans District Attorney
Jim Garrison implicated him in the assassination of
John F. Kennedy, and he allegedly worked for the
Central Intelligence Agency (CIA).

Whether this was an elaborate hoax or
not, it incorporates conspiracy, an MIB visitation,
disappearances, double bluffs, sabotage, death and
assassination, which all became regular features of
ufology over the following years.

Officially, Air Materiel Command at Wright Field
mainly dealt with UFO reports under the command
of Lieutenant General Nathan F. Twining. After a
conference with aviation experts to review the
evidence, he sent a memorandum to Brigadier
General George Schulgen, Chief of the Air Intelligence

ABOVE: William Hartmann,
an astronomer working for the Condon Committee,
was convinced the McMinnville pictures showed
an artificial, metallic object several metres in diameter.
Fortean Picture Library

Requirements Division. The memo, dated 23 September 1947, sets out a list of conclusions about the phenomenon and makes some recommendations. The first point in the memorandum is that the flying discs are 'something real and not visionary or fictitious'. It goes on to state that the discs are similar in size to man-made aircraft, some sightings might be caused by natural phenomena, such as meteors, and they are highly manoeuvrable, indicating they 'are controlled either manually, automatically, or remotely'. He notes that the descriptions of the craft have the following characteristics:

1. Metallic or light-reflecting.
2. Absence of trail, except in a few instances when the object apparently was operating under high performance conditions.
3. Circular or elliptical in shape, flat on bottom and domed on top.
4. Several reports of well-kept formation flights varying from three to nine objects.
5. Normally no associated sound, except in three instances a substantial rumbling roar was noted.
6. Level flight speeds normally of above 300 knots are estimated.

Given these factors, there were three main considerations. One was that the discs were of domestic origin, constructed under such high levels of security that even the investigators did not know about it. Another possibility was that they were nuclear propelled craft operated by a foreign nation. And thirdly, there was as yet no undeniable evidence 'in the shape of crash recovered exhibits'.

In response, Brigadier General Schulgen set

out the characteristics of this flying saucer-type aircraft in a memorandum dated 28 October 1947. He was of the opinion that the sightings were of 'a manned aircraft, of Russian origin, and based on the perspective thinking and actual accomplishments of the Germans.' In particular, it was thought that the Russians had taken over the development and production of a flying wing-type aircraft inspired by the work of the Horton brothers. Two of these jet-propelled aircraft were built and flight-tested by the Germans, but it never went into mass production.

Operatives in Berlin soon tracked down brothers Reimer and Walter Horton. The agents summarised their findings in a long memorandum dated 16 December 1947. Basically they found them 'exceedingly peculiar and can be easily classified as eccentric and individualistic.' As far as they could tell, they had never been in contact with the Soviet Air Force, though it was possible that others involved with the design of the Horten IX aircraft during World War Two supplied their designs to the Soviets. However, it seemed unlikely that the Soviets had created a fleet of Horten-type craft in such a short period, and even if they had it would be unlikely that they would invade US airspace in such a blatant manner.

Project Sign

Project Sign was launched on 22 January 1948 to 'collect, collate, evaluate and distribute to interested government agencies and contractors all information concerning sightings and phenomena in the atmosphere which can be construed to be of concern to the national security.' It was headed by Captain

BELOW: Carl Hart Jr took this picture of the 'Lubbock Lights', Texas, on 30 August 1951. One explanation was that they were reflections from a flock of birds.
Fortean Picture Library

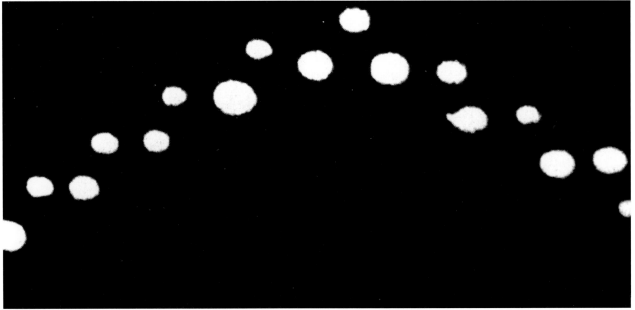

ABOVE: Nicolas
Mariana used a
16mm camera to
capture two bright
circular objects
travelling swiftly
over Great Falls,
Montana, on 15
August 1950. The
film was classified
for several years.
Fortean Picture Library

Robert R. Sneider and based at Wright Patterson
(formerly Wright Field) Air Force Base, Dayton, Ohio.

The Estimate of the Situation was a Project Sign
report written in September 1948. It concluded that
the UFO reports they received indicated that a real
craft was observed and that it displayed abilities
beyond anything built by any nation on Earth. This
meant that they had to accept the idea that UFOs had
an interplanetary origin.

This conclusion did not go down very well with
General Hoyt Vandenberg, Chief-of-Staff of the USAF.
Its extreme conclusions led to its incineration and no
copy has survived for posterity.

Project Twinkle

In December 1948 and February 1949, mysterious
and spectacular green fireballs were frequently seen
in northern New Mexico. Dr Lincoln La Pez of the
University of New Mexico's Department of Meteoritics,
stated that:

1. The trajectory of the green fireballs was too flat
   compared to normal meteor falls.
2. Their colour was too green.
3. After tracking their trajectories he could not find
   any fragments where they should have landed.

When more sightings occurred near Holloman Air
Force Base and Vaughn, New Mexico, in February
1950, an outlook post with two personnel was set up
at Holloman. They were armed with a theodolite,
telescope and camera to gather factual data about
the fireballs.

The following month it was decided to set up a
formal project to track the fireballs. This was called
Project Twinkle and run by the Air Force's Cambridge
Research Laboratory. They planned to use:

1. Askania instrument triangulation by Land-Air Inc.
2. Observations with a Mitchell camera using
   spectrum grating by Holloman Air Force Base
   personnel.
3. Electromagnetic frequency measurements
   using Signal Corps Engineering Laboratory
   equipment.

The project ran from 1 April 1950 to 31 March 1951,
but according to Edward J. Ruppelt it was 'a bust',
since their meagre resources were divided between
Holloman and Vaughn – a distance of 150 miles
(241.4km). The electromagnetic measurements were
never made because they were too expensive, and
the cameras were always moved too late to capture a
UFO on film. By the autumn of 1951 sightings of the
fireballs had dwindled away, and Project Twinkle
went into oblivion.

ABOVE: After leaving Project Blue Book in 1953 Edward Ruppelt wrote *The Report on Unidentified Flying Objects* in 1956. Before his sudden death in 1960, he became sceptical about the ET origin of UFOs.
Fortean Picture Library

ABOVE: In 1951–52 Edward Ruppelt directed the USAF's Project Grudge.
Fortean Picture Library

Project Grudge

After being sympathetic to the open-minded investigation of UFO reports, the USAF did a complete U-turn with Project Grudge, which took over from Project Sign on 12 February 1949. As the name suggested, they set out to explain and debunk UFO reports at every opportunity.

A 600-page *Project Grudge Technical Report* concluded that UFO sightings are created by:

1. Misinterpretation of various conventional objects.
2. A mild form of mass-hysteria and war nerves.
3. Individuals who fabricate such reports to perpetrate a hoax or to seek publicity.
4. Psychopathological persons.

Since they found that UFOs were not of foreign origin and 'constitute no direct threat to the national security', the report was used as an excuse to scale down their activities.

The project was dormant for a year and then it was reactivated in July 1950. Lieutenant Edward Ruppelt, who had a reputation for problem solving, was put in charge of Project Grudge in late 1951, and went on to head the New Project Grudge from October 1951 until its dissolution in March 1952. Ruppelt insisted on using the term UFO, rather than flying saucer or disc. To obtain essential details of UFO sightings from witnesses he introduced a standardised interview questionnaire that was developed by Ohio State University, and he employed the Battelle Memorial Institute to carry out a statistical analysis of the UFO data. Ruppelt took an open-minded approach to the subject and dismissed anyone from his team who was too sceptical or too obsessed by a single theory.

The Robertson Panel

A wave of UFO sightings concentrated over Washington DC hit the headlines in July 1952. UFOs over the nation's capital meant that something had to be done about the matter, and in January 1953 a panel of experts was set up by the CIA to review the subject. Dr Howard P. Robertson, director of the Defense Department Weapons Evaluation Group, chaired it.

After four days of meetings they came to the same conclusions as the Project Grudge report. Their main concern, however, was that false sightings and the 'morbid national psychology' could be skilfully used by enemy nations to clog up channels of communication and confuse air defences. At a time when long-range Soviet bombers could unleash atomic weapons upon the USA, this was of pressing importance.

The panel recommended that UFOs be stripped of their 'aura of mystery' and that the public should be better educated to be able to recognise the difference between truly hostile aircraft and UFOs. It was also advised that civilian UFO groups be monitored 'because of their potentially great influence on mass thinking ... the apparent irresponsibility and possible use of such groups for subversive purposes should be kept in mind.'

Unfortunately, the policy to debunk UFOs only made it seem that the government was covering up the subject and knew more about it than they were willing to say.

At the end of 1953 the CIA decided to keep track of UFO research carried out by the USAF and other agencies rather than carrying out their own investigations. However, the CIA would continue to monitor UFO reports from Communist Bloc countries, as they might indicate the introduction of non-conventional air vehicles with military applications.

LEFT: In the August 2010 edition of *Fortean Times*, Mark Pilkington looks at the role of the CIA in connection with the UFOs seen over Washington DC in 1952.
Fortean Times

LEFT: Photograph of a 100ft (30.4m) long airship-like UFO taken by customs officer Domingo Troncoso, in Puerto Maldonado, on the border of Peru and Bolivia, circa 1951/2. It left a trail of dense smoke in its wake.
Fortean Picture Library

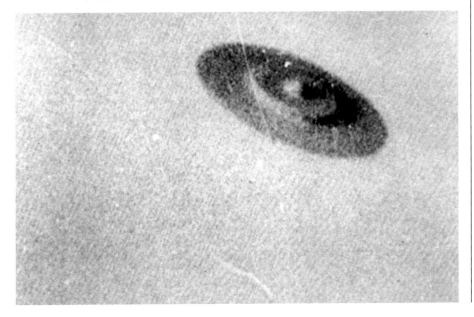

RIGHT: On 7 May 1952, Ed Keffel, a press photographer, took five pictures of this UFO near Barra da Tijuca, Brazil.
Fortean Picture Library

Project Blue Book

Project Blue Book came into existence on 25 March 1952. It replaced Project Grudge, but Ruppelt (now a captain) remained in charge. He continued with investigating cases and introduced better means of analysing them. Things changed after the Robertson Panel meeting, when the policy of demystifying UFO reports began to bite.

In February 1953 the Air Force issued Regulation 200-2, which ordered airbase officers not to give any publicity to unsolved UFO sightings and to only discuss cases that had a mundane explanation. At the same time, any sightings with intelligence or national security implications were farmed out to the 4602nd Air Intelligence Service Squadron (AISS), and Blue Book was left to investigate less significant cases. Furthermore, Regulation JANAP-146 imposed a fine of $10,000 and ten years' imprisonment on any military personnel who made UFO information

public without permission. Blue Book was also ordered to reduce the number of unsolved cases in its annual listings.

With the reduction of his powers to investigate UFO reports and his team reduced from ten to two subordinates, Ruppelt became disillusioned with the project and resigned in August 1953. The following year an updated Air Force Regulation 200-2 stated that UFOs (or UFOBs, as it called them) were 'any airborne object which by performance, aerodynamic characteristics, or unusual features, does not conform to any presently known aircraft or missile type, or which cannot be positively identified as a familiar object'.

Blue Book still remained the public face for official UFO investigations, but it mainly operated as a repository of information and an outlet for debunking cases. After collecting 12,618 sighting reports, of which 701 remained unsolved, it closed down on 30 January 1970 due to the findings of the Condon Committee.

LEFT AND ABOVE: On the afternoon of 29 July 1952, George Stock took five photographs of this UFO from his backyard in Passaic, New Jersey. The bluish-grey object photographed at Passaic was estimated to be 20ft (6m) in diameter.
Fortean Picture Library

LEFT: The Passaic photographs hit the headlines in the 1 August 1952 edition of *The Morning Call*.
Fortean Picture Library

The Condon Committee

After a wave of UFO sightings and Congressional UFO hearings in April 1966, the Air Force agreed to have their Blue Book files re-examined and to conduct a multidisciplinary study of the UFO subject to determine if a major problem existed. After considering several universities, the University of Colorado was selected to carry out the work in November 1966.

Under the scientific direction and leadership of Professor Edward U. Condon, the committee originally received help and support from the NICAP and APRO civilian UFO groups. This changed when a memorandum by Robert Low, the committee's coordinator, dated 9 August 1966, was discovered that contained these damning words: 'The trick would be, I think, to describe the project so that, to the public, it would appear a totally objective study, but to the scientific community would present the image of a group of non-believers trying their best to be objective but having an almost zero expectation of finding a saucer.'

When Condon learnt on 7 February 1968 that two of his team members, Dr David Saunders and Norman

Levine, had leaked this memo, he promptly fired them. Saunders went on to co-write a book *UFOs? Yes! Where The Condon Committee Went Wrong: The Inside Story by an Ex-Member of the Official Study Group*. As its title indicates, this criticised the workings of the committee. Its main argument was that there was a government conspiracy to keep the truth from the public, and the committee was unwilling to consider that UFOs could be extraterrestrial vehicles.

Despite the controversy, the committee submitted a 1,400-page typewritten report to the Air Force in November 1968, entitled *The Final Report of the Scientific Study of Unidentified Flying Objects*, often referred to as the Condon Report.

Section I of the report pulled no punches: 'Careful consideration of the record as it is available to us leads us to conclude that further extensive study of UFOs probably cannot be justified in the expectation that science will be advanced thereby.

'It has been argued that this lack of contribution to science is due to the fact that very little scientific effort has been put on the subject. We do not agree. We feel that the reason that there has been very little scientific study of the subject is that those scientists who are most directly concerned, astronomers, atmospheric physicists, chemists, and psychologists, having had ample opportunity to look into the matter, have individually decided that UFO phenomena do not offer a fruitful field in which to look for major scientific discoveries.'

Since UFOs did not, therefore, represent any national security threat in the form of foreign or extraterrestrial vehicles, and did not merit further scientific investigation, the Air Force used the report's findings as an excuse to close down Project Blue Book and, at least in public, wash their hands of ufology altogether. Their recommendation to any UFO witness is to contact their local law enforcement agency.

ABOVE: Three classic flying saucers photographed over Italy on 26 September 1960. Probably a fake.
Fortean Picture Library

LEFT: Captain Hugo F. Niotti, who served in the Argentinean Air Force (AAF), was driving from Yacanto towards Cordoba, Argentina, when he snapped this picture of a UFO on 3 July 1960.
Fortean Picture Library

Majestic 12

The most infamous set of leaked documents pertaining to UFOs relates to a US government project called Operation Majestic Twelve (MJ-12), codenamed MAJIC. Some sources claim it was really called Majority 12. It came to the attention of ufologists in 1984, and so far about 3,500 pages of documents relating to this project have become known.

These documents seemed to confirm that the US government did indeed recover a crashed saucer at Roswell in the summer of 1947, and that President Harry Truman formed the Majestic 12 committee on 24 September 1947 to investigate the implications of this incident. Since then more MJ-12 documents have surfaced that indicate the US has secretly worked with aliens and utilised their technology.

The first set of MJ-12 documents was released to the public by William Moore in the USA, and Timothy Good in Britain during May 1987. Since then research has shown that the early documents were probably doctored versions of real documents, and even Timothy Good admits that they are fabrications. Good, however, contends that they still give vital clues about the US government's involvement with aliens.

MJ-12 seems to have evolved from a US government disinformation project. This centred on an electronics expert called Paul Bennewitz, who believed that aliens were sending out signals to people who had implants inside their brains.

To test his theory he tried to intercept electronic low frequency (ELF) transmissions. Unfortunately, instead of intercepting alien signals he stumbled upon ELF signals from the nearby Kirtland Air Force Base, which was conducting secret experiments for the Strategic Defense Initiative (SDI) 'Star Wars' project.

When the USAF discovered Bennewitz's activities, they warned him to stop. When persuasion did not work, the Air Force Office of Special Intelligence (AFOSI) started discrediting him by feeding him disinformation that encouraged his preconceived ideas about aliens.

This disinformation included a fake document that

LEFT: Timothy Good, author of the best-selling *Above Top Secret* book that features the MJ-12 documents.

Dennis Stacy/Fortean Picture Library

detailed the activities of Project Aquarius and mentioned an 'MJ Twelve'. Richard Doty, who was a counterintelligence officer with AFOSI, gave this to Paul Bennewitz in November 1980. The AFOSI also enrolled UFO researcher William Moore to help them. He admitted that a top secret group of military intelligence personnel, who called themselves the 'Aviary' – which probably included Richard Doty and was part of an AFOSI project – had contacted him. In return for spying on Bennewitz and other ufologists, Doty gave Moore a mixture of fake and genuine UFO documents.

Doty also gave disinformation about cattle mutilations, implants and abductions carried out by the aliens in league with the US government, operating from underground bases, to journalist Linda Moulton Howe. Using this material, she produced an influential television documentary called *A Strange Harvest* in 1980.

Project Serpo

The Internet is great for spreading rumours, hoaxes and disinformation about alien encounters. One of the most widespread has been about Project Serpo. The story says that human astronauts were sent to planet Serpo in the Zeta Reticuli solar system.

In November 2005 a contact called 'anonymous' started sending information about an extraordinary alien exchange programme. Basing his claims on a 3,000-page document written in the late 1970s, he boldly claimed that six aliens were recovered from the Roswell crash.

Claims that aliens living and/or dead were recovered from the Roswell crash are nothing new, but in this case it was stated that an alien survivor from the crash, called EBE 1, helped to organise 12 specially trained people to visit his home planet, Serpo. This mission occurred in 1965, and they remained there until 1978. Two of them died during their stay, two remained behind on the planet and the rest, after returning to Earth, have died because of the high levels of radiation they were exposed to on Serpo.

This information was originally distributed and edited by Victor Martinez via a private email list. Bill Ryan also gained information from 'anonymous', who apparently worked in the US Defense Intelligence Agency (DIA) and had been nominated as the spokesperson for a group of six DIA employees. This material can be found on the 'Serpo.org: The Zeta Reticuli Exchange Program' website, which claims its mission is 'intended to facilitate the gradual release of confidential documents pertaining to a top secret exchange program of twelve US military personnel to Serpo, a planet of Zeta Reticuli, between the years 1965–78'.

Serpo material suddenly stopped arriving in August 2006, and the website notes that: 'Logically there are four possibilities: 1) Anonymous is a prankster and the reported data is either all invented or culled from other sources and added to a wild novelistic story. 2) Anonymous is operating to a planned agenda and the information is deliberately distorted, but contains a core of extraordinary truth. 3) Anonymous is doing his best to report data from an indirect source (personal notes, his own short or long-term memory, or another person), but accidental errors, omissions and additions have occurred. 4) Anonymous is reporting everything faithfully and accurately as best as he can present it.'

Ryan's own conclusion was that 'the Serpo story is a mixture of disinformation (i.e. truth mixed with added fictional elements) and naturally occurring compounded errors ... surrounding a core of extraordinary truth'.

Doubts have been cast on this story since former AFOSI agent Richard Doty has supported it. Apparently as early as 1983 he had previously told Linda Moulton Howe a variation of this story. In this version, only three humans were sent to the Zeta Reticuli system. One died during the mission, one went insane and the last one returned home safely but was kept in isolation.

It is hard to determine whether Doty is working on leading the way for full public disclosure of the government's secret involvement with aliens, or is weaving complex stories to spread confusion amongst gullible ufologists for his own enjoyment.

United Kingdom

In the 1960s and 1970s, Julian Hennessy wrote hundreds of copious letters to various authorities throughout the world to seek out UFO evidence.

His persistent enquiries to the British Ministry of Defence (MoD) eventually led them to review their UFO policy in 1967. Previously they had destroyed all UFO records that were more than five years old, but now they decided to keep all the remaining records dating from 1962 onwards.

The catch was that these files would only be released to the public after a period of 30 years, although they did concede that a major scientific organisation could apply for immediate access to them before this date.

With the cooperation of J. Allen Hynek and his Center for UFO Studies (CUFOS), Hennessy applied to look at the files, but they were turned down because it would be a drain on the MoD's financial and human resources. Hennessy also ran a NICAP European sub-committee, and set up Euronet, a project to obtain sighting reports from European airlines.

Dr David Clarke, Andy Roberts, Gary Anthony and Joe McGonagle have been far more successful. From the 1980s onwards they have obtained many UFO-related files from the Public Record Office (PRO) and the MoD.

In 1997 Dr Clarke discovered that in October 1950 Britain set up a Flying Saucer Working Party that liaised with the CIA. Influenced by the CIA's mission to debunk UFO sightings, the six-page final report by the Working Party in June 1951 concluded that delusions, hoaxes and misidentification were the main sources of UFO sightings. This showed that not all UFO files dated before 1962 were destroyed, and more could still be lurking in the archives.

Another discovery was the MoD's Project Condign, which was so secret that it only distributed 11 copies of its four-volume report. It was funded by the MoD Intelligence Staff (DIS), section DI55, in the late 1990s and was completed in 2000.

The report's full title is *Unidentified Aerial Phenomena in the UK Air Defence Region*. After discounting hoaxes, common natural phenomena and misidentifications, it concluded that there are rare sightings of what it labelled Unidentified Aerial Phenomena (UAP). UAPs are rare plasma balls in the upper atmosphere, which can be seen by human observers but are undetectable by radar. Meteors, or other unknown and unpredictable events, create UAPs, and are 'attributable to physical, electrical and magnetic phenomena'.

When the report was made public in May 2006 it was underlined that UAPs are not hostile, intelligently controlled, extraterrestrial or associated with any

Project Magnet

The Canadian Department of Transport agreed to form an official UFO investigation project at the suggestion of Wilbert B. Smith, a senior radio engineer at the Department of Communications. It began life on 21 November 1950 under the Project Magnet name. Three years later, Smith reported that 'we are faced with a substantial probability of the real existence of extraterrestrial vehicles, regardless of whether they fit into our scheme of things. It is therefore submitted that the next step in this investigation should be a substantial effort toward the acquisition of as much as possible of this technology.'

This led to the establishment of a UFO detection station at Shirleys Bay, near Ottawa, Ontario. Based on Smith's theory that UFO propulsion systems manipulate gravity, his instruments were tuned to detect any changes in the local gravity field. On 8 August 1954 the detectors went wild, but the sky was overcast and no UFO or any other reason for triggering them was visible. When Smith reported this to the media his claims embarrassed the government, leading them to cancel the project. Smith was left to investigate UFO reports on an unofficial basis.

From 1952 Canada ran Project Second Story to examine whether UFO reports needed a more large-scale investigation. In 1969 the UFO files were transferred to the National Research Council, where they became available for public inspection.

particular nation. From 1991 to 1994 Nick Pope ran the MoD's 'UFO desk', where he was responsible for seeing if UFOs were any threat to the UK or of a more general defence interest. He explains that: 'The terms of reference and investigative methodology were based on the USAF's Project Blue Book, though unlike the US, we never gave our work a formal project name. This confused the UFO community, because over the years MoD's UFO programme has been embedded in a veritable alphabet soup of different MoD sections, including S4, S6, DS8, Sec (AS) and DAS. Sometimes there's been an RAF lead and sometimes a civilian lead.

'While the methodology and conclusions of Project Condign were fundamentally flawed, the most interesting points were missed by the media and the UFO community. Firstly, the realisation that whatever the true nature of the UFO phenomenon, the flight safety aspects need to be taken seriously. Secondly, the fact that MoD was interested in the "novel military applications" that might result from a better understanding of the phenomenon. More fundamentally, Project Condign demonstrates that all the time MoD was downplaying its interest in the subject and telling Parliament, the media and the public that UFOs were of "no defence interest", behind the scenes, some of us thought otherwise and were conducting more in-depth and highly classified work than people realised.'

Beginning in May 2008, the MoD started a phased transfer of all their UFO-related documents to The

National Archives (TNA) to make them available for public viewing. Dr Clarke has worked as a consultant with the TNA to release tranches of these files on the TNA's UFO website, which has attracted several million visitors.

The 'UFO desk' at the MoD was terminated in 2009. However, Nick Pope notes: 'UFOs are still being seen, reported and – occasionally and depending on the circumstances – investigated. But this is being done on an ad hoc basis, by the chain of command, outside the scope of any formally-constituted research effort. And those concerned are using phrases such as "unusual aircraft" and "unconventional helicopter" so as to avoid the baggage that comes with the term UFO and – perhaps – to make it less likely that any of this will be picked up by future Freedom of Information Act requests.'

France

Under the auspices of the Centre National d'Études Spatiales (CNES, in English, National Centre for Space Studies), a group was formed to study UFO reports in 1977. Since 2005 it has gone under the title of GEIPAN (Groupe d'Études et d'Informations sur les

ABOVE:
Dr David Clarke used the Freedom of Information Act to make official UK government files public.
David Clarke

LEFT: Nick Pope ran the British Ministry of Defence's 'UFO desk' and has authored several books on the subject.
Nick Pope

RIGHT: A fisherman took this photograph at Lake Tiorati, New York, on 18 December 1966. The UFO left in the direction of Stockbridge Mountain.

Fortean Picture Library

Phénomènes Aérospatiaux Non-identifiés – Unidentified Aerospace Phenomenon Research and Information Group). It is run by two full-time staff and has 20 trained volunteers in France, Corsica and Martinique, who can investigate the most interesting reports in more detail. It can call on CNES resources and experts, and UFO reports are received directly from the public or passed on to them from the Gendarmerie.

In 1999 a 90-page report entitled *UFOs and Defence: What Should We Prepare For?* was released by a committee of experts to review all the available UFO evidence. It is mainly known as the COMETA Report, and it concluded that 5% of cases are inexplicable and could be of an extraterrestrial origin.

Worldwide

Many other nations that have conducted secret UFO investigations are now making their files publicly available and are putting them online. These include China, Russia, Australia, New Zealand, Spain, Argentina, Brazil, Denmark, Chile and Peru.

Many of these files contain communications between departments and fairly low-grade material. This contrasts with the high expectations of ufologists and supporters of the exopolitics movement, as Nick Pope explains: 'Ufologists constantly talk about "Disclosure" – a ufological trope where the President announces that extraterrestrial visitation is a reality. In fact, countries all around the world are releasing their UFO files. However, because there's no "spaceship in a hangar smoking gun", ufologists regard these

releases either as disinformation or as acclimatisation, ahead of the real announcement. Because I'm often the person people see being interviewed in the media about these releases, this fuels the fire with conspiracy theorists, in view of my government background.'

In the context of the British Ministry of Defence (MoD) files, Dr David Clarke notes: 'As the MoD "UFO desk" is now defunct there will be no further files generated post November 2009, so pretty much everything that has been released (apart from a few stragglers) is all that is likely to emerge. As you will realise if you have examined the content, 90% is complete rubbish – in that most reports consist of a piece of paper containing a brief description of what was seen, where, when etc and a standard letter in response setting out MoD's lack of interest. Therefore no proper "investigations" have been done in recent years. As I have read all the surviving files (remember the stuff released on the TNA [The National Archives] website is all post-1984 and a similar amount of files pre-1984 exist only in paper format in the TNA at Kew), it's fair to say that the last really detailed investigations conducted by MoD – in terms of field investigations – date from 1968. So pretty much the MoD's interest died around the same time the USAF closed Blue Book and transferred their files to the US TNA. Ever since then the British have been looking for an excuse to do the same ... but they didn't feel confident to do so until 2009 when austerity gave them the opportunity.

'But I think the value of the MoD archive lies in what it tells us – in totality – about the people who see and believe in UFOs and where they got their ideas from (i.e. media/UFO literature/Internet).'

References

Ghost rockets

Carpenter, Joel. *Guided Missiles and UFOs*, at: www.project1947.com/gr/grchron3.htm. Contains considerable information on the official investigations into the Swedish ghost rocket sightings.

The Ghost Rockets. Swedish television documentary website reporting on search for a ghost rocket, at: www.ghostrockets.se/.

Vembos, Thanassis. *The Greek Ghost Rockets of 1946*, at: www.vembos.gr/Greek_Ghost_Rockets.htm.

USA

'Kenneth A. Arnold' website, at: www.kennetharnoldufo.com/kenneth-arnold.html.

Good, Timothy. *Above Top Secret* (Sidgwick & Jackson, London, 1987).

Project Blue Book

The official website for the United States Air Force contains a fact sheet about the project at: www.af.mil/information/factsheets/factsheet.asp?id=188.

The Fund for UFO Research (FUFOR) and other civilian researchers are making all the Blue Book files available online, at: www.bluebookarchive.org.

United States Department of Defense

A large file of UFO sightings reported to the National Military Command Center (NMCC) in the mid-1970s as well as other UFO documents are available at: www.dod.mil/pubs/foi/homeland_defense/UFOs/.

NSA, National Security Agency

Over 40 pdf files of international reports and assessments, released after a court case in 1980, are supplied at: www.nsa.gov/public_info/declass/ufo/index.shtml.

FBI, Federal Bureau of Investigation

The FBI files include reports concerning cattle mutilations, Roswell, Majestic 12 and Project Blue Book. There are several large pdf files covering UFO sightings and theories sent to them by members of the public, at: vault.fbi.gov/unexplained-phenomenon.

Redfern, Nick. *The FBI Files: The FBI's UFO Top Secrets Exposed* (Simon & Schuster, London, 1998).

CIA, Central Intelligence Agency

The CIA's involvement with UFO investigations is reviewed at: https://www.cia.gov/library/center-for-the-study-of-intelligence/kent-csi/vol40no5/html/v40i5a09p.htm.

NASA

Attempts have been made to get NASA to admit that astronauts have seen UFOs, and to get NASA to investigate sightings, but so far they have refused on both counts. See: www.nasa.gov/centers/glenn/technology/warp/warpfaq_prt.htm#UFO.

Henry, Richard C. *UFOs and NASA*, at: www.scientificexploration.org/journal/jse_02_2_henry.pdf.

The official website of the United States Air Force

Several fact sheets and reports about UFOs are available here. There is a page about a USAF study of the Roswell incident, which was initiated by the General Accounting Office (GAO), at: www.af.mil/information/roswell/index.asp.

US Government Accounting Office (GAO)

Majestic 12, at: archive.gao.gov/f0102/154832.pdf.

Roswell, at: www.gao.gov/products/NSIAD-95-187.

United States Navy

Their Naval Historical Center website surveys US research into UFOs and provides a list of published sources and the records kept by Project Blue Book. It also contains documents about the Bermuda Triangle and the alleged disappearance of a US Navy destroyer in 1943 – the so-called Philadelphia Experiment. See: www.history.navy.mil/faqs/faq29-1.htm.

Bermuda Triangle, at: www.history.navy.mil/faqs/faq8-1.htm.

Philadelphia Experiment, at: www.history.navy.mil/faqs/faq21-1.htm.

Contrails – Paul V. Gavin Library, Illinois Institute of Technology

This site contains links to official reports on the pros and cons of the Roswell incident: contrails.iit.edu/history/roswell/.

Project Twinkle

Elterman, Louis. *Project Twinkle. Final Report*, 27 November 1951, at: www.project1947.com/gfb/twinklereport.htm.

Ruppelt, Edward J. *The Report On Unidentified Flying Objects*, at: www.project1947.com/gfb/rufos4u.htm.

Canada

Canada's *UFOs: The Search for the Unknown*, at: www.collectionscanada.gc.ca/ufo/002029-2200.01-e.html.

Project Magnet Report, at: www.collectionscanada.gc.ca/ufo/002029-1401-e.html.

United Kingdom

McGonagle, Joe. 'Julian Hennessy: Portrait of A British UFO Pioneer', *Magonia no 92*, June 2006, at: magonia.haaan.com/2010/julian-hennessey/.

MoD, Ministry of Defence

UFO reports received by the MoD can be found at: www.gov.uk/government/publications/ufo-reports-in-the-uk.

The Project Condign UFO report is at: webarchive.nationalarchives.gov.uk/20121026065214/http://www.mod.uk/DefenceInternet/FreedomOfInformation/PublicationScheme/Search PublicationScheme/UapInTheUk AirDefenceRegion ExecutiveSummary.htm.

TNA, The National Archives

pdf files of annual UFO reports are available at: www.nationalarchives.gov.uk/ufos/.

Dr David Clarke, Andy Roberts, Gary Anthony and Joe McGonagle were mainly responsible for getting the Public Record Office (PRO) and the MoD to make their files public. A review of their work and links to the files they have uncovered at: drdavidclarke.co.uk/national-archives-ufo-files-7/.

Clarke, David. *The UFO Files: The Inside Story of Real-life Sightings* (Bloomsbury, London, 2012).

France

Groupe d'Études et d'Informations sur les Phénomènes Aérospatiaux Non-identifiés Their website contains archives, analysis, information about how to identify a UFO and sighting report forms, at: www.cnes-geipan.fr/index.php?id=385.

The COMETA Report and related documents can be found at: www.ufoevidence.org/topics/Cometa.htm.

Worldwide

List of countries that have disclosed alien and UFO documents, 'Educating Humanity' website, contains links to archives or news reports on new releases, at: www.educatinghumanity.com/2011/01/list-of-countries-that-have-disclosed.html.

Olmos, Vicente-Juan Ballester. *State-of-the-Art in UFO Disclosure Worldwide* is an excellent and detailed review of the release of UFO archives, at: www.ikaros.org.es/disclosure.pdf.

3

Waves, flaps, hot spots, polls and patterns

FO sightings seem to cluster in temporal clumps and are attracted to specific locations. A sudden eruption of sightings is known as a 'flap' or 'wave'. Flaps are more short-lived and localised, whereas waves can spread throughout a whole country or even the whole world. Places that UFOs regularly visit are known as 'window areas', 'Ufocals' or 'hot spots'.

It was only with the introduction of the umbrella term 'flying saucer' that ufologists slowly rediscovered the full extent of the pre-1947 waves and realised that UFOs are not a very new phenomenon. Indeed, as today, there has always been an underlying steady trickle of UFO sightings throughout the world that for various reasons turn into a flap or wave.

Ufologists have considered several theories to explain what triggers a flap, and why and how it spreads into a wave, but equally puzzling is why some places are UFO hot spots, and what is it that attracts UFOs to these areas?

From the very beginning the USAF and other government agencies were concerned that top secret enemy flying saucers were infiltrating the nation's airspace, for the purpose of espionage, surveillance or psychological warfare. It was particularly worrying that UFOs were often seen near nuclear bases, missile sites and military installations.

As reports flooded in they had to determine whether the sightings were of real and unusual vehicles with the ability to fly at high speeds and easily outmanoeuvre any known aircraft. This meant that they had to weed out all the misidentified sightings and study the remaining unexplained sightings to define the characteristics of such craft.

In 1955 *Project Blue Book Report No 14* summarised the findings of the Battelle Memorial Institute, which in 1952 had been contracted by the USAF to conduct a statistical analysis. 3,201 cases were recorded on IBM punch cards and run through a computer to divide them into three categories – 'known', 'unknown' and 'insufficient information'. Four experts independently decided which cases should go into each category, and all of them had to agree for a case to be deemed 'unknown'.

The sightings were divided into six categories according to these characteristics:

1. Colour of the UFO.
2. Number of UFOs seen.
3. Length of observation.
4. Brightness of the UFO.
5. Shape of the UFO.
6. Estimated speed of the UFO.

Furthermore, the quality of each sighting was assessed on a scale ranging from excellent to poor. An excellent sighting would include a case that had supporting evidence such as photographs or radar data, multiple witnesses to the same event, or trained or reliable witnesses such as pilots. The characteristics of the knowns and unknowns were compared to see if there were any statistical differences or comparisons.

The main outcome was that they identified 69% of the cases as known, 9% contained insufficient information for analysis, and 22% were judged unknown. In the identified category aircraft, balloons and celestial events caused 86% of the sightings and only 8% were regarded as hoaxes.

BELOW: The Cradle Hill skywatching area as seen from Battlesbury Hill. A digital recreation of the infamous 'Amber Gamblers' seen in the area during the 1960s and 1970s.
Kevin Goodman

Worldwide UFO waves since 1947

1947	USA
1950	South America
1952	Eastern USA
1954	Europe, principally France
1957	Southwestern USA, South America
1958	Japan
1959	Papua New Guinea
1960	New Zealand
1962	Brazil, Argentina
1964	USA
1965	Midwestern USA
1966	Soviet Union

1966–67	USA
1967	United Kingdom
1968	Spain
1970	Malaysia
1972	USA, South Africa, Latin America, Canada, Australia, Europe
1973	South America, USA
1973–74	France
1975	USA
1977	United Kingdom
1977–78	Northern Brazil, Australia, New Zealand, Chile, Italy, Middle East

1978	Italy
1979	Philippines
1982	South America
1985	Italy
1988	United Kingdom
1989–90	Belgium
1991	Mexico
1993	Israel
1996	United Kingdom
1997	USA
1999	Malaysia, China
2008	United Kingdom
2011	USA

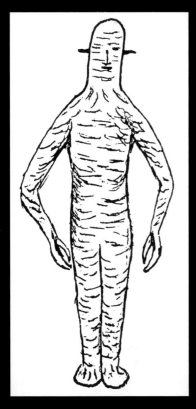

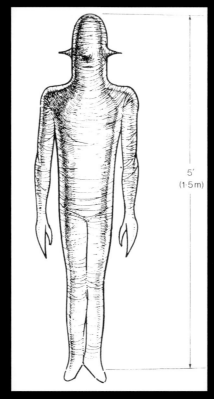

5′
(1·5 m)

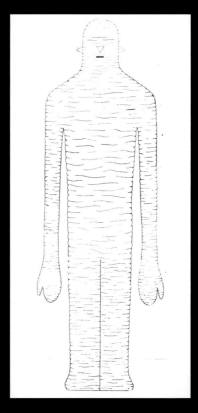

Low levels of UFO activity
US UFO researcher Richard Hall discovered four periods when worldwide UFO activity was at its lowest:

1948 to 1951
1958 to 1960
1970 to 1972
1979 to 1981

The report, one of the most detailed of its kind, uses 240 charts, maps and graphs to come to the conclusion that it is 'highly improbable that any of the reports of unidentified aerial objects … represent observations of technological developments outside the range of present-day knowledge.'

The USAF presented this to the public in October 1955 with the claim that they only discovered 3% unknowns, and that these too would be capable of explanation if more information was available. This was the continuing mantra of the USAF until it publicly washed its hands of the subject in 1969.

Analysing the unknowns

Beyond the USAF, amateur groups and civilians have worked hard to separate the identified knowns from the unknowns to obtain evidence of 'true' UFOs. The amount of true unknowns in most studies has varied widely, but it has not stopped ufologists from trying to determine correlations and patterns in respect to 'true' UFO behaviour.

As the fear of top secret aircraft faded away, the possible extraterrestrial origin of UFOs became more prominent. In this context, ufologists found correlations between UFO waves and the closeness of Mars. This superficially indicated that they were travelling from Mars, but as arch-sceptic Donald Menzel pointed out, a Martian visitor would take time to get to Earth and would not appear here at the exact time of a Mars–Earth opposition. For Menzel it was either a coincidence or people were mistaking the brighter appearance of Mars itself for a UFO, thereby causing the correlation. The Mars–UFO hypothesis has since lapsed, mainly because it does not consistently correlate with UFO waves.

Although the USAF dismissed the idea that UFOs were spying on their sensitive military bases, ufologists tend to think this is true, as it indicates that the UFOs are of an alien origin and are monitoring our activities. Alternatively, in the case of the infamous Area 51 it is believed that the USAF is actually flight-testing retrieved UFOs or using UFO wreckage to reverse-engineer advanced aircraft. On the other hand it can be argued that military personnel, especially during stressful times, are more likely to misidentify mundane phenomena for UFOs. In addition, sometimes the authorities encourage the belief in UFO activity near their bases as a cover for other nefarious activities, knowing that the ridicule factor surrounding ufology will discourage any serious investigation.

Cycles of activity

In 1971, using the UFOCAT computer catalogue, Dr David Saunders discovered that the US UFO waves occurred in five-yearly cycles: 1947, 1952, 1957 and 1967. They built slowly to a peak and then quickly fizzled away. He also noted that they moved progressively 30° in longitude eastwards. The 'missing' 1962 wave occurred in Brazil and Argentina. Using this information he was able to predict UFO waves in 1972 and 1977. However, they did not correspond exactly to the longitudes he predicted (or, as he argued, not enough data was available) and no further work on this hypothesis has been conducted.

The controversial US journalist and UFO researcher John Keel collected several hundred UFO reports for the period between 1966 and 1968, and discovered that 20% of them occurred on a Wednesday. He noted:

'No one except the US Air Force had attempted even a superficial statistical analysis of UFO sightings before, so my findings were greeted with howls of derision by the scientists who posed as experts on the phenomenon. Then Dr David Saunders of Colorado University fed several thousand sightings into a computer and found the Wednesday phenomenon remained stable. That day produced the largest number of sightings, well beyond the laws of chance and averages.'

Keel also used his data to find that the best time to see a UFO is between 8:00pm and 11:00pm on a Wednesday. Saturday night is the next best day to see or encounter a UFO at close quarters. Besides the Wednesday phenomenon, he found that UFO sightings are more likely to occur in areas where there

BELOW: Avebury in Wiltshire is a prehistoric henge monument with a circular bank and ditch enclosing a large stone circle, inside which there are two smaller circles.
Janet & Colin Bord/ Fortean Picture Library

is a magnetic fault. He called UFO hot spots 'window areas', which can be 322km (200 miles) wide. Furthermore, psychic and other paranormal events also seemed to follow the same geographical and temporal patterns, which indicated to him that they were interrelated and had at their core 'an electromagnetic basis'.

Based on his findings, Keel put forward the idea that there are specific window areas on our planet that allow visitors from other dimensions to enter our physical world. A similar idea is Dr Bernard E. Finch's concept of gateways or points in space that enable space visitors to travel from one dimension into another. Instead of being fixed at specific localities on Earth, he postulated that gates are dotted around the Sun. As the Earth orbits the Sun it will encounter these gates on an annual basis, and when they enter our gravitational field it allows UFOs to flood into our skies. The gates pass through our atmosphere so they are only open to visitations for a relatively short period.

A variant on Finch's theory was put forward by Malaysian researcher Ahmad Jamaludin, who suggests that there is a 'Source X' that emits gravity waves as it moves in an eccentric orbit between Mars and Jupiter. These waves allow UFOs from other dimensions to ride along them and visit Earth. Since

RIGHT:
Glastonbury Tor, Somerset: is it a portal into other dimensions?
Philippa Foster/ Fortean Picture Library

BELOW: Aerial view of Glastonbury Tor. The St Michael ley runs from Cornwall to East Anglia, and passes through Glastonbury and Avebury.
Fortean Picture Library

the waves pulsate on a roughly ten-year cycle, this explains why we get sudden waves and troughs of UFO appearances. Furthermore, the gravity waves trigger earthquakes on Earth when they hit weak geophysical fault lines.

Some ufologists and writers, like John Michell and F.W. Holiday, have also suggested that prehistoric constructs were built where inter-dimensional vortexes or portals exist. At these locations there were high levels of UFO activity, and sites like Stonehenge were built as representations of flying saucer craft and meeting places to facilitate contact with aliens and/or places where aliens might be worshipped. This links with the Ancient Astronaut theories that in our distant past aliens frequently visited us and built structures like Stonehenge and the Great Pyramid in Egypt.

Glastonbury is certainly a UFO and paranormal hotspot. Originally a megalithic structure used for astronomical and religious purposes adorned the summit of Glastonbury Tor, long before it was replaced and Christianised in the 12th century by St Michael's Church. Dan Green, a researcher and author based in Lincoln, has climbed to the top of the Tor on several occasions. He believes that:

'With over 2,000 years of civilisation, we still haven't fully grasped the potential of the brain nor understand the hidden natural Laws of the planet, combining both absences explains our ignorance concerning Portals.

'We are looking at symbolic Doorways by which we can journey to other realities that exist within us.

'I do think that at certain geographical power points, especially the Tor, we can randomly have an experience triggered off by electromagnetism – akin to an unknown epileptic seizure – that allows us access into unknown areas of the brain that can "transport" us to other dimensions. We can experience weeks of our spatial time away, before recovering consciousness in moments.'

Leys

UFOs were frequently seen over Glastonbury in the 1960s, leading John Michell to discover that the Tor stands on the longest ley in Britain. The ley is thought to carry psychic energy and forces in a line that joins many ancient sacred sites, including Stonehenge, from Land's End to East Anglia.

Alfred Watkins originally postulated ley (lines) in 1921; he believed that in Neolithic times, travellers used geographical features and megaliths to guide them through the landscape. Michell was one of the first to regard these lines as mystical lines of energy that surge through the land, much like the Chinese concept of feng shui. With its origins in Chinese astronomy, feng shui practitioners use the stars and landscape features to find the perfect location to construct a building.

ABOVE: Multi-coloured balls of light are regularly seen over Glastonbury Tor.
Janet & Colin Bord/ Fortean Picture Library

LEFT: Alfred Watkins, the pioneer of ley hunting.
Paul Devereux

FAR RIGHT: Old Sarum ley starts north of Stonehenge and travels through Stonehenge, Old Sarum and Salisbury Cathedral.
Fortean Picture Library

RIGHT: Aerial view over Saintbury ley in Gloucestershire, which runs from Saintbury Cross through ancient barrows to Wells Farm. Ghostly activity is linked with this 5.6km (3.5 mile) ley.
Paul Devereux/ Fortean Picture Library

Exactly 40 years after Watkins, Tony Wedd linked UFOs with leys that represented 'magnetic lines and centres'. He found that at such locations you could feel strange tingling and sensations produced by these forces, and that people could plot them using dowsing rods.

Wedd linked the leys he discovered with UFO flight-lines that were discovered by French ufologist Aime Michel, who called the subject 'Orthoteny'. After looking at the reports generated during the French 1954 wave, he found that in every 24-hour period the locations of the sightings, when plotted on a map, followed straight lines. The concept generated a lot of interest at the time but has since fallen into disrepute, for reasons discussed at the end of this chapter.

Whilst Michell was looking at Glastonbury in the late 1960s, New Zealand researcher Bruce Cathie used mathematical equations to plot a vertical and horizontal grid-pattern that covers the Earth, which he thought is the power source for flying saucer propulsion systems. When he visited strategic points on this grid, he often found secret government establishments bristling with aerials. He was told that a top secret international group of scientists ran these bases. Roberts and Gilbertson in their bleak book *The Dark Gods* also allege that leyline researchers throughout the world have found microwave towers on or near important leys. With chilling logic, they wrote: 'Microwaves are among the waves most often mentioned in terms of behaviour modification!'

Cathie's harmonic calculations relate to 'light, gravity and earth magnetic field values', and such sites as the Great Pyramids and Stonehenge are built in alignment with them, showing that ancient civilisations were aware of this grid network.

ABOVE: Alfred Watkins published his findings about ancient alignments in *The Ley Hunter's Manual* in 1927.
Fortean Picture Library

RIGHT: Plan of Old Sarum ley in Wiltshire. Old Sarum was the site of an Iron Age hill fort and was a settlement as far back as 3000 BC.
Fortean Picture Library

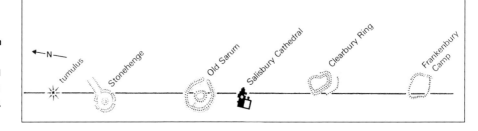

ABOVE: Cradle Hill, Warminster, at sunset.

Kevin Goodman

Warminster: an anatomy of a hot spot

When you visit Warminster, Wiltshire, it immediately strikes you as an ordinary market town. There are the usual shops, pubs and houses. Nothing on the surface tells you that this was THE centre of British – indeed, worldwide – UFO activity from the mid-1960s to early 1970s.

There are several reasons why UFOs might take an interest in this particular area. First of all, there is a strong military presence. Army manoeuvres are frequently conducted on nearby Salisbury Plain, which is restricted from public access; and not far away was the Aeroplane & Armament Experimental Establishment at Boscombe Down. Furthermore, maps do not give any details about these military training ranges that are situated to the east of the town.

The surrounding countryside consists of rolling hills and great views of the sky from horizon to horizon, making it ideal for spotting any roaming UFOs. The landscape also has links with Britain's mystic past; in particular, Stonehenge is only a few miles away to the west. The nearby Cley Hill and Battlesbury Hills are also said to be ancient burial sites.

Furthermore, the town itself has the infamous and well-named Cradle Hill. You can drive nearly to the top of this, and then it is just a short walk to its summit. In 1965, at the peak of the UFO activity, thousands of people would gather on this hill to take part in skywatches. There, UFOs were spotted literally every night, and people wondered if this was a prelude to a mass landing.

Intriguingly the 'Warminster Thing', as it was called, began with loud and mysterious noises from the sky that rattled rooftops and literally scared people from their beds. The aural attack began significantly enough in the early hours of Christmas Day 1964. They were described as being like the sound of giant hailstones, or a shockwave of violent force, clattering and droning. No suitable mundane explanation could be found for them.

In either April 1964 or February 1965, a flock of dead pigeons was found in Five Ash Lane. A local resident called David Holton alleged that they had been killed by the mysterious sounds. The troublesome noises continued throughout 1965 but had faded away by June 1966. As they took their exit, the 'Thing' manifested itself in the form of UFOs.

David Holton predicted the arrival of the UFOs in a TV feature broadcast in March 1965. He boldly claimed that the noises were created by alien spacecraft that were targeting Warminster. In May UFOs were duly spotted in the form of cigar-shaped objects high in the sky.

Holton had several letters published about his theories regarding the Thing in the town's local newspaper, *The Warminster Journal*. In the 4 June 1965 edition he wrote: 'Sufficient evidence has been discovered to enable me to assure readers that these occurrences will be reported more frequently in the future, perhaps with observations even more startling than those made hitherto.'

After this, the letters page of the *Journal* carried many letters about UFOs, mainly asserting that they are of alien origin, and the newspaper began reporting local sightings. In June and July it published letters from *Flying Saucer Review* contributor (later to become its editor), Gordon Creighton.

The Thing could have drifted into oblivion at this stage, but two major events brought it to national and international attention. On Friday 27 August 1965, conveniently at the start of a Bank Holiday weekend, a public meeting was organised to discuss the matter. TV crews and journalists from the *News of the World* and the *Daily Mirror* covered the event, where some UFO witnesses recounted their sightings and a panel of UFO experts pontificated on them. David Holton, who had been most vocal in advocating the extraterrestrial reality of the Thing, avoided the event and called it a 'pseudo-circus'.

The meeting proved inconclusive and a waste of time for those who wanted hard and fast answers to the Warminster mystery, but 7,000 visitors came to the town on that weekend to look for UFOs. For the first time since World War Two the local pubs ran dry of beer, and the souvenir shops did a roaring trade.

A local journalist, Arthur Shuttlewood, explained that 'Witnesses have come to Warminster, knowing we can guarantee a sighting.' Shuttlewood claimed that as a hard-boiled journalist he was initially sceptical about the reality of UFOs, but as reports of sightings filled his notebooks he finally conceded that there was something to them. What really tipped the balance for him was that he finally saw one for himself on 28 September 1965.

The Warminster experience

The Thing began as a sonic roof rattler and progressed to appearing as an aerial craft or lights in the sky (LITS). These UFOs ranged in shape from cigar to 'classic' saucer types. Literally hundreds of UFOs were seen before the end of the decade.

THE WARMINSTER
MYSTERY
Eyewitness accounts of
dramatic UFO sightings in England

ARTHUR SHUTTLEWOOD

Photographs and a few other forms of evidence backed up the witness testimonies. A young chap called Gordon Faulkner took the most iconic image of the Thing. This was given international coverage and appeared prominently in the *Daily Mirror* newspaper. It was also used on the cover of Shuttlewood's book, *The Warminster Mystery*. It is now widely regarded as a fake.

Other photographs of the Thing can be categorised as deliberate fakes or photographs of streetlights or other mundane objects or light sources.

Shuttlewood often scoured the hilltops surrounding Warminster in the search for landing marks, ground traces or disturbed crops. He did find a few saucer 'nests' that averaged 9.1m (30ft) in diameter and consisted of flattened crops. It can be seen that these presaged the notorious crop circles that proliferated in this region during the 1980s and 1990s.

Shuttlewood speculated that Warminster was targeted to forewarn people that the UFOs' occupants would reveal themselves to the world in the near future. They picked Warminster because of its ancient links with Cley Hill, Avebury and Stonehenge.

Shuttlewood was impressed by a witness who saw a UFO firing a device into Cley Hill, which suggested to him that this was a form of homing beacon being buried inside the hill for the benefit of UFO navigators. He was also intrigued by the discovery that at least 12 leys pass through Warminster. These leys indicated that the aliens used them as navigation aids or that the leys carried some form of energy that the UFO propulsion systems could utilise.

For British ufologists Warminster is still a place of pilgrimage, though it has never maintained or approached its former glory. Steve Dewey and John Ries, in their book *In Alien Heat*, note that several factors created the Warminster phenomenon:

1. Trigger events, in this case unidentified noises in the night.
2. The persistence of these events attracted the attention of the local population.
3. Letters to the local newspaper put these events in the context of UFOs and extraterrestrial visitors.
4. The public meeting and Gordon Faulkner's photograph heightened the expectations of the local population and visitors to the area.
5. Arthur Shuttlewood acted as a charismatic focal point who was able to channel UFO reports and stories to the national media and through his books.

It can also be added that Warminster has easy access to skywatching areas, such as Cradle Hill, where ufologists can gather to watch UFOs and trade stories.

LEFT: Kevin Goodman and Steve Dewey have both authored books about the Warminster mystery.
Kevin Goodman

LEFT: Kevin Goodman with his book *UFO Warminster*, which recounts his experience of the phenomenon over several years.
Kevin Goodman

LEFT: Mike Oram, author of *Does It Rain In Other Dimensions?*, and Kevin Goodman.
Kevin Goodman

LEFT: Kevin Goodman with a hardback edition of Arthur Shuttlewood's first book about UFO encounters in Warminster.
Kevin Goodman

Earth lights

The linking of leys and Earth energies with UFO activity in the 1960s was part of the New Age movement of the period; by the late 1970s the time was ripe to subject them to the scrutiny of more rigorous investigation. In Canada, Michael Persinger and Gyslaine Lafrenière made a statistical study of the correlation between UFO sightings and seismic-related locations. Their book *Space-Time Transients and Unusual Events* put forward evidence suggesting that tectonic strains in the Earth's crust produce enough energy to create columns of electrical energy and glowing balls of light in the atmosphere. This Tectonic Strain Theory (TST) explains why UFOs appear at window areas or certain hot spots.

At the same time British researcher Paul Devereux had been making a detailed study of ancient sites,

UFOs, paranormal incidents, geology and meteorology in the county of Leicestershire. He then went on to examine such phenomena throughout the UK and worldwide. He concluded that aside from misidentifications there is a solid rump of unexplained phenomena that constitute unidentified atmospheric phenomena (UAPs). These consist of anomalous luminescences and what have become known as 'Earth lights' (ELs), which have similar characteristics to ball lightning and earthquake lights.

Since UAPs are composed of plasma they glow at night and appear metallic in daylight, or they can even appear black. They cast out electromagnetic (EM) fields that can initiate poltergeist-like events (such as objects being thrown about) and they can even react to witnesses as if acting in an intelligent or playful manner.

Michael Persinger has gone on to consider and experiment with the possibility that the EM fields of

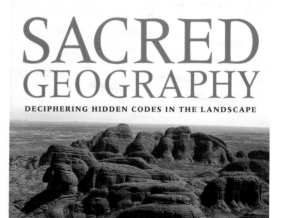

SACRED GEOGRAPHY

DECIPHERING HIDDEN CODES IN THE LANDSCAPE

Paul Devereux

LEFT: A pre-Columbian linear feature in Death Valley, California, where Paul Devereux has studied ancient ground markings. This is thought to relate to ancestral Shoshone shamanism.
Paul Devereux

BELOW: Pre-Columbian ground markings at Tie Creek, Manitoba, Canada. Paul Devereux notes: 'There aren't any leys. There are only physical alignments of different types, relating to various purposes, cultures, time periods. But there was a widespread belief in the ancient world of spirit paths – some physical, some virtual. These were often straight (especially the virtual, folk mind, ones), and that is where scholarly ley research led – to an authentic research area.'
Paul Devereux

BOTTOM: Paul Devereux, testing rocks at Carn Menyn, the Preseli Hills, Pembrokeshire, Wales, source area of the Stonehenge bluestones.
Paul Devereux

UAPs can trigger hallucinations or trance states in people who get too near to them. This would explain the many stories of 'alien' abductions and other strange encounters that are experienced after a witness has seen a light in the sky.

Paul Devereux explains that in the light of new research, 'There aren't any leys. There are only physical alignments of different types, relating to various purposes, cultures, time periods. But there was a widespread belief in the ancient world of spirit paths – some physical, some virtual. These were often straight (especially the virtual, folk mind, ones), and that is where scholarly ley research led – to an authentic research area.'

This indicates that there is a combination of geophysical and geopsychological factors at work that can produce 'high strangeness' UFO experiences. Dr David Clarke, who has investigated several Earth light hot spots in Britain, reflects that in his view 'a small (very small) percentage of those cases that remain unidentified may possibly (though not definitely) be caused by a range of very unusual natural atmospheric phenomena.

ABOVE: Will-o'-the-wisp created by a goblin who tries to lead an unsuspecting person off the path and into danger.
Richard Svensson/ Fortean Picture Library

RIGHT: Will-o'-the-wisp at Issy in France, June 1871.
Fortean Picture Library

BELOW: Nineteenth-century depiction of will-o'-the-wisp or ignis fatuus.
Fortean Picture Library

'This may or may not include a lot of things related and unrelated, both to meteorology (atmospheric plasmas, ball lightning) and geology (earthquake lights, Earth lights, will-o'-the-wisps etc), although these two categories may in themselves be related in ways we don't understand.

'Since the '90s when I co-operated with Paul Devereux my views have become more inclusive on this issue, in that I was hoping some hard science would emerge to validate the EL phenomenon. Experience has taught me that no one theory can explain everything – and I feel the EL theory was being used to do just that.

'In retrospect I realise there isn't a UFO phenomenon, there are lots of "phenomena", some understood others not, some identified others not, and it's the media and the UFO industry that transform these disparate bits into "the UFO mystery".'

Solar activity

There have been several attempts at correlating UFO sightings and sunspots. These areas of intense magnetic activity send out solar flares and coronal mass ejections (CMEs). The plasma of CMEs, consisting of electrons and protons, reach Earth at the rate of one every five days during solar minima and three a day at solar maxima. On reaching Earth, they compress the dayside of our magnetosphere and extend the magnetic tail on the night side. The release of solar energetic particles in the upper atmosphere can cause power failures, disrupt radio transmissions and damage orbiting satellites. Intriguingly, power failures and disruptions of electronic equipment are often associated with UFOs. CMEs can also produce powerful aurora displays in the northern and southern hemispheres. Another recently discovered phenomenon associated with the Sun is flux transfer events (FTEs). David Sibeck of the Goddard Space Flight Center states that using evidence obtained by the European Space Agency's fleet of four Cluster spacecraft and NASA's five THEMIS probes, the existence of FTEs is incontrovertible. They are created every eight minutes as the Earth's magnetic field briefly merges with the Sun's magnetic field. In these moments a magnetic cylindrical portal, as wide as the Earth, forms, allowing tons of high-energy particles to flow through before it closes again.

FTEs can breach the defences of our magnetosphere and load it with so much plasma that it will help trigger power outages, auroras and disturbances much like CMEs. These events might well produce UAP sightings with similar characteristics to UAPs produced by tectonic strains in the Earth's crust.

When there was a concentrated wave of UFO sightings in the 15km (9.3-mile) Hessdalen valley, Norway, researchers took the opportunity to use a range of instruments (including a magnetometer, radio spectrum analyser, infrared viewer and cameras) to make an intensive study of this phenomenon. Starting on 21 January 1984, Project Hessdalen ran uninterrupted for 36 days. It found from radar and magnetometric data that this mysterious luminous phenomenon was associated with radio emissions and magnetic disturbances. It also had some correlation with daily solar activity, which suggested that high-energy particles from the Sun might create luminous plasma balls in the upper atmosphere. An alternative view was that the solar activity merely overlapped this phenomenon and was not a factor in its creation.

Taking a more nuts and bolts viewpoint, it has been suggested that solar activity, which was at its peak in 1947, dragged a hypothetical Bracewell space probe out of orbit, making it crash at Roswell, New Mexico. (Bracewell probes are theoretical unmanned interplanetary spacecraft that might be launched by extraterrestrial civilisations to search out life-bearing planets and initiate contact with intelligent species.) This is an intriguing idea, and it would hold water if it related to only one or two really high-quality reports, but it does not explain why there have been thousands of sightings before and after 1947. Unless, of course, our solar system is full of Bracewell probes.

Statistics and plotting

Plotting UFO sightings on maps and correlating them with solar activity and leys takes us from the reaches of outer space to our most ancient history and legends. The basic problem with such studies is

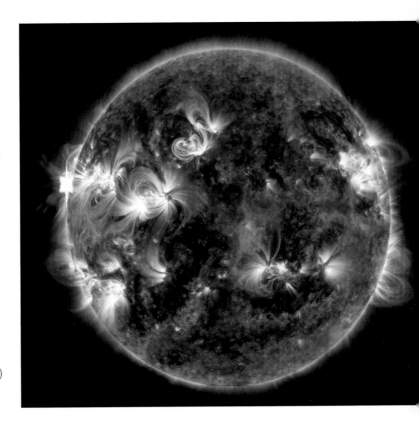

ABOVE: On 12 May 2013 an intense flare erupted from the Sun, and an associated coronal mass ejection sent billions of tons of solar particles into space.
NASA/SDO/AIA

Paranormal triangles

Most people have heard of the Bermuda Triangle, located in the North Atlantic Ocean, where ships and aircraft have mysteriously disappeared. Yet there are many similar less well-known paranormal triangles throughout the world.

A wave of UFO sightings in 1977 occurred in a triangular region formed by Pembroke, Cardigan and St David's in West Wales. This was quickly dubbed the Welsh Triangle, and even prompted a secret MoD investigation into the matter.

Since 1992 UFO sightings have centred on Bonnybridge, Scotland. This has been promoted as Scotland's UFO capital and is part of the Bonnybridge, Stirling, Edinburgh 'Falkirk Triangle'.

In the south-eastern region of Massachusetts, USA, everything from UFOs and cattle mutilations to bigfoot sightings and poltergeists have clustered in the Bridgewater Triangle. Not surprisingly, there is a Nevada Triangle that is formed by Area 51, Fresno and Reno.

It is not known why such events should cluster in triangles rather than any other shape. Perhaps, like the term 'flying saucers', the label 'triangle' provides a convenient term for a wide range of paranormal events.

UFO hot spots

USA
Brown Mountain, North
    Carolina
Gulfbreeze, Florida
Marfa, Texas
Mount Shasta, California
Rachel to Groom Lake
    (Area 51) along
    Highway 95, Nevada
Roswell, New Mexico
Sedona, Arizona
Stephenville, Texas
Yakima Indian
    reservation,
    Washington

United Kingdom
Banbury,
    Oxfordshire
Barmouth, Wales
Bonnybridge,
    Falkirk,
    Scotland
Broad Haven,
    Pembrokeshire,
    South Wales
Cannock Chase,
    Staffordshire
Epping Forest,
    North-East
    London
Glastonbury,
    Somerset
Pendle Hill,
    Lancashire
The Pennines
Rendlesham Forest,
    Suffolk
Warminster, Wiltshire

Elsewhere
Hessdalen, Norway
Hoia-Baciu Forest,
    Romania
Mexico City, Mexico
Sam Clemente, Central
    Chile
Wycliffe Well,
    Australia

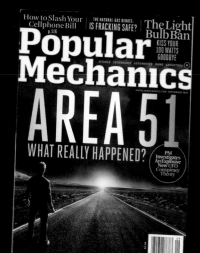

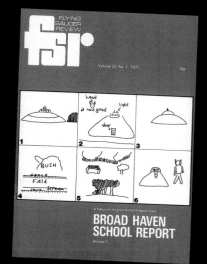

that they are only as good as their sources of data. In the context of the British MoD files and Project Condign, Dr David Clarke states:

'There is absolutely no value in my view in the data from the point of view of looking at trends in the numbers of red objects seen over Bognor Regis on Thursday nights at 9pm, etc. You can draw some basic conclusions, ie that swarms of floating orange lights in clusters spotted post-2003 are likely to be Chinese lanterns. But the raw data – because it is so contaminated – is pretty useless for statistical analysis.'

The same criticism can be extended to Persinger and Lafrenière's *Space-Time Transients and Unusual Events*, as it relied on UFO and Fortean data from magazines and books. Even worse, the evidence for Michel's Orthoteny study was based mainly on newspaper clippings. His most famous straight-line correlation was called BAVIC, because six sightings on 24 September 1954 fell on a line running from Bayonne to Vichy. He even used this line to prove that it linked with Palaeolithic caves, which contained UFO-type drawings, and he linked it with the birthplaces of famous people. This all implied that our ancestors were well aware of the UFO phenomenon and that it somehow influenced the improvement of humanity. Unfortunately, two of these sightings fell on a different date and one was 4.3km (2.7 miles) from the line. Nonetheless, other BAVIC-type lines

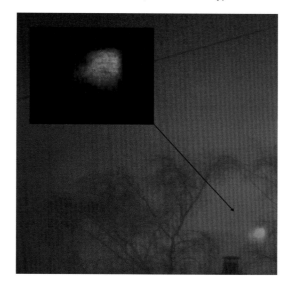

**ABOVE: Nigel Mortimer and his wife Helen,
discovered the Sun Dial Portal at Castleberg,
near Settle, North Yorkshire. It was the
location of an ancient megalithic structure,
and even today, the energies associated with
it seem to produce or attract UFOs like the
one photographed here.**
Nigel Mortimer

have been discovered throughout the world and Orthoteny encouraged the study of leys.

As can be seen with the flap phenomenon in Warminster, it only takes one or two UFO investigators, groups or promoters to highlight UFO activity in one particular area. Another area might have just as many UFO sightings, but if there are no active ufologists there and/or local media that ignores such stories, then they will never get any attention. This begs the question of which comes first, the UFO or the ufologist?

Even if the data sources are correct there is a problem with plotting them on a map. Even on a large-scale map of a small area, a pencil line will represent a 10m (32.8ft) wide ley. To create a ley you not only have to define its width and influence on people interacting with it, but you have to define the specific size of the significant points it passes through, to get any form of accuracy.

When dealing with UFO statistics the situation is equally difficult. As French ufologist Claude Mauge puts it, 'the richness and precision of a report, and the confidence of the witness who makes it, are no guarantee of its reliability; witnesses who are correct and witnesses who are mistaken present just as many details and are just as positive about what they saw.' For this reason alone it is extremely difficult to separate knowns from unknowns. Indeed, even within ufology one person's 'true' UFO is another's hoax or misidentification of Venus.

ABOVE: Artwork by Nigel Mortimer inspired by his visits to the Sun Dial Portal. His discoveries at the site are detailed on his www.openingportals.co.uk website.

Nigel Mortimer

References

'Bad Archaeology' website, at: www.badarchaeology.com/?page_id=878.

Clarke, David. The Welsh Triangle, at: www.uk-ufo.org/condign/secfilwelsh1.htm.

Devereux, Paul. Seeing the Light, Fortean Times website, at: www.forteantimes.com/features/articles/58/unidentified_atmospheric_phenomena.html.

— Spirit Roads: An Exploration of Otherworldly Routes (Collins & Brown, London, 2007).

— with Clarke, David; Roberts, Andy; and McCartney, Paul. Earth Lights Revelation (Blandford, London, 1989).

Dewey, Steve and Ries, John. In Alien Heat: The Warminster Mystery Revisited (Anomalist Books, New York, 2006).

Giant Breach in Earth's Magnetic Field Discovered, at: science1.nasa.gov/science-news/science-at-nasa/2008/16dec_giantbreach/.

Goodman, Kevin and Dewey, Steve. UFO Warminster: Cradle of Contact (Fortean Words, Exeter, 2012).

Green, Dan. Glastonbury Tor – Did a Portal Open on 26/02/07, at: ellisctaylor.homestead.com/cjglastonburytor.html.

Hall, Richard. 'Signals, Noise, and UFO Waves' International UFO Reporter, Winter, 1999, at: www.cohenufo.org/UFOWaves-RoleofNICAP-byRichardHall.htm.

Magnetic Portals Connect Earth to the Sun, at: science1.nasa.gov/science-news/science-at-nasa/2008/30oct_ftes/.

Mauge, Claude. 'UFO Statistics' in Evans, Hilary and Spencer, John (eds), UFOs: 1947–1987 (Fortean Tomes, London, 1987).

Mauge, Claude. 'UFO Statistics' in Evans, Hilary and Spencer, John (eds), UFOs: 1947–1987 (Fortean Tomes, London, 1987).

McCue, Peter. *Zones of Strangeness* (Author House, UK, 2012).

Michell, John. The Flying Saucer Vision (Abacus, London, 1974).

Military Bases suspected of UFO Activity are listed at: www.theforbiddenknowledge.com/hardtruth/military_bases_ufos.htm.

Persinger, Michael and Lafrenière, Gyslaine. Space-Time Transients and Unusual Events (Nelson Hall, Chicago, 1977).

Project Blue Book Report No 14, at: www.ufocasebook.com/pdf/specialreport14.pdf.

'Project Hessdalen' website, at: www.hessdalen.org.

Roberts, Anthony and Gilbertson, Geoff. The Dark Gods (Hutchinson, London, 1980).

Saunders, D.R. 'A Spatio-Temporal Invariant for Major UFO Waves' in Dornbos, N. (ed). Proceedings of the 1976 CUFOS Conference (Center for UFO Studies, Evanston, Illinois, 1976).

Shuttlewood, Arthur. The Warminster Mystery (Tandem, London, 1973).

Strand, Erling and Teodorani, Massimo. Data Analysis of Luminous Phenomena in Hessdalen, at: www.itacomm.net/ph/hess_e.pdf.

'UFO Warminster' website, at: www.ufo-warminster.co.uk/.

The Wanderling. The Great 1947 Sunspot, Roswell, and Coronal Mass Ejections, at: www.angelfire.com/indie/anna_jones1/roswell-sunspots.html.

The Warminster Files, the Magonia website, at: magonia.haaan.com/the-warminster-files/.

Watkins, Alfred. The Old Straight Track (Methuen, London, 1925).

4

Classifying and identifying UFOs

UFO reports can be collected from numerous sources. Some can be collected from friends or family, and all types of media provide rich sources of information. Local newspapers, radio and television often report sightings, and in recent years the Internet has expanded the range of local and international news. Internet search engines can quickly provide you with a long list of UFO websites and search engines like Google can provide you with daily or weekly email alerts based on keywords such as 'UFO sightings' or 'alien'.

Posters or flyers placed in local libraries, colleges and shops can encourage people to report sightings to you by either telephone or email. Indeed, several UFO organisations used to run dedicated 24/7 UFO reporting telephone hotlines, but they have been supplemented or replaced by UFO websites that allow witnesses to report their sighting via an online form or email address.

Since 1974 the non-profit-making National UFO Reporting Center (NUFORC), based in Seattle, USA, has run a fully staffed 24-hour telephone hotline ([206] 722-3000). Its main aim is to collect, record and document UFO reports. Over the years it has received thousands of phone calls, and law enforcement agencies, National Weather Services offices, military facilities, NASA and other official agencies routinely direct UFO witnesses to its hotline.

The Center has been so successful because it is independent from other UFO organisations

ABOVE: On 16 November 1973 two boys saw a domed disc in a field in Lemon Grove, California. After one of the boys knocked on the UFO with his torch, it flew away. On the same evening, local residents reported unusual TV interference and two telephone lines were fused. Investigators found three indentations at the site. This was ranked as a CE-II encounter.

Fortean Picture Library

ABOVE: A 1950s artistic representation of an investigation group at work collecting, mapping, recording and classifying UFO reports.

Mary Evans Picture Library

MUFOB

Merseyside UFO Bulletin   Volume 5 / Number 5

Editorial Panel: John Harney; John Rimmer; Peter Rogerson; Alan Sharp.

REPORT NO. 31725
DATE 11/3/73
INVESTIGATED BY *Albert Figgis*
RESULT *Identified.*
✓

IDENTIFYING UFOs

and it guarantees anonymity to all its callers. This policy is continued on the online UFO Sighting Report Form contained on its www.ufocenter.com website. They also summarise all the information they receive in monthly listings on the website, which shows that they get hundreds of reports every month, and they are willing to pass information on to serious UFO investigators.

A British equivalent is the UK 'UFO Sightings' website (www.uk-ufo.co.uk/), which also has an online report form. This non-profit-making group doesn't run a telephone hotline, but despite that they do get hundreds of reports every week, which they post on their website. They have also launched a 'UFO Sightings Near You' app that allows you to search their database of over 6,000 UFO reports on your mobile phone. Since the website was launched to allow members of the United Kingdom public to share their experiences online, 95% of the database consists of UK sightings that are listed by county boundaries, while the remaining 5%, consisting of worldwide reports, are listed by country. They receive up to 30 new reports a day that are uploaded within 72 hours of their receipt, and

comments about each case can be added by members of the public or experts.

The Mutual UFO Network came into existence in May 1969, when it set up a network of field investigators throughout the Midwestern states of America. According to its website, it now has a nationwide network of 800 trained field investigators, an underwater dive team and a rapid response team for investigating high priority cases. Like UK UFO, MUFON has a mobile phone app and a website that carries UFO news, investigations and sighting reports from the public. On the www.mufon.com home page you can access their live UFO event map, which as the title denotes, plots the location of UFO and alien sightings on a searchable map of the USA. The same page also carries the latest sighting reports along with statistics and trends.

MUFON's mobile telephone app is called UFO Connect (www.ufoconnect.com), and has two major features. One allows you to find information about UFOs and to navigate MUFON's online content, while the other is called Skywatch Alert, which allows you to view the latest sightings in map or listing format. Not only that, if you see a UFO and take photographs or video of it you can immediately report this information on this app, and alert anyone in the area who has the app that a UFO is present. With this you can be aware of a sighting within minutes, rather than in hours or days. No doubt similar apps will become available beyond the USA soon.

Although these apps and websites obtain lots more reports and data about sightings in a quicker and more efficient manner, they also collect lots of junk. The problem is that hoaxers and pranksters can easily send sighting reports all over the Internet, so we cannot really trust this type of data unless follow-up investigations are made to determine their validity.

Other than through the Internet, UFO witnesses often report their sightings directly to the police, air bases, coastguards and similar official and semi-official or amateur organisations, such as local astronomy groups. Rather than passively waiting to see a report in the media, you can ask these organisations to pass on any information they get from the public directly to you. Most organisations are usually willing to help, and, in return, media outlets are keen for you to pass on any newsworthy reports to them. Local media particularly welcomes UFO reports and stories, as they often arouse controversy and debate.

You should be cautious about what you say to the media, as they can easily use your words out of context, make you look silly or simply misquote you. Given that most media work to tight deadlines, they always want to obtain an explanation for a sighting before you even have a chance to meet the witness or examine the evidence. When pushed, it is certainly unwise to say that a sighting of a light in the sky is definitely the regular 10:00pm interstellar space shuttle from Alpha Centuri. So you have to resort to explaining what the witness might have seen and that you cannot give a definitive answer until you have studied the case in more detail. Since sensation sells, the more outlandish or cultish UFO experts and/or weirdest UFO stories get the most headlines and air space.

These factors mean that a relatively simple UFO sighting reported in a local newspaper can be distorted and inflated when the national tabloids get hold of it. This can make UFO investigators and UFO witnesses quoted in these stories look stupid, and can sometimes have quite serious repercussions.

A sensational UFO report will bring investigators, reporters, curiosity seekers, believers, cultists and sceptics to the doorstep of the witness. Some will confirm that the witness saw an extraterrestrial spaceship and believe everything about their story; others with a sceptical bent will try to find a conventional explanation for the sighting. The parade of characters is bewildering and can be extremely irritating and annoying, as can the associated emails and letters. In addition the witness and the rest of their family can be subjected to ridicule, and if they have an important job in the community they can face reprimand or dismissal for undermining the credibility of their position. These possible outcomes make scientists, police officers and pilots particularly reluctant to report their sightings.

Overall it is hard for a witness to know whom to trust, and they might well regret telling anyone about their experience. Thankfully most media sensations of this type don't last long before the circus moves on to other obsessions. Generally, however, most UFO witnesses are never put under the spotlight of such media frenzies, but they should be made aware of what might happen to them if they agree to have their name and photograph associated with their report. As a rule it is best to obtain permission from the witness to use their real name; if they refuse then you should respect their wish to remain anonymous.

On the one hand, UFO investigators consider UFO witnesses, especially those who publicly report an abduction experience, to be heroes willing to suffer social stigma and rejection to promote our understanding of this phenomenon. On the other hand, debunkers regard those who report sensational experiences to be suffering mental illness, delusions and the like, or merely publicity seekers willing to sell their granny to appear on TV and obtain their '15 minutes of fame'.

BELOW: Stephen Michalak was at Falcon Lake, Manitoba, Canada, when he saw two UFOs fly overhead on 20 May 1967. One landed nearby, but as he approached the craft it blasted off. The hot 'exhaust' from the UFO left grid-like burns on his chest, burned his cap and shirt, and melted his glove. A CE-II encounter.
Fortean Picture Library

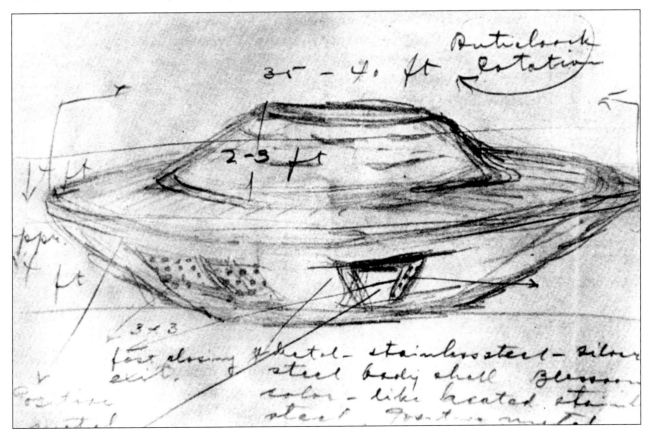

RIGHT: *Official UFO* magazine, January 1976, told its readers how to report and investigate UFO reports.

N. Watson

BELOW: To eliminate the 'plague of poor reports', *Official UFO* magazine suggested that the direction and angular elevation of a UFO are important pieces of information to collect from witnesses.

N. Watson

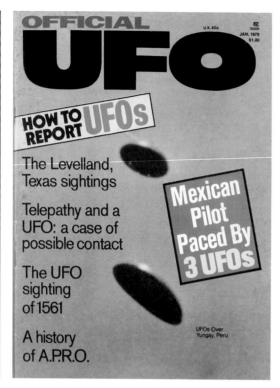

OFFICIAL

UFO

U.K. 40p
JAN. 1976
$1.00

HOW TO REPORT UFOs

The Levelland, Texas sightings

Telepathy and a UFO: a case of possible contact

The UFO sighting of 1561

A history of A.P.R.O.

Mexican Pilot Paced By 3 UFOs

UFOs Over Yungay, Peru

Directional Data Diagram

Angular Estimation Chart

Sky Map

Date Of Sighting: _____
(Day)   (Month)   (Year)
Location: _____
Notes: _____
_____
_____
_____

90°
Zenith
60°
60°
30°
30°
225° 270° 315°
SW W NW
0°
0°
180° 135° 90° 45° 0°
S SE E NE N

Sighting report forms

It is always better if you can obtain information about a UFO sighting as soon as possible, because memories quickly fade and become distorted.

Sighting report forms are useful for collecting information and provide a basis for analysis and further investigation. The very first sighting report forms were created by the British government during World War One. These were distributed to every police force in the country and were meant to be filled in by any witness who reported seeing what might be an enemy aircraft or any other type of aerial threat. The completed forms were sent to the MI5 headquarters in London for analysis, and if they considered that any such sighting posed a threat to national security they would sanction a more thorough investigation. Forty years later the British Ministry of Defence had a similar attitude towards the UFO phenomenon.

Even if adequate information is gathered from forms or interviews there can be differences of opinion about what was actually seen. This was underlined when enemy aircraft were seen over Los Angeles in 1942. The US Navy and US 4th Air Force concluded that there had been no enemy aircraft over the area in question, and that the sightings were caused by suggestion and expectation. In contrast, the US Army evaluated the same reports and concluded that, hidden within the cloud of confusion and rumour, enemy aircraft had actually visited the Los Angeles area.

The USAF created an extensive sighting report form that was developed by the Battelle Memorial Institute non-profit-making science and technology company. The analysis is carried out in their Sixth Status Report submitted to the Air Intelligence Technical Center, Wright Patterson Air Force Base (www.bluebookarchive.org/page. aspx?PageCode=NARA-PBB86-493). It notes that in September and October 1952 they tested out a questionnaire that would be suitable for non-technical witnesses and would have the flexibility to obtain as much information as possible with a view to machine-coding the data. It included questions that would detect the 'over-imaginative individual'. Anyone who described 'unknown creatures or interplanetary visitors' was not regarded as 'a discerning observer', and their report would be eliminated from any further analysis. The forms collected three main categories of information:

1. Date, time and location of the witness.
2. A description of the weather and viewing conditions at the time.
3. A description of the UFO.

Subsequent sighting report forms have generally followed the format of those created in the 1950s. The types of question posed in standard sighting report forms are listed in Appendix 1, along with references to where you can find more advanced types of report forms.

Such forms gather a lot of information, but they are not a total substitute for a face-to-face interview with the witness. Indeed, the maverick US ufologist John Keel suggested that they are useless, as astronomers and pilots designed them for the sole purpose of identifying a conventional explanation for such sightings. Keel noted from his own experience that witnesses are notoriously bad at estimating the direction, height and speed of objects seen in the sky. He advocated the use of in-depth interviews with the witness and that we should gather more information about their beliefs and experiences prior to and after their sighting. In this manner, wider aspects of the UFO phenomenon could be revealed beyond the strict confines of a sighting report form.

To make sense of the nature of the UFO phenomenon by separating identified sightings from the 'genuinely' unexplained sightings, and to detect any patterns of UFO behaviour, numerous UFO classification systems have been introduced with varying levels of success.

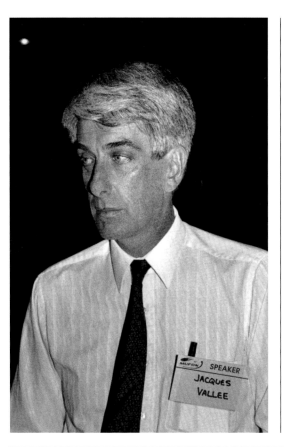

LEFT: Jacques Vallée, a computer scientist, astronomer and influential ufologist, originally analysed UFO data to determine if they were of an extraterrestrial origin. In the 1970s he regarded UFOs in the context of folklore and psychic phenoma.
Dennis Stacy/Fortean Picture Library

Classification systems

The French astronomer and computer scientist Jacques Vallée created the first significant UFO classification system in 1961. It was created as a means to study the hundreds of sighting reports gathered in France, and to help test different hypotheses without bias. Instead of classifying sightings by how the witness described the physical appearance of the UFO, Vallée decided to classify sightings according to how the UFO behaved in the sky.

Vallée's system consists of five major categories.

TYPE I

Type I sightings are divided into four subcategories:

Type Ia: UFOs seen to travel near to the ground or that land on the ground.
Type Ib: UFOs seen close to bodies of water.
Type Ic: Occupants of a UFO taking an interest in human signals or gestures.
Type Id: A UFO taking an interest in a terrestrial vehicle.

TYPE II

Classifies observations of cloud cigars. These were commonly seen throughout Europe in 1954, but are now so rare that Vallée has discarded this category.

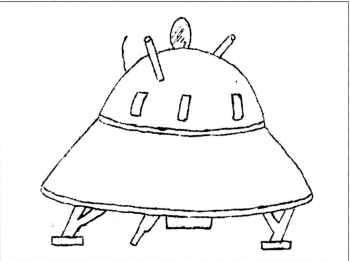

Type IIa: Cigar-type UFO seen erratically moving in the sky.
Type IIb: Cigar-type UFO stationary in the sky that sends out secondary objects.
Type IIc: Cigar-type UFO surrounded by secondary objects.

TYPE III

This includes sightings of spherical or elliptical UFOs that stop, hover or carry out any other interrupted or discontinuous flight trajectory.

ABOVE: Twelve-year-old William Holland drew this UFO that he saw on 22 July 1963 when he was playing with friends in Merseyside. It had a red flashing light on top. A CE-I encounter.
Fortean Picture Library

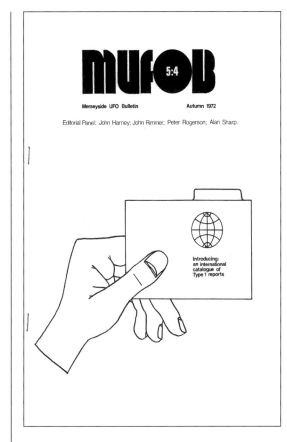

Merseyside UFO Bulletin   Autumn 1972

Editorial Panel: John Harney; John Rimmer; Peter Rogerson; Alan Sharp.

Introducing: an international catalogue of Type 1 reports

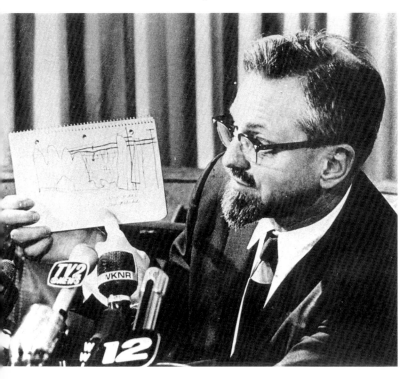

Type IIIa: UFO engages in a pendulum motion or carries out a 'falling leaf' manoeuvre.
Type IIIb: UFO interrupts its flight to hover for a few moments before continuing its flight.
Type IIIc: Whilst hovering the UFO changes its luminosity or shape or discharges a secondary object.
Type IIId: A swarm of UFOs that move around each other.
Type IIIe: UFO moves slower over a certain area, moves in circles or changes course.

TYPE IV

Features sightings of UFOs that follow an uninterrupted flight path.

Type IVa: Continuous flight of a UFO.
Type IVb: UFO changes course due to the presence of a conventional aircraft.
Type IVc: UFOs that fly in formation.
Type IVd: UFOs that follow a wave-like or zigzag trajectory.

TYPE V

This categorises UFOs that do not look like they have a solid structure.

Type Va: Extended apparent diameter, non-point source luminous objects.
Type Vb: Star-like objects, motionless for extended periods.
Type Vc: Star-like objects rapidly crossing the sky, possibly with peculiar trajectories.

Astronomer Dr J. Allen Hynek, who worked as an advisor on Project Sign, Project Grudge and Project Blue Book, devised a rival classification system that emphasised the distance and behaviour of the UFO rather than its flight characteristics. It achieved worldwide fame in 1977 when Steven Spielberg used the 'close encounters of the third kind' category designated by Hynek as the name for his Hollywood blockbuster about UFOs. The Hynek system consists of six major divisions, which have been extended since its creation in the 1970s:

NL
NOCTURNAL LIGHTS

This is the most commonly reported type of UFO. The movement and appearance of these lights is significantly different from conventional light sources.

DD
DAYLIGHT DISCS

As the name suggests these are sightings of disc- or oval-shaped metallic objects that have the ability to hover, and can accelerate out of sight very rapidly.

RV
RADAR-VISUAL UFO CASES

Unidentified radar 'blips' that can be correlated with visual sightings of a UFO.

CEI
CLOSE ENCOUNTERS OF THE FIRST KIND

UFOs seen within 500ft (152m) of the witness.

CEII
CLOSE ENCOUNTERS OF THE SECOND KIND

A UFO that leaves markings on the ground, causes burns or paralysis to humans, frightens animals, interferes with car engines or TV and radio reception.

CEIII
CLOSE ENCOUNTERS OF THE THIRD KIND

A UFO and its occupants are seen in close proximity to the witness.

Ufologist Ted Bloecher gave a finer definition of the different varieties of CEIII encounters:

A: An entity is explicitly seen inside the UFO, either through windows, portholes, doorways or translucent domes on the craft.

B: An entity is observed emerging from and/or entering the UFO.

C: An entity is seen in the vicinity of a UFO, but not going in or out of it.

D: An entity is seen but no UFO is visible nearby. UFO activity is reported by independent witnesses in the local area, implying the entity is connected with the UFO sightings.

E: An entity is seen independently of any nearby UFO or UFO activity in the area.

F: The witness does not see a UFO entity or UFO but experiences some kind of direct or psychic communication from an alien source.

G: This coincides with the CEIV category. Either the witness is voluntarily or involuntarily taken inside a UFO; this might not include an encounter with entities.

H: An alien is injured, captured and/or killed.

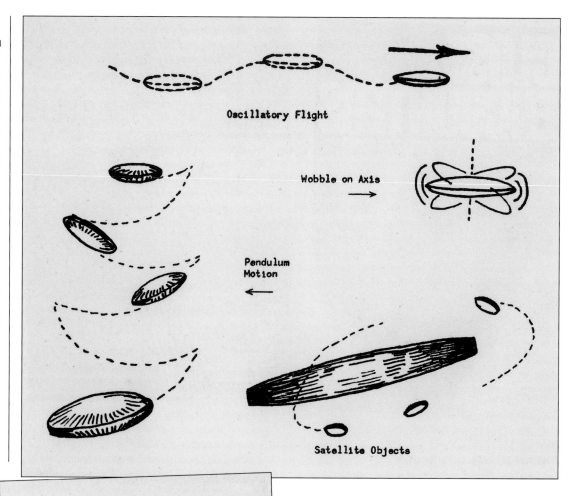

THE NATIONAL INVESTIGATIONS COMMITTEE ON AERIAL PHENOMENA (NICAP)

THE UFO EVIDENCE

EDITED BY RICHARD H. HALL

Close encounters of the fourth and fifth kind were not included in Hynek's original classification scheme. This was because he wanted to present a serious and scientific picture of the UFO phenomenon and was reluctant to include any mention of the appearance of aliens or any other type of UFO-related entity:

CEIV
CLOSE ENCOUNTERS OF THE FOURTH KIND
An encounter with a UFO and abduction of the witness.

Ufologists have tended to favour Hynek's system over Vallée's, and as ufology has embraced ever-stranger types of case the categories have been expanded to accommodate them. These later categories are not as universally used or accepted:

CEV
CLOSE ENCOUNTERS OF THE FIFTH KIND
A mutual interaction between human and extraterrestrial intelligence via telepathy or channelling.

CEVI
CLOSE ENCOUNTERS OF THE SIXTH KIND
Murder or injury of animals and humans allegedly caused by aliens. This includes cattle mutilation cases.

CEVII
CLOSE ENCOUNTERS OF THE SEVENTH KIND

Human/alien hybrids created by an alien breeding programme.

A few more categories were added by Hynek's Center for UFO Studies (CUFOS):

AM: Animal mutilation reports, except cases involving cattle.

BH: Black or mystery helicopter sightings.

BVM: 'Blessed Virgin Mary' visions.

CM: Cattle mutilation reports.

CR: Crashed discs and their retrieval.

DL: Daylight lights (previously grouped with Hynek's DD/Daylight discs).

DO: Daylight objects (previously grouped with Hynek's DD/Daylight discs).

ND: Nocturnal discs (previously grouped with Hynek's NL/Nocturnal lights).

NO: Nocturnal objects (previously grouped with Hynek's NL/Nocturnal lights).

RR: Radar-only UFO reports.

TC: Trace cases, such as crop circles that do not involve a UFO sighting.

UX: Unexplained auditory events such as explosions or sonic booms.

Even with all these categories, none has been created to include alien underground or underwater alien bases, alien implants or encounters with Men in Black.

Hynek highlighted the fact that these categories seek only to differentiate the types of witnesses' perceptions of UFOs, and do not assume that they are necessarily of physically real objects. The system also does not attempt to determine the nature or origin of UFOs.

The Vallée and Hynek systems and their variations are widely used to tackle the huge quantities of information generated by UFO reports, since their classifications facilitate the coding of elements of a UFO report on a computer database so that patterns can be discerned and analysed. However, this very much depends on the quality of the data. Also, since they do not help us determine the validity of sightings Hynek proposed the adoption of a 'Strangeness/Probability' rating that would highlight the most important cases worthy of further investigation.

The Strangeness Rating tries to measure the information in a UFO report that goes beyond our common-sense expectations. A nocturnal light moving across the sky would get a low numerical Strangeness Rating, whereas a close encounter with a disc-shaped craft that sends out a light that burns the witness in the face would get a high rating.

The Probability Rating gives a numerical value

to the reliability and consistency of the UFO report. If the witness or witnesses seem unreliable the case should get a low Probability Rating, while a high numerical value should be given to a case that has reliable witnesses and supporting evidence.

The US Computer UFO Network (CUFON) developed a Strangeness/Probability rating system to code their UFO report database:

S – STRANGENESS

This can be rated from 1 to 5 as follows:

1: Explained or explainable.
2: Probably explainable with more data.
3: Possibly explainable, but with elements of strangeness.
4: Strange. Does not conform to known principles.
5: Highly strange. Definitely indicative of intelligent guidance.

P – PROBABILITY

This is rated 1 to 5 depending on the credibility of the witnesses and the soundness of the evidence supporting their claims:

1: Not credible or sound.
2: Highly unreliable or probably a hoax.
3: Somewhat credible or indeterminate.
4: Credible and sound.
5: Highly credible, leaving almost no doubt.

LEFT: The cover of the June 2008 edition of *UFO Magazine* depicts a graphic close encounter of the third kind.

UFO Magazine

Using this system a sighting of an aircraft by a credible witness would rate as an S1/P4, and a close encounter reported by an unreliable witness would be rated as S5/P2.

Jacques Vallée created a similar 'SVP' rating system, which gives a numerical value to three aspects of a UFO report:

S (SOURCE RELIABILITY RATING)
0: Unknown or unreliable source.
1: Report attributed to a known source of unknown or uncalibrated reliability.
2: Reliable source, second-hand.
3: Reliable source, first-hand.
4: First-hand personal interview with the witness by a source of proven reliability.

V (SITE VISIT RATING)
0: No site visit, or answer unknown.
1: Site visit by a casual person not familiar with the phenomena.
2: Site visited by persons familiar with the phenomena.
3: Site visit by a reliable investigator with some experience.
4: Site visit by a skilled analyst.

P (POSSIBLE EXPLANATIONS RATING)
0: Data consistent with one or more natural causes.
1: Natural explanation requires only slight modification of the data.
2: Natural explanation requires major alteration of one parameter.
3: Natural explanation requires major alteration of several parameters.
4: No natural explanation possible, given the evidence.

BELOW: Artist's depiction of a UFO seen over Sweden. A CE-I encounter.
Richard Svensson/ Fortean Picture Library

If a single report scores more than two in each rating it indicates that it is a significant case worthy of further study. Although useful, these types of ratings are very subjective and have not been universally adopted by ufologists.

Jenny Randles and Peter Warrington proposed the introduction of a further rating system to determine the 'Investigation Level' of published UFO reports, which would indicate their validity and probability. The Investigation Levels were coded as follows:

LEVEL A
A report that has received an on-site investigation by experienced investigators.

LEVEL B
Investigators conducted an interview with the witness or witnesses but there was no follow-through investigation into the case.

LEVEL C
The witness has simply completed a standard UFO sighting report form. No interviews conducted with the witness.

LEVEL D
The report consists solely of some form of written communication from the witness.

LEVEL E
The report is based on information received second-hand (such as a newspaper account). There has been no follow-up investigation at all.

However, since its suggestion in 1979 ufologists or ufological publications have not used this rating system, though it is a handy reminder of what we should consider when we read a UFO report. With the Internet, it is now easier for anyone to report a UFO sighting to the whole world, and far easier for anyone to make up a story that amounts to a Level D case.

The French GEIPAN organisation developed an easy-to-use system that classified reports according to the level of difficulty required to explain or identify UFO sightings:

TYPE A
The phenomenon is fully and unambiguously identified.

TYPE B
The nature of the phenomenon has probably been identified but some doubt remains.

TYPE C
The report cannot be analysed since it lacks precision, so no opinion can be formed.

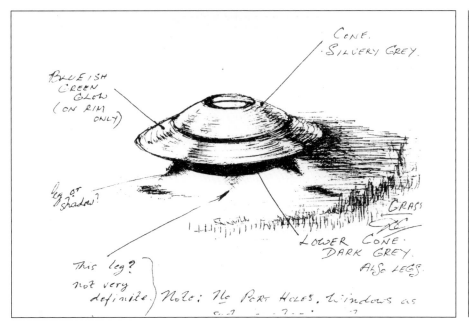

RIGHT: Dennis Crowe drew this UFO that he saw land at Vaucluse Beach, Sydney, Australia, on 19 July 1965. A CE-II encounter.

Fortean Picture Library

CONE.
. SILVERY GREY.

BLUEISH
GREEN
GLOW
(ON RIM
ONLY)

leg or
shadow?

GRASS

This leg?
not very
definite.) Note: No PORT HOLES. Windows as

LOWER CONE.
DARK GREY.
ALSO LEGS.

TYPE D

The witness testimony is consistent and accurate but cannot be interpreted in terms of conventional phenomena.

Type A and B cases are also subdivided into categories of explanation, such as mundane astronomical and aeronautical causes. Mini-investigations were carried out on Type B and C cases, and full investigations were reserved for Type D cases.

As psychic and paranormal phenomena became more commonly associated with UFO sightings and abductions, Vallée attempted to consolidate his classification system with Hynek's and to incorporate these newer elements. In this scheme he has four major categories:

AN: Anomalous phenomenon.
MA: The behaviour of the UFO.
FB: Fly-by characteristics of the UFO.
CE: Close encounters.

Each category is rated according to five criteria:

1. Sighting.
2. Physical effects.
3. Encounter with an alien or entity.
4. Transformation of the sense of reality, transport to another realm or abduction by UFO.
5. Injury or death caused by the encounter.

The CE category is analogous to Hynek's system, the MA and FB ratings conform to Vallée's 'Type' scheme, whilst the AN ratings include such anomalies as crop circles, interaction with entities and unexplained injuries.

"I never saw my father so scared." Tom Carey reports.

UFO
magazine

ABDUCTIONS
BY BEINGS
FROM THE SKY
IS MANKIND'S
OLDEST STORY.

JACQUES
Vallee
Aubeck
CHRIS

Vol. 24 No. 3   Issue # 156

LEFT: Jacques Vallée and Chris Aubeck on the May 2011 cover of *UFO Magazine*, to promote the publication of their book *Wonders in the Skies: Unexplained Aerial Objects from Antiquity to Modern Times.*

UFO Magazine

References

The J. Allen Hynek Center for UFO Studies (CUFOS) website, at: www.cufos.org/HynekClass.html.
Vallée, Jacques F. *A System of Classification and Reliability Indicators for the Analysis of the Behavior of Unidentified Aerial Phenomena*, at: www.jacquesvallee.net/bookdocs/classif.pdf.

5

Identifying Type I cases

---

here is a long list of possible explanations for UFO sightings, especially if they come under Hynek's 'Nocturnal lights', 'Daylight discs' and 'Close encounters of the first kind' (CEI) categories. Although the figure is disputed and depends on what database you use, between 90% and 98% of all 'UFO' sightings can actually be explained, making them 'identified flying objects' (IFOs).

With varying levels of certainty, up to 10% remain unidentified, although sceptics would be quick to point out that this is due to having insufficient information to identify them, or that they are due to extremely rare phenomena that have nothing to do with aliens from outer space. For others, the remaining 2% to 10% of sightings are of 'true UFOs' that are produced by exceptional and exotic phenomena beyond the grasp and understanding of modern-day science.

Sightings can be identified under the following categories:

1. Man-made terrestrial objects.
2. Natural terrestrial phenomena.
3. Natural celestial phenomena.
4. Man-made celestial objects.

1 Man-made terrestrial objects

Aircraft

During daytime, aircraft in the distance can easily reflect light and give the impression that a ball of light is moving through the sky. An aircraft, especially if it is flying towards or away from the horizon at a far

distance, can also look like a domed flying saucer, as it is hard to distinguish the craft's wings from its fuselage. As an aircraft turns or moves towards or away from the observer it can look as if it is hovering in the sky.

At night the navigation and landing lights of aircraft can also generate UFO sightings. Aircraft are usually identified as such by their engine noise, but loud background sounds or the distance of the UFO and wind direction can hide them from the witness. The lights of a large tanker aircraft refuelling several small jet aircraft can look like an impressive formation of UFOs.

One example of a classic UFO case caused by aircraft involves sightings of what are now known as the 'Phoenix Lights'. On the night of 13 March 1997, a 'V' formation of five UFOs was seen moving rapidly over the state of Arizona from 8:30pm to 8:45pm.

ABOVE: Contrail of an aircraft in the distance.
Tim Printy

LEFT: An aircraft reflecting light in the distance.
Tim Printy

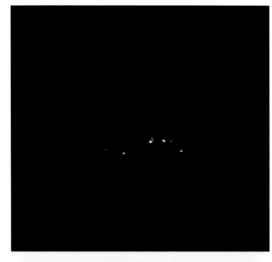

RIGHT: Aircraft lights at night, giving the impression of a V-shaped formation of UFOs or a single triangular UFO.

Tim Printy

RIGHT: Long exposure of aircraft landing lights, produces a picture of a luminous, cigar-shaped craft.

Tim Printy

BELOW: The Moon is often mistaken for a UFO. When travelling in a car it can appear to be following you.

Tim Printy

Many witnesses thought they saw a black triangle supposedly carrying these lights, but two witnesses who viewed them through a telescope identified them as a formation of high-altitude aircraft. The lights passed over Phoenix at 8:30pm, and at 10:00pm more supposed UFOs were seen over the city that were actually caused by an aircraft dropping flares.

Several websites carry information about civilian air traffic routes and the location of airports and airfields. If these are of no help in explaining such sightings, local flying or gliding clubs can tell you if they logged any flights at the time they were seen.

Military flights are harder to track as they are often not made public, and in the United Kingdom the Royal Air Force is not always aware of aircraft operated by the USAF. In addition you have to take into account illegal, unscheduled or unrecorded flights.

In a report entitled *The CIA's Role in the Study of UFOs, 1947–90*, Gerald K. Haines claims that half of all UFO reports in the USA from the late 1950s to the 1960s were due to the manned, high-altitude flights of U2 and SR-71 aircraft (operated under Project Oxcart). Flying at 60,000 feet, they reflected sunlight that made them look like fiery fast-moving objects in the sky. Since they were top secret, the USAF explained away the sightings as temperature inversions.

In the 1970s Allan Hendry, working for J. Allen Hynek's Center for UFO Studies (CUFOS), claimed that a quarter of night-time UFO sightings could be identified as being due to advertising aircraft. Seen at low altitudes in populated areas, their illuminated signs give the impression of a hovering craft with rotating lights.

Model aircraft

Many individuals and clubs fly remote-controlled aircraft, and because it is difficult to judge distance and size these can be mistaken for larger craft, and at night can look even more exotic. Pranksters are likely to use them to generate UFO sightings.

Helicopters

Helicopters have the ability to travel quickly, vertically and horizontally, and can hover over areas, making their combination of manoeuvres puzzling to observers, especially at night when they might be carrying lights or directing a searchlight downwards. The main giveaway is that they are very noisy and tend to fly at low altitudes.

Sightings of so-called 'black helicopters' – craft lacking any insignia or markings – were associated with cattle mutilation cases in the USA during the 1970s, and in northern England there was a wave of phantom helicopter sightings from early 1973 to the beginning of 1974. Mysterious helicopters have been reported to take an interest in UFO witnesses and UFO investigators, and are linked with sinister government surveillance operations by conspiracy theorists.

Drones

Unmanned drones are remotely controlled aircraft. Unmanned aerial vehicles (UAVs) were originally used by the military in battlefield areas and are now increasingly used for civilian purposes. They can vary in size and have relatively quiet engines. An outstanding feature is that they can remain in the air for several hours or days without having to land or refuel.

Flares

Flares are deployed by the military during training operations or in combat to divert heat-seeking missiles. They are suspended from parachutes, and it can take half an hour before they burn out. When dropped as a cluster they can give the appearance of a hovering craft with lights and portholes on its side. Flares are given as the explanation for the second set of UFO sightings of the Phoenix Lights. Apparently an A10 Thunderbolt jet fighter aircraft belonging to the 104th Fighter Squadron, a unit of the Maryland Air National Guard, dropped the flares at the end of a training flight.

LEFT: Although very noisy, helicopters can be mistaken for UFOs, or are connected with covert operations linked to UFO sightings and cattle mutilations.
Tim Printy

ABOVE: NASA's Ikhana drone carries science and navigation instruments in the bulging fairing at the front of its fuselage.
NASA/Tony Landis

LEFT: Two Golden Hawk drones at NASA's Dryden Flight Research Center.
NASA/Tony Landis

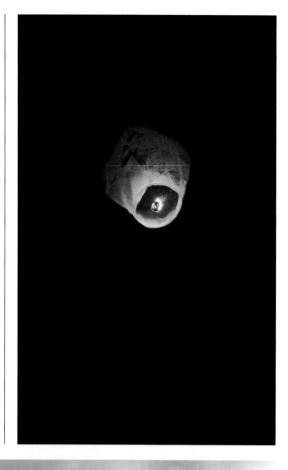

Aircraft carrying out photographic reconnaissance work often use flares or strobe lights to illuminate the ground. Aircraft that take infrared photographs are equipped with noisy turbine generators that make a whining sound. Most of these types of flights are carried out in the morning by aircraft that fly at a low speed and altitude.

Fireworks, either set off individually or as part of a display, can also trigger UFO sightings – especially if they are seen from a distance or are unexpected.

Chinese lanterns

These are simple fire balloons that have an illuminated heat source suspended beneath a paper or plastic bag. The heat causes the lantern to rise in the air, where it can drift with the winds to a height of 1.6km (1 mile). They are visible for several minutes as an orange glowing object floating in the night sky. A number of lanterns are often sent aloft at the same time to celebrate national holidays, weddings and parties. To an observer they can look like a formation of UFOs silently flying overhead. In the past few years they have probably become the most common cause of UFO sightings in the United Kingdom.

Weather balloons

Approximately 900 weather balloons are simultaneously launched at noon and midnight Greenwich Mean Time throughout the world. They carry an instrument called a radio sonde, which senses temperature, humidity and atmospheric pressure. Radar or global positioning systems (GPS) are used to track their flight path to get data about the prevailing wind conditions. During their average flight time of two hours such balloons might travel as far as 200km (125 miles) from their launching point. On reaching a height of 35,000m (115,000ft) the balloon is designed to burst, and a parachute is released to return the radio sonde back to Earth in one piece.

The latex balloons are filled with helium and at launch they are approximately 1.8m (6ft) in diameter; before bursting at their maximum height range the balloons can be 6m (20ft) in diameter. A lightstick is attached to the balloon for night-time launches so that it can be visually tracked until a radio signal is clearly received.

During daylight hours they can be spotted as silvery conical or triangular objects that move slowly and can make dramatic changes in direction due to the influence of winds and thermal updrafts.

Military balloons

Significantly, in 1947 the US Navy began testing large polyethylene balloons that could travel to a height of 30km (100,000ft) and expand to a diameter of 30m (100ft). Under Project Skyhook, over 1,500 balloons of this type were launched during the 1950s.

A Skyhook balloon was believed to have been responsible for the death of Captain Thomas F. Mantell, who crashed his P-51 Mustang aircraft whilst trying to chase a UFO on 7 January 1948. Since this was a top secret project the USAF preferred to explain the incident as being due to the misidentification of Venus.

Under Project Mogul the US Army Air Force sent high-altitude balloons over the Soviet Union from 1947 to 1948 to detect ballistic missile and atomic bomb testing. Mogul Flight number 4, launched from Alamogordo, New Mexico, on 4 June 1947 was targeted by a USAF report in 1994 as the primary source of the Roswell UFO crash-landing rumours.

Solar balloons

These consist of thin black envelopes that are heated by the Sun. The warm air expanding inside the envelope enables them to rise to altitudes as high as 9,000m (30,000ft). They can be virtually any shape, including triangular, disc and cigar-shaped, and although they are usually tethered they can escape and travel vast distances.

In the UK there have been many sightings and video recordings of objects in the sky that might have been caused by solar balloons, which can be easily made from black bin bags taped together or purchased in high street shops or online. Indeed, some are even sold as 'flying saucer' shaped craft.

Balloons of most types can be identified by the following criteria:

1. Shape – this can vary from teardrop, cylindrical and conical to oval, round or disc shapes. Tetrahedral balloons can appear delta-shaped and create the illusion of vertical surfaces.
2. Its brightness and colour can vary according to the type of material it is made from and the time of day. At sunrise and sunset it can appear orange. The reflection of city lights or moonlight from a balloon can also make it look more self-luminous and eerie.
3. Duration – a sighting of a balloon is likely to last from a few minutes up to a few hours.
4. Movement – generally they travel slowly, but can reach speeds of 241kph (150mph). As it rises, the balloon will increase in size and might move

LEFT: A Project Mogul balloon being prepared for launch.
Fortean Picture Library

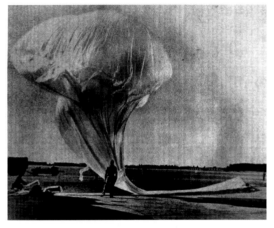

LEFT: Huge Skyhook balloons like this were regularly launched from the west coast of the USA. The balloon would become egg or disc shaped as it undulated in the air currents.
Fortean Picture Library

LEFT: Project Mogul originally used rubber meteorological balloons, but replaced them with more durable polyethylene balloons.
Fortean Picture Library

erratically. Wind currents at a higher altitude are different from those at ground level, making the observer think it is 'going against the wind'.

5. The balloon's rotation can make it look like it is a bright flashing light in the sky.

6. A cluster of balloons can look like a formation of UFOs moving in unison.

7. The parachute recovery of the payload or the rapid descent of a balloon envelope can appear like a UFO crashing to the ground.

8. Temperature inversions can create the illusion of a second balloon in the vicinity.

9. Having no engines, balloons are completely silent, although manned balloons do carry a noisy burner.

Kites

Kites can fly to high altitudes and come in a wide range of sizes and shapes. They are mostly flown during daylight, but at night they can appear more mysterious, especially if they carry lights.

Blimps

Those like the famous Goodyear blimps are helium-filled, non-rigid airships. They fly at a slow speed at low altitudes, and when illuminated at night can give the impression of a huge flying saucer. They have engines that can be heard if they get relatively close to the observer.

Smaller tethered blimps are also used for advertising purposes. If illuminated at night these can also give rise to UFO sightings.

Searchlights and lasers

Outdoor 'sky laser' lights are used by such venues as nightclubs, cinemas, festivals, celebrations and music concerts. The lasers produce circles of light that are reflected off clouds. They can be seen many miles away and can look like a dark round craft with lights around its edges. Conventional searchlights can also produce UFO reports when they reflect off clouds at night, and can give the impression of sending light downwards rather than upwards into the sky.

Hand-held laser pointers have also become more common and easy to buy. The US Federal Aviation Administration (FAA) has recorded 3,000 incidents of them being pointed at aircraft in the past 20 years. So far they haven't caused any serious accidents, but they do startle and distract pilots and aircrew. They could easily be mistaken for UFOs, especially if used by pranksters and hoaxers.

2 Natural terrestrial phenomena

Clouds

Surprisingly even clouds can be mistaken for UFOs. Some ufologists claim that UFOs either disguise themselves as clouds or hide behind them. There is some justification for thinking lenticular clouds are UFOs, since they take on classic flying saucer shapes and can have brightly coloured edges. They are turbulent clouds that usually, but not always, form near mountain ranges. Lenticular clouds regularly gather over Mount Shasta, a UFO hot spot, and over Mount Rainier, where Kenneth Arnold saw his formation of UFOs in 1947.

At night in the polar regions, when the Sun is below the horizon, bluish-coloured noctilucent clouds are visible at altitudes up to 85km (53 miles). They are a relatively recent phenomenon and climate change seems to be making them more frequently seen at lower latitudes.

Clouds are more likely to initiate UFO sightings by reflecting searchlights and the headlight beams of cars travelling uphill, which give the impression of moving illuminated objects in the sky. If the cloud is at a high altitude it might well move in a direction opposite to the wind direction experienced on the ground. Such reports can be checked by visiting the locality or checking a map for roads on the slopes of hills, and by finding out if searchlights are used in the vicinity.

Mirages and temperature inversions

Mirages are optical illusions created by the bending of light rays. This happens when light travels through layers of air that have different temperatures.

Inferior mirages are produced by hot air near the ground that has cooler dense air above it. In deserts such a mirage reflects the sky above it, which looks like a patch of water in the distance. The same effect causes the tarmac on roads to look as if it's shimmering.

Superior mirages are produced by relatively rare temperature inversions, which are layers of hot air above cooler layers of air. They refract light from the ground and are more likely to produce UFO-like mirages. These types of mirage can distort, enlarge and multiply the appearance of stars or other light sources on or under the horizon. Indeed, ships or cities have been seen 'flying' above the horizon due to this effect.

LEFT: A lenticular cloud over Ayers Rock, Australia.
Fortean Picture Library

LEFT: Mount Shasta, North California, USA, is the location of many myths, legends, Fortean phenomena and UFO sightings.
Rene Dahinden/Fortean Picture Library

BELOW: Mount Shasta is famous for the lenticular, flying saucer-like clouds, which form above its summit.
Rene Dahinden/Fortean Picture Library)

In the United Kingdom, Steuart Campbell has been one of the biggest advocates of mirages as an explanation for nearly all 'intractable' UFO sightings. He explains away the sighting of a giant UFO buzzing a Japanese Boeing 747 aircraft in November 1986 as a superior mirage of the runway lights of a military airfield 450km (280 miles) away. A similar mirage refracted the light from nine snow-capped mountain peaks in the Cascade Range to produce the UFOs seen by Kenneth Arnold. His own aircraft's movements in relation to the mirage created the illusion that the UFOs were travelling at high speed.

Swamp gas

Dr J. Allen Hynek used swamp gas as the explanation for numerous sightings of red, yellow and green lights over swampy ground near Ann Arbor, Michigan, during March 1966. When he announced this at a press conference the witnesses and media roundly ridiculed his explanation, and he became a laughing stock.

Swamp gas lights are thought to be created by the decomposition of plants beneath watery, marshy areas of land, where they release methane gas. The gas spontaneously ignites when it meets the oxygen in air and burns with a bluish light.

Many cultures have legends surrounding lights that inhabit marshy regions. In Britain such lights are known as will-o'-the-wisps or ignis fatuus. They drift with the wind and tend to be confined to certain localities connected with local legends of ghosts and spirits.

Birds

In bright sunlight the underbodies and wings of birds at a high altitude can create the illusion of white flickering discs in the sky, and at night birds can reflect street lighting or other light sources.

The Condon Report explained the classic sighting and 16mm movie footage of brilliant disc-like objects moving about over Tremonton, Utah, on 2 July 1952 as due to a flight of birds.

On an Internet page, 'Ray Rational' notes that in 2012 a brightly moving object in the sky impressed his neighbour and several other people. In the overcast sky, bright sunlight managed to shine through a gap in the clouds on to some nearby cornfields. He pointed out to the gathering that the moving object was probably a goose or some other type of bird reflecting the light from the fields. They were unimpressed with this explanation until the gap in the clouds closed, and the bird became clearly visible.

This certainly shows that in the right circumstances birds could well explain many sightings.

Reflections

Strong sunlight reflected off all manner of objects and structures, from glass-clad buildings to water surfaces, can cause UFO sightings. For example, in November 1948 US Navy Commander W.J. Young observed numerous 'flying discs' on several occasions when flying over the Willamette valley and the plains of eastern Washington and Oregon. The sightings occurred on bright days, and he determined that they were caused by sunlight reflecting from the aluminium roofs of farm buildings situated a great distance away. This suggested that similar reflections could have generated Kenneth Arnold's sighting that occurred in similar circumstances.

Lightning

Streaks, chains and sheets of lightning during thunderstorms can look impressive and can provide the conditions in which ball lightning can be created. In 1989 it was discovered that at heights of 56km to 129km (35 to 80 miles) specific types of thunderstorms generate short bursts of light. These are called 'sprites', and can be several miles wide and stretch to a height of 72km (45 miles).

Giant expanding halos of electromagnetic radiation pulses (EMPs), called 'elves', emanate from some lightning discharges but only last for a fraction of a second. 'Blue jets' can also appear from thunderstorms and shoot from cloud tops to a height of 25 miles at speeds up to 100 miles per second. Unlike elves, blue jets can be seen from the ground and appear like cones or blobs of light leaving trails behind them.

'Super bolts' are types of upward lightning that jump up to a mile above their parent cloud. This type of lightning lasts a few seconds and appears like bright white channels.

Ball lightning and plasma balls

Ball lightning is likely to appear in association with thunderstorms. These colourful balls of static electricity can appear for several minutes and move at random or are attracted to metal objects, such as aircraft. They quickly disperse, or on occasion can explode. They are still nearly as mysterious to science as UFOs.

One hypothesis is that conventional lightning strikes cause vaporised mineral grains to be released from soil to form ball lightning. Another idea, championed by Australian astrophysicist Stephen Hughes, is that meteor fireballs can increase the flow of current between the ionosphere and ground for a few seconds to create a plasma ball.

LEFT: A drawing of ball lightning.
Henrik Klinge Pedersen/SUFOI/ Fortean Picture Library)

LEFT: A possible photograph of ball lightning taken in summer 1978 by Werner Burger at Sankt Gallenkirch, Vorarlberg, Austria.
Werner Burger/Fortean Picture Library)

LEFT: The June 1916 edition of *The Electrical Experimenter* features ball lightning being created in the laboratory.
Fortean Picture Library

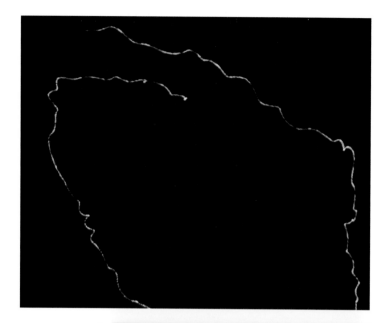

Experiments have been conducted involving firing intersecting microwave or infrared beams to create plasma balls for military purposes, so secret testing of such equipment might be responsible for some UFO sightings. It is possible that the sightings of 'foo fighters' during World War Two might have been generated by the use of German radar interacting with radar systems carried by Allied aircraft.

3 Natural celestial phenomena

Stars

Although to our eyes stars are mere pinpoints of light, they do have different levels of brightness and colouration. The brightness of a star is rated according to its stellar magnitude, with the dimmest having a high rating and the brightest a low rating. A bright star, such as Sirius, has a magnitude of -1.46, and dimmer stars like Altair are rated +0.77. The magnitude of a star remains constant as they slowly travel east to west across the sky. However, their colouration can give the illusion that they are flashing, especially when they are near the horizon.

A bright star might look closer than surrounding dimmer stars. There is also what is known as the autokinetic effect, which is caused when staring at a light against a featureless background. The lack of visual stimulation causes the mind to 'see' the light darting about. Unseen clouds in the night sky can also part to reveal a bright star, giving the illusion that it has suddenly appeared in the sky; likewise, clouds can cover a star making it look as if it has suddenly switched itself off or zoomed away from the observer.

When viewed through binoculars or telescopes atmospheric distortions can magnify and distort stars so that they look like triangular, domed or cone-shaped objects.

If a 'UFO' is seen for a long time in the same area of sky this generally indicates that it is a star.

The planets

The planets look like stars but they become brighter according to how close they are to Earth. The main planetary contenders for being mistaken as UFOs are Mars, Venus, Saturn and Jupiter. Venus is the brightest, with a maximum magnitude of -4.60; Mars has a maximum magnitude of -2.91, whilst the maximum magnitudes of Saturn and Jupiter are respectively +0.43 and -2.49.

ABOVE: A five second exposure of the star Sirius. During the exposure time, the camera was moved around to create this pattern.
Tim Printy

RIGHT: A photograph of comet Hale-Bopp taken on 7 April 1997. Its arrival triggered the mass suicide of the Heaven's Gate UFO cult.
Tim Printy

RIGHT: Jupiter seen from an aircraft.
Tim Printy

Whilst the stars remain in the same order of constellations as they travel across the sky, planets move against this background. Over several nights planets will appear in a slightly different position in the sky, and combined with their brightness seem like something out of the ordinary. Furthermore their brightness can make them look a lot larger, and if viewed through binoculars or windows they can look like a cross-shaped object. Two bright planets visible in the same area of the sky can often give rise to a flood of UFO sightings.

As with stars, clouds or other atmospheric phenomena (eg fog or mist) can make planets suddenly appear and disappear. If the witness is walking or travelling, changes in the terrain can make it look like the star or planet is following them.

The Sun

The Sun is the brightest celestial object in our skies, with a magnitude of -26.74. When its rays filter through breaks in the clouds they can look like laser beams from a UFO striking down to the ground.

Sundogs, also known as 'mock suns', are halos around the Sun or bright spots of light either side of it, and are sometimes mistaken for UFOs. They are created by ice crystals in high clouds that refract the Sun's light, usually when it is near the horizon.

The Moon

The full Moon rates a bright -12.74 magnitude and is generally unmistakeable. However, if fast-shifting clouds pass by it the illusion can be given that the moon is moving rather than the clouds; and if obscured by thin clouds that allow its light to shine through it can resemble an odd-shaped luminous UFO. Similarly, travellers in a vehicle sometimes mistake the moon for a large, bright UFO that is pacing or following them. This is especially true if the moon is low on the horizon and is viewed from a car moving along winding roads, as it will seem to appear in different directions in the sky. In reality it is the witness whose direction of movement is changing, not the Moon/UFO's.

'Moondogs' are created in the same manner as sundogs. They are rarer and less bright, but like sundogs can also be mistaken for UFOs.

Comets

The nucleus of a comet is composed of rock, dust and ice, and can range in size from 100m to 40km. They follow highly elliptical orbits that can take

LEFT: Mock sun is visible to the left of the real sun.
Tim Printy

BELOW: Aurora visible on the horizon. These displays are caused by the collision of atoms and charged particles at a high altitude in the atmosphere.
Tim Printy

LEFT: The Moon rising over the horizon looks unworldly and can inspire UFO experiences.
Tim Printy

ABOVE: An impressive picture of comet Hale-Bopp taken on 16 March 1997.
Tim Printy

RIGHT: Comet Hale-Bopp was moving away from the Earth when this photograph was taken on 7 April 1997.
Tim Printy

RIGHT: Meteor visible streaking across the background of stars.
Tim Printy

hundreds or millions of years to go round the Sun. As comets travel closer to the Sun its radiation causes gas and dust to leave their nuclei, which can be viewed as distinctive tails.

On average a comet will come close to the Earth once every decade, and will be visible even to the casual observer in daylight. Close-approaching comets are known as 'great comets' and look like a plume of light that is stationary in the sky. Such events might account for some UFO sightings, although comets of this type usually gain a lot of publicity and would be easy to identify by most people.

In the past people believed that comets were the harbingers of war, pestilence and great world-shattering changes, and even in more enlightened times rumours have spread that an approaching comet would have a dramatic impact on the world. For example, when Biela's Comet was expected to pass within 20,000 miles of Earth in 1832 alarmists claimed that vapours from its nucleus would destroy all animal and vegetable life.

In 1910 the fear that the tail of Halley's Comet would release poison gas into the Earth's atmosphere spread across the world. Scientists argued about it and people held all-night parties and prayer vigils on 18 May when it was expected to make its closest approach. Exaggerated and sensational newspaper and magazine articles initiated most of this panic.

In our own time comets can still have a powerful influence on our minds. One tragic case involves the Heaven's Gate UFO cult that was led by Marshall Herff Applewhite, who believed that an alien spacecraft from the Kingdom of Heaven was following the Hale-Bopp comet. As it made its nearest approach to Earth on 26 March 1997, all 39 members of the cult committed suicide in the belief that their spirits would transfer or reincarnate aboard the spaceship to reach a higher evolutionary level. Evidence for the UFO came from a dubious photograph of the alleged craft following the comet that was confirmed as an extraterrestrial craft by 'remote viewers'. Heaven's Gate did not care whether such evidence was valid or not, as they regarded the comet as a 'marker' to take their 'boarding pass' out of this world.

Record numbers of UFOs were reported in 1996 and 1997 to the British Ministry of Defence, during the period when Hale-Bopp was visible to the naked eye. This was attributed to the publicity surrounding Hale-Bopp, making people look to the skies, rather than to misidentifications of the comet itself.

Meteors and fireballs

Meteors look like falling or shooting stars, but they are mainly composed of stone (aerolites) or iron (siderites) that originate from the tails of comets or the asteroid belt, and can be as small as a grain of sand. They enter the Earth's atmosphere at a velocity of up to 71km per second, causing a rapid compression of the air in front of them that produces a trail of gases.

At certain times of year the Earth enters a cloud of debris that causes meteor showers, which radiate from specific constellations. For example, in November showers appear from the Leo constellation and are named Leonids.

Every day thousands of meteors descend into our atmosphere. Fortunately most burn up or disintegrate and only about 500 per year of any size reach the Earth's surface, when they are labelled as meteorites. Ancient civilisations often regarded these stones from heaven as sacred objects, though it was not until the 19th century that scientists accepted that they came from outer space.

Meteors have a magnitude of about 0, whereas larger meteors that produce a magnitude of at least -3 are regarded as fireballs. Out of about 1,000 observations, only one will have a magnitude of -3. Meteors are visible as a short streak of light lasting a few fractions of a second, whilst fireballs are blue/ green or orange balls of light that have a fiery tail, and are visible for several seconds. Exceptionally bright fireballs with a magnitude of -14 are known as bolides.

Meteors and fireballs can be associated with a crackling, whooshing, swishing or rumbling sound followed by a sonic boom a few seconds after it goes out of view. Spectacular fireballs can be seen even in daylight, and because they start glowing at a height of 160km (100 miles) and travel a similar distance, they are visible to many witnesses on the ground. Indeed, in many cases several independent witnesses have been able to photograph or video a fireball as it has crossed the sky. For example, 16 people independently videoed, and thousands saw, a -13 magnitude fireball travel over the eastern United States on 9 October 1992, before it crashed at Peekskill, New York.

On the morning of 15 February 2013 a huge 20m (65ft), 11,000-ton asteroid plunged through the Earth's atmosphere over Russia. It appeared brighter than the Sun and exploded at a height of 25km (16 miles) near the city of Chelyabinsk, causing a rain of meteor fragments. Numerous videos were captured of its spectacular and unexpected appearance. Although it was not mistaken for a UFO, there have been claims that a UFO shot at and exploded the fireball to help minimise the damage it would caused if it had directly hit the ground.

Meteors are often mistaken for crashing aircraft or perceived as cigar shapes, saucers or spheres descending through the skies. Their brightness can cause observers to think that the meteor is flying at a low trajectory, and the breaking up of a meteor can give the impression that it is a formation of UFOs.

LEFT: Meteors generally appear to come downwards towards the Earth, but in some cases, they appear to be moving upwards.
Tim Printy

BELOW: Meteors are usually seen for a few fleeting moments and can easily surprise witnesses.
Tim Printy

ABOVE: A 30-second time exposure showing the International Space Station crossing the sky.
Tim Printy

RIGHT: The launch of an Intercontinental Ballistic Missile (ICBM) captured on film.
Tim Printy

4 Man-made celestial objects

Orbiting artificial satellites

Satellites orbiting the Earth are at the limit of visibility by the naked eye. They look like moving stars, and their size and brightness can vary as they cross the sky for a period of on average four to six minutes. One of the brightest satellites is the International Space Station (ISS); details of when and where you can see it and many other satellites are available on NASA's Human Space Flight (HSF) website, which can also supply data about satellite orbits in the past, which is handy for checking against any UFO reports.

When docked with a space shuttle spacecraft in September 2009 the ISS was very bright, and even though the event was publicised many witnesses thought they were seeing a UFO. Besides the ISS, a multitude of iridium telecommunication satellites can cause UFO sightings as their aluminium panels suddenly catch and reflect sunlight earthwards. These bright flashes of light (up to -8 magnitude) last for about eight seconds and are known as 'iridium flares'. These satellites are expected to remain in service until 2020.

Tumbling satellites or geostationary satellites can also reflect sudden 'glints' of light. Once they enter the Earth's shadow they suddenly blink out of view, and they can look as if they are moving in a jerky fashion or hovering due to a phenomenon called 'autostasis'. Instead of making a stationary object look like it is moving, as with autokinesis, autostasis makes a moving object look like it is stationary. All these factors can make artificial satellites puzzling to an observer on the ground.

Re-entry of satellites and rockets

The re-entry of satellites can cause spectacular displays over large areas of territory visible to literally thousands of witnesses. In appearance they look much like descending meteors or fireballs, but remain visible for a few minutes rather than a few seconds.

When the unmanned Soviet Zond IV lunar spacecraft re-entered the Earth's atmosphere over Kentucky and Pennsylvania on the night of 3 March 1968, many differing reports were sent to the USAF's Project Blue Book. Most got the facts of the sighting correct, but it was how these facts were interpreted that made them seem more UFO-like. Several witnesses reported it as a craft or vehicle with a fuselage and windows that passed silently and low overhead.

In the early hours of 19 September 1976 King Hassan II of Morocco and many others saw what he described as a 'silvery luminous circular shape and [it] gave off intermittent trails of bright sparks and fragments, and made no noise' that travelled from the southeast to the northwest. A memo was sent to the US Secretary of State on his behalf to find out what it was, but the US could only reply that it was not due to any of their activities. Years later it was discovered that the sightings were caused by the re-entry of a Soviet rocket booster.

When a Russian Tsyklon rocket booster 22586U re-entered the Earth's atmosphere a few minutes after 1:00am on 31 March 1993, after putting a Cosmos 2238 satellite into orbit, witnesses in Ireland, Wales, the Midlands, Devon, Cornwall and northern France viewed it. An MoD police patrolman at RAF Cosford reported the most detailed sighting. He said he saw 'a vast triangular shaped craft flying at about 200ft [61m]' that made a low-frequency humming sound and swept the ground with a narrow beam of light. For this reason, this has become known as the Cosford Incident.

Russian rocket launch accidents have also produced spectacular illuminated spiral shapes in the sky, that have panicked witnesses into thinking it was some type of UFO display. One event of this type occurred over northern Norway on 9 December 2009; another was witnessed on 7 June 2012 over Russia, Iran, Israel, Turkey, Jordan, Lebanon and Cyprus. On 4 June 2010 another spiral was seen over Australia, which was attributed to the second stage booster of a Falcon 9 rocket launched from Florida.

Space expert James Oberg has noted that the Soviets often used UFOs as a smokescreen for secret missile and rocket tests. The testing of a Fractional Orbit Bombardment System (FOBS) – which sent a missile in a loop over the Earth and back to a target area – near the lower Volga River was no doubt responsible for mass sightings of a huge crescent-shaped object on 17 July, 19 September and 18 October 1967.

On 3 December 1967 the exhaust plumes from a rocket launched from a newly opened top secret space centre at Plesetsk, to the north of Moscow, also generated sightings of a UFO that sent out cones of light to the ground. The same base was responsible for many UFO sightings, including the classic 'Petrozavodsk Jellyfish UFO' seen on 20 September 1977, which was due to the launch of Cosmos 955. It was described as a huge star that sent down tendrils of light like a 'huge jellyfish' as it moved towards Petrozavodsk.

LEFT: The fiery exhaust gases blasted out by a Delta rocket shortly after launching.
Tim Printy

LEFT: Rocket high in the sky after launching.
Tim Printy

BELOW: Night launch of a Titan rocket.
Tim Printy

Multiple explanations

A simple light in the sky, which can be identified using the information above, can trigger a UFO sighting. Often the sighting can become stranger if there is a combination of factors at work. For example, an aircraft in the distance might trigger a sighting and then a star or balloon might come into view that is regarded as the same UFO flying in the sky.

Humans are not perfect recording devices, and there can be a big difference between what is seen and how it is perceived. As a UFO investigator you need to get as much information as possible about a sighting before you can attempt to identify what caused it.

It is also worth noting that obtaining a satisfactory explanation for a sighting is often difficult. For example, in the case of the Kenneth Arnold sighting it has been 'satisfactorily' explained as being caused by a flight of pelicans, meteors, mirages or reflections. Given this room for ambiguity and doubt, it is no wonder that explanations which are far more exotic can all too easily find their way into the equation.

ABOVE: Kenneth Arnold shows an illustration of one of the 'flying saucers' he saw on 24 June 1947.
Fortean Picture Library

BELOW: An identification chart showing how mundane objects can be perceived as UFOs.
N. Watson

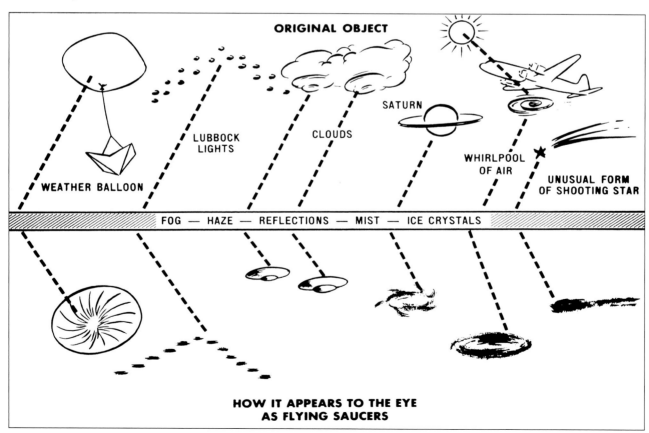

ORIGINAL OBJECT

LUBBOCK LIGHTS   CLOUDS   SATURN   WHIRLPOOL OF AIR   UNUSUAL FORM OF SHOOTING STAR

WEATHER BALLOON

FOG — HAZE — REFLECTIONS — MIST — ICE CRYSTALS

HOW IT APPEARS TO THE EYE AS FLYING SAUCERS

References

Aircraft
The Investigation of UFOs – Central Intelligence Agency: type 'UFO' in the search box, at: www.cia.gov/index.html.

Helicopters
Black Helicopters ... Watching You?, at: usahitman.com/nwo-helicopters/.

Searchlights and lasers
Laser Hazards in Navigable Airspace, at: www.faa.gov/pilots/safety/pilotsafetybrochures/media/laser_hazards_web.pdf.

Clouds
Lenticular Clouds, at: www.crystalinks.com/lenticular.html.
Noctilucent Clouds, at: www.ouramazingplanet.com/1593-night-shining-noctilucent-clouds-season-here.html.

Mirages and temperature inversions
The Science of Mirages, at: www.astronomycafe.net/weird/lights/aamirages.htm.
20 Most Incredible Lenticular Clouds, at: www.environmentalgraffiti.com/nature/news-20-most-incredible-lenticular-clouds?image=0.
The Weather Doctor, at: www.islandnet.com/~see/weather/elements/supmrge.htm.

Lightning
Atkinson, Nancy. *UFOs or High Altitude Lightning?*, at: www.universetoday.com/26094/ufos-or-high-altitude-lightning/#ixzz2R77jty71.
Learn More About Lightning, at: www.ec.gc.ca/foudre-lightning/default.asp?lang=En&n=82FC562C-1.
Sprites, Blue Jets, Elves and 'Superbolts', at: www.sky-fire.tv/index.cgi/spritesbluejetselves.html.

Ball lightning and plasma balls
Hambling, David. Unfriendly Fire – Ball Lightning and UFOs, at: www.forteantimes.com/features/articles/225/unfriendly_fire_ball_lightning_and_ufos.html.

The Sun
Melina, Remy. *Strange & Shining: Gallery of Mysterious Night Lights*, at: www.livescience.com/16188-strange-mysterious-lights-gallery.html.

Meteors and fireballs
'International Meteor Organization' website, at: www.imo.net/.

General celestial explanations
Given the right time, date and location of the witness and the position of the UFO in the sky, you can easily check astronomy software and websites to see if it can be identified as a celestial object.

Downloadable realistic planetarium software, which enables you to view the night sky at the time and coordinates of a UFO sighting, are available at:

Stellarium – www.stellarium.org/.
Home Planet – www.fourmilab.ch/homeplanet/.

Numerous apps are available for iPhones, iPads and smartphones that when you point your device at the sky will show you the constellations and other data about that specific region of the sky. Some allow you to change the date and time to see what the sky looked like in the past, which is ideal for trying to identify any potential celestial object that could explain a UFO sighting.

The excellent 'Heavens Above' website, at www.heavens-above.com/, provides lots of useful information about the position of celestial objects and satellites.

Another great resource for astronomical and atmospheric information is 'AstroPilot', a grass-roots site for aircraft navigators and pilots, at: www.astropilot.info/index.htm.

Orbiting artificial satellites
NASA's 'Human Space Flight' (HSF) website, at: spaceflight.nasa.gov/realdata/sightings/index.html.
'Heavens Above' website, at: www.heavens-above.com.
IFO University: Satellites, at: home.comcast.net/~tprinty/UFO/SUNlite2_3.pdf.

Re-entry of satellites and rockets
Clarke, David. *The Cosford Incident*, at: drdavidclarke.co.uk/secret-files/the-cosford-incident/.
Oberg, James. *The Great Soviet UFO Coverup*, at: www.debunker.com/texts/soviet_coverup.html.
Plait, Phil. *Update on the Norway Spiral*, Bad Astronomy blog, at: blogs.discovermagazine.com/badastronomy/2010/01/20/update-on-the-norway-spiral/#.UXPbbrWcfK0.
— *Oh, those Falcon UFOs!*, Bad Astronomy blog, at: blogs.discovermagazine.com/badastronomy/2010/06/05/oh-those-falcon-ufos/#.UXPZ67WcfK0.

Multiple explanations
Printy, Tim. *Witness Perception Issues*, at: home.comcast.net/~tprinty/UFO/Perception.htm.
Tim Printy's *SUNlite* ezine provides an excellent guide to identifying and explaining UFO sightings, it is available to download at: home.comcast.net/~tprinty/UFO/SUNlite.htm.

6

Physical evidence

Investigating and identifying close encounters of the first kind (CEIs) is time-consuming. Even if you can't find a possible mundane explanation for a case, you still don't have any hard evidence to prove that it is something with an exotic pedigree.

CEI cases are given more credence if they are reported by several independent witnesses and/or by witnesses who are deemed reliable and have any skills or training related to viewing the sky (such as pilots or astronomers). Unfortunately even skilled observers can be mistaken, so it is better if a CEI-type sighting is backed up by photographic or radar evidence.

Radar cases

UFOs have been tracked on radar since the 1940s, but these cases have become less common in recent years. Their reduction might be attributed to the increasing reliability and sophistication of radar equipment and its ability to filter out 'false' or unwanted returns produced by flocks of birds or temperature inversions. Another factor is that the US was secretly testing and operating U2 spy planes and high-altitude skyhook balloons during the 1950s and 1960s, and UFOs served as a good cover for these activities.

Radar works by sending out beams of radio waves or microwaves. When the waves encounter an object, they are reflected and scattered. The radar receiver detects the return echoes and can then provide information about their range, altitude, direction and speed. Most radar systems use plan position indicator (PPI) screens that show the antenna at the centre of the circular display. The screen represents a map-like picture of the area the radar beam covers, and a radial sweep moves around its centre. Targets are represented by spots of light known as pips, or blips, which remain visible on the long-persistence screen until the sweep passes over them and shows their new position.

Air traffic control (ATC) screens mainly show aircraft that are fitted with transponders, so that they are easier to detect and monitor. Their systems use software that eliminates false echoes, precipitation, contrails, birds, ground features like hills and any other extraneous returns.

As might be expected, radar operators are mainly concerned with keeping air traffic running smoothly without causing any potentially fatal accidents, and do not have the time or inclination to investigate any irrelevant or strange blips on their screens.

All the data gathered from radar sites in the US is collected and electronically stored by the En Route Intelligence Tool (ERIT). In response to a Freedom of Information Act (FOIA) request in 2010, the US Federal

BELOW: A fake UFO, created using a model.
Andy Radford/Fortean Picture Library

Aviation Administration (FAA) determined that it cannot release this raw data, but it can release less sensitive and more specific constant data recording (CDR) information.

Prior to the digital age, radarscope cameras were used to record each revolution of the radar antenna represented on the PPI screen, and these images could be analysed either frame-by-frame or as a time-lapse film.

Early radar/visual UFO cases include the sighting of a mysterious aircraft over Australia in 1942.

In the 9 May 1946 issue of *The Western Mail* (Perth, Australia), a review of the role of radar in Australia during World War Two notes that it was a very monotonous task. The operators stared for long hours at a cathode ray tube display, and they felt that looking for hostile targets was like looking for a needle in a haystack. At that time radar operators were only just learning the role of temperature inversions and other weather conditions that could affect their equipment. Differing conditions on some occasions caused Australian radar sites to pick up echoes of ships many miles away, and on one occasion a whale delousing itself in shallow water caused a false alarm.

An unidentified aircraft, given the identification tag X5, was seen on radar at 2:00am one morning in 1942 as it travelled northwards parallel to the radar station in Geraldton, Western Australia. Eyewitnesses also saw the aircraft following the coastline, which confirmed the movement of the echo seen on radar. The aircraft went away to the east, and a detailed inquiry could only suggest it was a small plane launched by a Japanese submarine.

In the same year, at 1:44am on 25 February, an unidentified target moving in a south to east flight path over the Pacific Ocean was tracked by three radar sites on the Californian coast. Assumed to be an enemy Japanese aircraft heading for Los Angeles, the city was quickly put on alert. This led to sightings of formations of 'enemy aircraft' and a sustained anti-aircraft barrage, now known as the Battle of Los Angeles. Meteorological balloons, or balloons launched by a Japanese submarine, are the explanation for the object(s) that triggered the anti-aircraft fire, and the fear of an expected air raid might well have encouraged people to misinterpret objects in the sky as enemy aircraft.

The only sceptical explanation for the radar reports is that the equipment (SCR-270 and SCR-268-type radar systems) was unwieldy and needed considerable expertise to operate, and at a time of high expectation they misinterpreted anomalous blips. In addition, we do not know if the data from the three sites specifically related to the same target or not. After WW2 the Japanese said that they never launched any attack on Los Angeles on that date, so it still remains a curious episode from that period.

Certainly radar is a valuable tool to track objects in the sky, but the data it provides has to be interpreted by software and human operators. In the context of UFOs, it is more valid if an anomalous blip is tracked for a period of time, and if other radar systems track it

BELOW: An SCR-268 mobile radar system like this one picked up unidentified targets that suggested Japanese aircraft were on their way to attack Los Angeles in the early hours of 25 February 1942.

N. Watson

RIGHT: The 1 November 1945 edition of the *Walla-Walla Union Bulletin* notes that the Japanese say they never attacked Los Angeles on the night of 24/25 January 1942. That is true, since the 'UFO' scare occurred on the night of 24/25 February 1942.

N. Watson

Jap Denies Planes Over California

TOKYO (AP) — The battle of Los Angeles was a myth: the Japanese did not send planes over that city the night of January 24-25, 1942, a Japanese navy spokesman told the Associated Press Thursday.

The question was put because the fourth air force at San Francisco on October 28 said that planes, possibly Japanese, were overhead that night. Lt. Gen. John L. Dewitt, former commander of the western defense command at San Francisco, was quoted "it is my belief that those planes were launched from submarines somewhere close to shore under our detectors."

Captain Omae of the Japanese navy said, however, that a plane was launched from a submarine and sent over the southern Oregon coast on February 9, 1942, "to attack military installations, but the lone pilot was unable to discover any. Another purpose was to keep Americans worried over coastal attacks and force them to keep many planes at home This would cut down the air strength America could send overseas."

Omae said the reason the Oregon coast was selected was not indicated in navy files.

The submarine which shelled Fort Stevens, Oregon, near the mouth of the Columbia river approached its objective by remaining submerged during the day and surfacing late at night. Omae said the submarine commander had a full set of plans of Fort Stevens and his objective was to destroy the military installations.

The submarine which shelled the Goleta oil field near Santa Barbara, Calif. early in 1942 also sought military installations and to nail down American forces in the United States That attack also was made so the Japanese people could be told that one of their submarines easily reached the United States coast.

"When the submarine commander failed to find military installations he shelled oil property," Omae said.

Asked whether the Japanese had any plans to land troops on Hawaii or the United States, Omae flatly said "No."

LEFT: Artist's
impression of a pilot
witnessing a UFO
fly-past.

*Gary Marshall/Fortean
Picture Library)*

in the same position. As arch-sceptic, Philip Klass, often stated that we must be wary of radar/visual cases because 'it has been my repeated experience that once a radar crew has been told that there are unknown visual objects in the neighbourhood, they will invariably find "unidentified" targets on the radar, and vice versa. In the excitement of the moment, the visuals and radar sightings will seem to confirm one another, even though the visuals and radar blips may be in quite different locations.'

Photographic cases

A UFO picture tells a thousand lies. The basic problem is that if a UFO photograph is taken in daylight and looks close, clear and sharp, you suspect it is a fake; and if it is out of focus, distant and hard to define, then it could be a picture of anything in the sky, from a bird to a balloon.

The Condon Committee examined many photographs, and concluded that such cases should be selected and analysed according to the following criteria:

1. Subjective evaluation: How clear is the photograph? Does it present evidence of something unusual after astronomical, meteorological, photographic and optical effects are ruled out? Could it be due to misinterpretation?

2. Fabrications: Are light and shadows in the photograph consistent? If a film camera is used, has the negative been tampered with? Are the pictures taken before and after, and during, the UFO sighting in a continuous sequence, and do they agree with the eyewitness testimony? Are the sharpness and focus of the picture in agreement with the visual observations?

3. Consistency: Is the lighting in the photograph consistent with the time of day and direction of the UFO reported by the witness? Are the time intervals of a set of photographs consistent with the witness testimony?

4. Physical and geometric tests: Do the focus and contrast agree with the given distance of the object? In a series of pictures, can the flight path of the UFO be discerned? Can the size and distance of the UFO be discerned with reference to objects and landscape features either in front of or behind the UFO?

These basic questions can be used to determine the validity of a picture. Sometimes even an insect close to the lens – not seen by the photographer at the time – can produce a UFO picture. In addition, odd light reflections in the camera optics or in the scene itself can produce luminous, UFO-like images. Night-time photographs can turn stationary light sources into streaks of light – the longer the exposure time, the longer the streak. A flash unit attached to a camera can produce UFO-like pictures if it reflects off a window or other reflective surfaces; or, if the flash fails to go off in low-light conditions, objects in the dim light might look like UFOs.

RIGHT: You take a photograph, and later you find that there is a UFO lurking in the picture. In this instance the UFO is actually a bird, in flight over the gardens of Bodnant House, Conwy, Wales.
Janet Bord/Fortean Picture Library

RIGHT: This trio of UFOs was photographed at Conisborough, South Yorkshire, UK, on 28 March 1966. Fifteen-year-old Stephen Pratt snapped this picture as he and his mum returned home from a fish and chip shop. Some critics think it was a hoax.
Stephen Pratt/Fortean Picture Library

RIGHT: Dr J. Allen Hynek examined the negatives of the Jaroslaw pictures and was impressed by the tail structure and antenna of the craft. He did not think it was an obvious hoax.
Fortean Picture Library

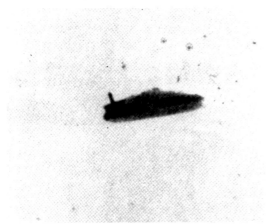

Photographs taken of birds or aircraft, balloons, kites etc, at a distance and at an odd angle, can appear UFO-like, and such pictures can be genuinely puzzling to the photographer.

In other cases fakery can be the explanation. In the past phoney pictures were made by photographing UFO models suspended or thrown into the air, double exposures, or by cut-out shapes of a UFO stuck to a windowpane. Today the latest digital technology makes it even easier to create and distribute faked UFO photographs and moving images. There are many apps that enable the user to create fake UFO photographs on their smartphones, and computer software that can be used to manipulate photographs and moving images. Such images should be checked like any other photographs for their consistency. You can obtain camera details and other information about a digital still image on a computer, by right-clicking on it and selecting 'properties' on the drop-down box. This will give you information about the type of camera used, the time the photograph was taken and many other details that can help your investigation.

It is significant that on the extensive listing of 'Best UFO Pictures' on the 'UFO Casebook' website, the number of best pictures has drastically reduced because people are now taking videos of UFOs on their mobile phones or with video cameras.

LEFT: This impressive daylight disc was photographed at Zanesville, Ohio, USA, on 13 November 1966. Analysis showed that the 'UFO' was only a few feet away from the camera and was just a few inches in diameter.
Fortean Picture Library

BELOW: This picture was taken on 19 November 1954 at Taormina, Sicily, by Giuseppe Grasso. It has been explained as being caused by a double exposure, as a photograph of lenticular clouds, as a flaw in the film's emulsion, and as water condensation in the camera lens.
Fortean Picture Library

LEFT: The Jaroslaw brothers, who confessed that their UFO photographs were faked.
Fortean Picture Library

LEFT: Here a simple button was used to fake a UFO photograph. A Venezuelan airline pilot allegedly took it.
Fortean Picture Library

Phone app fakes

The prevalence of digital cameras and smartphones makes it easy to produce fake UFO photographs, and there are several apps available to help you do it!

One of these apps is called Area 51 UFO. It works for iPhone and iPads, and provides UFO images that are either computer-generated or based on real-life reports. To create the picture, you select a UFO image provided by the app, and paste it into a picture on your camera. The transparency and blending of the UFO image can be changed, as can its position, rotation and scaling. Once satisfied, you apply the UFO to your picture. Then you can email it to all your friends and amaze the world by posting it on the Internet.

Other apps of this type include Camera Hoax, Camera360, UFO Sightings Free and UFO Camera Gold.

These apps are certainly a nuisance to UFO websites. As an example, at the end of December 2012 exactly the same flying saucer image was captured flying in such exotic locations as the Dutch Caribbean island of Bonaire, the province of Sakhon Nakhon, Thailand, and California. In each example the picture was accompanied with convincing eyewitness testimony.

UFO added with Area 51 UFO for iPhone/iPad
© by Magno Urbano (www.addfone.com)

UFO added with Area 51 UFO for iPhone/iPad
© by Magno Urbano (www.addfone.com)

UFO added with Area 51 UFO for iPhone/iPad
© by Magno Urbano (www.addfone.com)

UFO added with Area 51 UFO for iPhone/iPad
© by Magno Urbano (www.addfone.com)

Moving images

These need to be studied according to the same criteria as still photographs. With a moving film or video camera, a UFO can be produced by zooming in and out on a distant luminous object, like a star or street light. By altering focus and moving the camera about, the stationary light will take on a life of its own. This is not a very sophisticated form of UFO trickery, but backed with suitable witness testimony it can seem quite impressive.

As with still photographs, objects filmed in unusual circumstances can be genuinely puzzling to the photographer, and the images need to be checked against all the possible known factors that can cause misidentifications. For instance, over the last decade there has been a plague of orange orbs filmed moving sedately across the sky that are actually nothing more than Chinese lanterns. They can look spooky to eyewitnesses, as they make no sound, and if they are far away they can look as if they are a fleet of UFOs or imagined to be attached to a large object.

In terms of creating fake footage, it is relatively easy to make small models of UFOs and suspend them with fine fishing line from a pole. The UFO can be swung out in front of the camera and moved to make it look as if it is flying around the neighbourhood. Fitted with small lights and flown at night it can look even more impressive, and less like a fake model.

As with smartphone apps, digital technology has made it much cheaper and easier to manipulate very convincing moving UFO images. In October 2012 a video titled 'UFO Over Santa Clarita' was posted on YouTube, accompanied by a claim that the witness had spotted these two UFOs as he was driving along. In fact, it is easy to see that they are CGI creations, and Aristomenis (Meni) Tsirbas of MeniThings Productions, in partnership with the Gnomon School of Visual Effects, soon admitted he had created this fake. What is more impressive is that everything in the video is fake, including the car, landscape and sky!

Even without computer manipulation, there are many intriguing examples of UFOs haunting our virtual reality. As an example, two particular versions of a short video of a flying saucer are presented on YouTube. The first to be downloaded, at www.youtube.com/watch?v=YdyQu5Zx8xw, claims that it is a 'UFO over a river in Italy', and has had more than eight million viewings since being posted on 16 February 2007. Another version, saying the Italian Air Force produced it, is provided at www.youtube.com/watch?v=GzJEIL0ko4s. This has had nearly 650,000 views.

In fact the video sequence is not that new. Italian UFO researcher and writer Paola Harris presented it in 2005 at the 36th Annual International MUFON

Symposium held in Denver, Colorado. The seventh generation video tape was given to her and other UFO researchers anonymously. No details were given about who shot it, but it is Harris' opinion that the craft is of terrestrial origin. She speculates that it is a military prototype.

In an email sent out by her on 17 April 2007, she stated: 'No! This [is] old film footage I have been showing for 3 years and it was given to us [by] Italian researchers ... Not by the Air Force ... It is our technology. I had the film analysed in Hollywood. It is a real object in the film. It has been shown in my MUFON and Laughlin presentations and someone put it on YouTube and Google! This all takes place in the Veneto region of Italy at a place called Ponte di Giulio, near Aviano NATO Base. It is a dry river bed where the military does manoeuvres and the photographer was on a tripod waiting for the object to come out of the woods. I doubt aliens appeared there!'

Comments about the original YouTube posting range from outright wonder to dogged scepticism. It is either regarded as the best-ever footage of a real flying saucer or a neat piece of CGI workmanship.

After covering these possibilities, a contributor called 'Star GateSG7' seemed to be on the right track: 'This film is filmed in Quebec just north of the military UAV facility of Bombardier (they also make the Peanut UAV). It's based on a 1986 design called Hystar originally designed as a lighter-than-air ship – they added multiple lightweight Rotax engines and thrust vectoring (see pods and vents in videos) and expensive gyroscopes and control software – ain't that hard to do though...'

In a later contribution, he states: 'Actually I have

made a mistake ... This footage was taken in France OR Italy but the aircraft is still based upon a 1986 Canadian Design called Hystar. The Engines are indeed Bombardier Rotax turbines and the craft is a French Dassault/Italian Avroni Motobecane/ Robert Bosch Germany and a Canadian Bombardier collaboration.'

So, was a Hystar (or LML, as it is now called) responsible for the Italian video? As Paola Harris noted, the camera was on a tripod and the cameraman seems to know that something is about to happen. Before the UFO becomes visible, the camera zooms in to the rough location where it comes into view. The craft seems to 'perform' in front of the camera and then it shoots away as the camera zooms out. The position and zooming of the camera and its distance from the UFO gives the impression

that this is something that suddenly came into view at an opportune moment, rather than being an official, professional recording of an aircraft test by the Italian Air Force.

Philip Mantle, who helped reveal the notorious 'Alien Autopsy' film footage to the public, notes: 'There are two ways to look at this type of thing. One is to get the footage out in the open in order to stimulate debate, uncover more details etc. The other is to keep it under wraps until full analysis has been conducted. There is no right or wrong way, it is just a matter of opinion. In the days before the Internet it was common practice to look at photographs and film/video in detail before releasing them. Today's world is much different with more and more people having computer access around the world. For the record, I have looked at the video in question, and this is just my opinion and nothing more, but I would err on the side of caution as I think the footage is highly suspect. It has the "feeling" of computer graphics to me.'

Nick Pope is equally cautious about this film: '"Interesting if true", as they say in the world of intelligence analysis. Determining the film's provenance will be difficult if not impossible, given the mix of UFO researchers and anonymous sources. In my official UFO investigations I could call on technical specialists who could analyse and enhance photos and videos. The fact that this video was shot in daylight and that other features are visible

means it should be possible to determine some characteristics of the object, including its diameter. It should also be possible to determine whether the film has been faked.'

For an expert opinion I contacted Michael George, senior consultant, forensic video/audio, for BSB Forensic Ltd (www.bsbforensic.com). He said: 'Original footage must always be examined to give clear and precise expert witness evidence. In this instance I assume access to original footage is a non-starter. The interesting point in this footage is at the end of the recording. The "off" (where the imagery ends and then shows a fighter jet) point on this footage shows it has been edited already. It also shows that the two clips have been produced from two separate cameras and edited together.'

Only a version on Google (that is no longer on the site) showed the tape break up followed by a fighter aircraft for a brief moment.

Nick Pope acknowledges that 'analysis of such footage is intriguing. Technology to create a realistic fake moves on, but so does the technology to spot one. Only industry insiders will be able to give you the current state of play and as in many fields, the experts may not all agree. It may not be possible to give a definitive answer on analysis alone, which is why I always recommend a holistic approach to such investigations: investigate not just the footage, but the story, the participants, the witness, etc.'

Henry 'Aviation Jedi' Eckstein (aka 'Star GateSG7'), in a long email to me, concluded: 'I think we can safely say this is NOT an Alien UFO and is DEFINITELY NOT out-of-this-world technology. The design is too mainstream and even some modern toys can emulate what was seen on the video. The problem part of the footage is the sudden burst of acceleration at the end of the footage, which to me is an editing/post-production effect intended to show future possibilities rather than show an actual performance envelope.'

Until we get any further substantial information about the circumstances of where, how and why this footage was recorded, we can only speculate about its validity. The footage does make us consider what constitutes UFO video evidence when computer software and models can be easily manipulated and constructed. In addition, the proliferation of Internet sites that allow you to anonymously post your work for worldwide attention means that faking UFO footage is a rich field of fun, and even income, for pranksters and hoaxers.

Such videos can only be taken seriously if they are backed up by reliable independent witnesses. Documentation recording the full details of how the images came to be captured should also be included. Otherwise such Internet videos are only of entertainment value.

Cattle mutilations

There was a huge wave of cattle mutilations in the USA during the 1970s. They were linked to the work of Satanic cults, CIA weapon testing operations, UFO activity and sightings of unmarked helicopters. John Lear put forward the idea that the US government was working in conjunction with the aliens to mutilate cattle. According to this suggestion the aliens apparently have a genetic disorder, and they need to obtain enzymes or hormonal secretions from the tissues of the dead animals. This still begs the question 'Why are the animals mutilated and left for people to discover? Why not just abduct the cattle, or even better breed them in secret for the aliens?'

A report on the problem by District Attorney Kenneth M. Rommel Jnr, entitled *Operation Animal Mutilation*, published in June 1980, attributed all the cases they examined as being 'consistent with predator action'. This hasn't stopped people believing that aliens or other forces are systematically mutilating cattle, sheep, goats, horses and other animals on a huge scale throughout the world.

ABOVE: New Mexico State Patrol Officer Gabe Valdez inspects a mutilated cow carcass.
Peter Jordan/Fortean Picture Library)

LEFT: UFOs and cattle mutilations were linked in this 1978 comic strip.
maryevans.com

Evidence for CEIIs

All the categories of identification, and the use of evidence from radar systems and images, can be applied to close encounters of the second kind (CEIIs). These encounters involve UFOs that actually cause an effect on the environment or leave some trace of their appearance, and are more likely to yield far more useful evidence than CEI cases.

ELECTROMAGNETIC EFFECTS

What are presumed to be side-effects of the UFOs' propulsion systems are due to gravitational or electromagnetic (EM) effects that cause interference with TV and radio signals, or even power blackouts. When motorists view UFOs, the vehicle engine can suddenly stop and all electrical power is lost; at other times UFOs are linked with causing interference to car radios, or causing them to switch off completely. Once the UFO moves out of sight, the car engine will restart without any problem, and the headlights and radio will switch back on.

Such cases are difficult to explain, because the interference is selective and inconsistent. There are many cases where UFOs have come very close to vehicles without affecting them at all, and cars that have been affected by a close encounter do not reveal any expected changes in their magnetic patterns. There is never any permanent damage to the vehicle, and it is significant that the effects never influence several cars at exactly the same time. Instead – being theoretically an accidental by-product of the UFO's propulsion system – perhaps the UFOs target a specific vehicle with a beam that can either stop it or interfere with its electrics.

Other theories are that rare balls of plasma have this ability to affect vehicles, or that the power of suggestion is at work. It might be pure coincidence that the radio crackles when a UFO is viewed, or the witness accidentally and unconsciously stalls their car at the excitement of seeing a UFO. The Condon Report notes that when radar was developed during World War Two, local motorists thought that the newly erected and top secret radar masts were causing their cars to stall, and wonders if the cars stopped stalling once the purpose of the masts was discovered.

UFOs also physically affect witnesses. The reported effects range from the sounds generated by the UFOs – from loud explosions to buzzing and bleeping – to the smells they give off. US ufologist James McCampbell put forward the idea that the smell of sulphur dioxide, like rotten eggs, is produced by pulsed microwaves or electrical

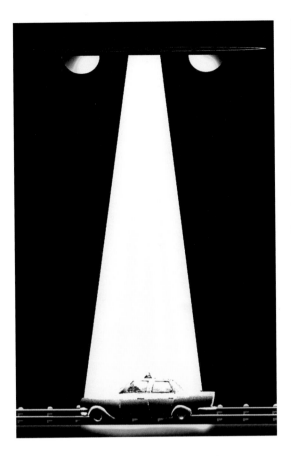

Angel Hair

Streams of sticky, hair-like substances falling from the sky were associated with UFO activity in the 1950s. Since then, 'Angel Hair' has become a footnote in UFO history, and reports of it have faded away, much in the way that it was said to evaporate and disappear when it touched the ground.

Whenever samples were collected small insects and spider threads were found to be responsible. Another explanation is that atmospheric electricity causes floating dust particles to collect and form long filaments. However, it has also been suggested that the propulsion systems of UFOs cause the surrounding air to ionise and produce Angel Hair.

LEFT: An artist's impression of 'Angel Hair' falling over Oloron, France, on the afternoon of 17 October 1952. The white hair-like substance appeared to rain down from a cylindrical object and 30 spherical UFOs. *Fortean Picture Library*

LEFT: A sample of 'Angel Hair' said to have been retrieved in Japan. *Fortean Picture Library*

discharges. This would indicate that the witnesses encountered either Earth light or ball lightning phenomena, or flying saucers using this type of technology. He also noted that microwaves could be responsible for causing the tanning or burning of witnesses exposed to UFOs, and speculated that they might cause the witness to be temporarily paralysed.

In Britain, Albert Budden has gone further, postulating that EM effects produced by everything from power lines to the electrical gadgets in our homes are causing electromagnetic pollution. In hot spots of this pollution, poltergeist activity can be experienced, and people with electromagnetic hypersensitivity can believe aliens have abducted them.

Roger Sandell, in the *Merseyside UFO Bulletin*, made the point that vehicle stoppage cases date back to the 16th century, long before the invention of the internal combustion engine: in Britain, for instance, local witches were said to have the ability to stop horse-drawn carts moving, and could use curses to stop machinery. Lonely, haunted spots were also said to be places where vehicles would stop for no reason. Sandell attributes accounts of vehicle interference cases to the release of *The Day the Earth Stood Still* film in 1952, which features an alien who has the power to disable all the world's weapons and machinery.

Traces

Unlike all the types of evidence we have looked at so far, traces are the next best thing to having an actual UFO in the laboratory. Yet, like radar and photographic evidence, things are never that clear-cut. Italian researcher Maurizio Verga notes that ground traces 'offer a complex conceptual problem'. There are four main reasons for this:

1. Having experienced a CEII sighting, witnesses are predisposed to tie in anything else that seems strange. Therefore they will search for ground traces or any other strange markings in the environment. These will be in accordance with their emotional state of mind and 'cultural belief system'.

2. The link between a UFO and any traces may be made by the witness, even though they know there is no connection between them.

3. UFO investigators, because of their own belief systems, may confirm the link between traces and a UFO sighting even if it seems dubious. An investigator might even find traces or similar evidence to link with a UFO sighting, in order to give it more credence.

4. Traces might be created to support a hoax, or unusual looking traces might be found that are then used to support a hoax UFO report.

RIGHT: Ground traces left behind by the landing pads of an egg-shaped UFO seen at Socorro, New Mexico. It was seen taking off like a rocket by Deputy Marshal Lonnie Zamora, on 24 April 1964.
Fortean Picture Library

As can be seen, ground traces can be caused by all sorts of activities, natural and artificial. These marks and traces come under three basic categories:

1. PRIMARY EFFECTS

A: Circular sites, which consist of burns, depressions or dehydrated material.
B: Rings, composed of burns, depressions or dehydrated material.
C: Irregular areas of burns, depressions or dehydrated material.
D: 'Nests', depressed crops or other plants in an oval swirling pattern.

2. SECONDARY EFFECTS

A: Imprints on the ground.
B: Damage to trees and flora.
C: Craters.
D: Footprints attributed to alien beings.
E: Signs that soil or flora has been removed.

3. RESIDUES

Powder, liquids or solids left behind by an alleged UFO landing.

It is best if a UFO sighting is closely linked with these effects, but there are many examples where such strange effects are assumed to be caused by UFO activity. One such case caused a great deal of media publicity in Britain during July 1963. A farm worker named Reginald Alexander found a large crater in one of his fields at Manor Farm, Charlton, Wiltshire (near Shaftesbury, Dorset). At first it was thought an unexploded World War Two bomb might have been responsible for it, and the British Army's Horsham Bomb Disposal Unit was called to the scene. They inspected the 2.4m (8ft) diameter, 0.9m (3ft) deep hole, and after spending ten days there they only found some metal at its core. This turned out to consist of magnetite, which is a naturally occurring iron oxide relatively common in that part of the country.

When TV astronomy pundit Patrick Moore visited the scene he saw four spurs of missing vegetation that radiated from the crater, and elliptical and round crop circles in nearby fields. He was misquoted as saying the metal recovered from the crater was a meteorite, although he did think it was possible that something from the sky probably caused the crater and the crop circles.

Roy Blanchard, the field's owner, firmly believed that it was 'obviously some craft from outer space, since it sucked out my barley and potatoes when it took off'. A character using the name Dr Robert J. Randall told the media he was an Australian astrophysicist, and he thought that the Charlton crater was caused by a 152m (500ft) wide, 600-ton (540-tonne) out-of-control flying saucer from Uranus. It had skimmed over the area, creating the crop circles, briefly landed to form the crater, and then flown away with its 50 crew, safe and intact. Besides the crater and crop circles, he pointed out some ash-covered leaves and some burnt grass in a nearby hedge, as further evidence of this extraterrestrial visitation. This was later attributed to mildew rather than the exhaust gases from a spaceship.

Needless to say, Dr Randall's credentials were not bona fide. His baseless pronouncements did make a good story, though, and for those with a conspiratorial viewpoint he was regarded as a government stooge who was wheeled out to discredit the whole story.

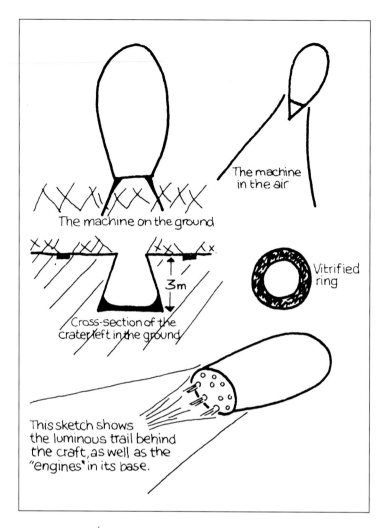

The machine in the air

The machine on the ground

3m

Cross-section of the crater left in the ground

Vitrified ring

This sketch shows the luminous trail behind the craft, as well as the "engines" in its base.

The local MP asked questions in the House of Commons on 29 July 1963, but no satisfactory explanation was put forward. Just as interest in the subject lapsed, John Southern, a television repairman, declared on 25 August 1963 that he and two friends were responsible for digging the crater. Southern and his friends had previously dug a crater near Haddington in Scotland, then they had dug the Charlton crater.

For a third crater, they had planned to drag a car towards its centre to give the impression that an enormous magnetic force had pulled it there. A laced shoe was going to be left in the car to indicate that someone had been wrenched from the spot, and after a few days Southern was going to appear to declare that he had been abducted and kept captive in a space station.

As the date approached for this planned crater/abduction hoax, Southern got more nervous and decided not to go ahead with it. Most, but not all, were happy to accept this hoax explanation; then, as a further twist, Southern confessed that his hoax explanation was a hoax. He had told the hoax story to flush out the real

hoaxer, but since this did not work he now thought that UFOs had caused the crater.

Another reason for not believing that a hoaxer was responsible for the crater – unless they were really opportunistic or clever – is that in the early hours of 16 July 1963, the night before the crater was found, witnesses saw streaks of orange light, and an 'explosion' was heard in the vicinity.

To shed light on this matter, Alan Sharp wrote an article for the *Merseyside UFO Research Group Newsletter* entitled 'Craters: Their Origin and Classification'. He puts them into two groups:

1. NATURALLY FORMED CRATERS

A: Natural impacts, caused by meteorites.
B: Natural explosions, caused by lightning or volcanic explosions.
C: Natural subsidence, caused by burrowing animals, caves or subterranean erosion.

2. ARTIFICIALLY FORMED CRATERS

A: Artificial impacts, caused by the crashing of satellite or rocket fragments.
B: Artificial explosions, caused by blasting, shelling or bombing.
C: Artificial subsidence, caused by mining or tunnelling activities.

At first he thought that the Charlton crater was caused by subsidence, but after further investigation found that 'in point of fact this was a classic example of the type of "crater" ascribable to the strike of lightning on open ground. It displays radiating surface marks, removal of material and a central hole. It was preceded by a violent thunderstorm accompanied by strong winds and was in an area of considerable storm damage to crops. The lightning struck the ground where there was evidence of a local elevation of the water table and pronounced detectable magnetic effects in the magnetite-bearing soil, similar to those recorded at Cockburnspath in Scotland.

'The strike occurred at a point on a previous field boundary where a large iron straining-post had once been embedded in the ground and secured by metal stays. The disappearance of plants was by no means complete, as had been alleged by one person, according to Mr Bealing, the Shaftesbury photographer whose photographs appeared widely in the Press at the time. Captain Rodgers of the Army investigation team also reported the finding of plant remains at the site.'

This explanation would account for the streaks of orange light and explosion seen prior to the discovery of the crater, and sounds more plausible than a spacecraft from Uranus or hoaxers being responsible for it.

Crop circles

On 19 January 1966, farmer George Pedley saw a dull object, like two saucers facing each other, rise above marshland at Horseshoe Lagoon near Tully, north Queensland. The 7.6m (25ft) long, 2.4m (8ft) deep craft rose 9m (30ft) above the ground and then quickly flew away. The sighting only lasted 15 seconds. When the witness went to the point where he had seen the UFO take off, he found a 9.7m (32ft) long by 7.6m (25ft) wide clockwise depression in the tall swamp grass. This became known as the first 'UFO nest', and set the agenda for ufologists to seek out similar ground traces elsewhere in the world.

The Royal Australian Air Force (RAAF) investigation into the case at first suggested that a helicopter was responsible for the sighting. Later it was thought that tropical air associated with thunderstorm activity had caused it. George Odgers, Director of Public Relations, Department of Defence (Air Office), explained that 'the most probable explanation was that the sighting was of a "willy willy" or circular wind phenomenon which flattened the reeds and sucked up debris to a height of about 30 feet, thus forming what appeared to be a "flying saucer", before moving off and dissipating. Hissing noises are known to be associated with "willy willies" and the theory is also substantiated by the clockwise configuration of the depression.'

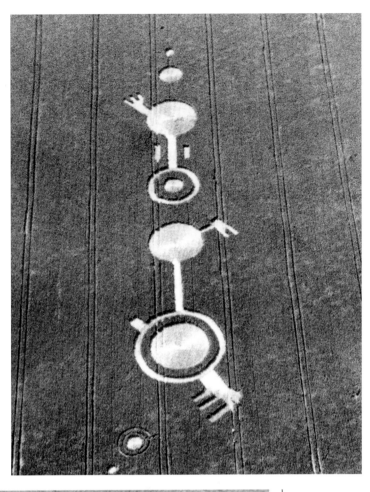

ABOVE: Another view of the huge Alton Barnes pictogram. Does it represent a sign or message from aliens?
Fortean Picture Library

LEFT: Crop circle at Cherhill, Wiltshire, in 1989.
Fortean Picture Library

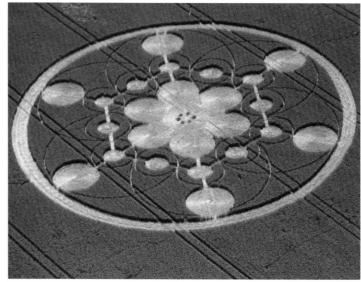

Simple circular 'crop circles' subsequently appeared in the English countryside, especially near Avebury and Stonehenge in the late 1970s, which brought about a new interest in ufology. In the following decade such circles became more complex, and cereologists regarded them as coded messages from aliens. In 1991 the bubble burst when Doug Bower and Dave Chorley confessed that they had used ropes and planks to create crop circles after being inspired by the Australian Tully 'UFO nest'.

Certainly hoaxers have created many of the hundreds of circles that have been reported throughout the world, but others could well have been caused by animal activity, insects, crop diseases, ball lightning, storms or even plasma vortexes. Then again, UFOs and entities have been seen near these circles, so they still represent one type of intriguing evidence for their existence. Supporters of such claims note:

1. Animals refuse to enter crop circle formations and can be sick after visiting a site.
2. Seeds from plants inside a crop circle grow five times faster than normal (control) seeds of the same type.
3. Cell walls near the seed-head of crops inside the circle become enlarged.
4. Electrical and mechanical equipment often fail to work in or near a crop circle. This can include vehicles, cameras and phones.

Wreckage

Wreckage from alleged UFOs is more promising than traces or residues, though here again the evidence is frustratingly inconclusive. One of the most famous instances concerns the story of a flying saucer that exploded over the beach at Ubatuba, São Paulo, Brazil, in 1957. Fragments were gathered by one of the witnesses and posted to a newspaper columnist. They were examined by the Brazilian Agriculture Ministry's Mineral Production Laboratory, which found that the samples were of magnesium of a high degree of purity. The Condon Committee also had the samples examined and concluded that they were not exceptional enough to suggest that they came from a flying saucer.

In the *Merseyside UFO Bulletin*, John Harney notes that rather than arguing about whether the samples could be created by terrestrial sources or not, we should question the veracity of their source. Other than the letter claiming a saucer was seen in conjunction with these samples being collected, the witnesses were never identified or interviewed. Harney states: 'The more rational conclusion in this case is, plainly, that the Ubatuba affair was a hoax. It must be regarded as one of the most successful hoaxes in the history of ufology, in view of the time and money spent and the amount of technical expertise lavished on it.'

As this case highlights, the 'better' the evidence used to support a UFO sighting, the more it is likely to have been produced by hoaxers or pranksters. David E. Pritchard has noted that any artefact, if it is to be convincing, must have unusual performance, composition and structure, which should be 'simple enough to be deduced, and yet impossible to duplicate naturally or in the lab.'

As with photographic evidence, the pedigree of the artefact is one of the most important factors. When dealing with any form of evidence for alien artefacts, we have to consider where and how it was found; who found it; and who analysed it? As Pritchard asserts, 'It is the whole story, confirmed by the artefact, which will do the convincing; not the artefact by itself.' So far no UFO traces, remains or wreckage have met these criteria to everyone's satisfaction.

References

Radar cases

Klass, Philip K. *UFOs: the Public Deceived* (Prometheus Books, New York, 1983), p109.

Printy, Tim. 'The Battle of Los Angeles UFO story' in *SUNlite* ezine, Vol. 3, No. 1, Jan–Feb 2011, p19, at: home.comcast.net/~tprinty/UFO/SUNlite3_1.pdf.

Thayer, Gordon O. 'Optical and Radar Analyses of Field Cases' in *Scientific Study of Unidentified Flying Objects*, section III, chapter 5, at: files.ncas.org/condon/text/s3chap05.htm.

Photographic cases

Ballester Olmos, V.J. UFO *Fotocat Blog*, a survey and catalogue of worldwide UFO photo events, at: fotocat.blogspot.co.uk/2012/05/20120601-en.html.

Hartmann, William K. 'Analysis of UFO Photographic Evidence' in *Scientific Study of Unidentified Flying Objects*, chapter 2, at: files.ncas.org/condon/text/s3chap02.htm.

'UFO Over Santa Clarita', at: youtube.com/watch?v=tFHSV4sMw6U.

'UFO Over Santa Clarita VFX Breakdown', at: www.youtube.com/watch?v=wRtqbM9kBi4.

Wallace, Lewis. *The UFO is Fake in Animator's YouTube Prank* — But so is Everything Else, 'Wired' website, at: www.wired.com/underwire/2013/02/ufo-video-fake-tsirbas/.

xman, mister. *How to Create Convincing but Utterly Fake UFO Photographs and Videos* video tutorial, at: practical-jokes.wonderhowto.com/how-to/create-convincing-but-utterly-fake-ufo-photographs-and-videos-387035/.

The electromagnetic effect

Budden, Albert. Electric UFOs: *Fireballs, Electromagnetics and Abnormal States*, (Blandford, London, 1998).

Craig, Roy. *Indirect Physical Evidence*, at: files.ncas.org/condon/text/s3chap04.htm.

McCampbell, James. 'Effects of UFOs upon People', in *UFOs 1947–1987* (Fortean Tomes, London, 1987).

Sandell, Roger. 'The Ghost in the Machine', *Merseyside UFO Bulletin* new series vol 3 (Summer 1976), at: magonia.haaan.com/2009/ghostinmachine/.

Ground traces

Harney, John. 'The Search for Physical Evidence: The Ubatuba Magnesium', *Merseyside UFO Bulletin* vol 4 no 2 (June 1971), at: magonia.haaan.com/1971/physical-evidence-the-ubatuba-magnesium/.

Laibow, Rima; Sollod, Robert; and Wilson, John (eds). *Anomalous Experiences & Trauma*: *Current Theoretical, Research and Clinical Perspectives. Proceedings of TREAT II* (Dobbs Ferry, New York: The Center for Treatment and Research of Experienced Anomalous Trauma, 1992), p190.

Sharp, Alan. 'Craters: Their Origin and Classification', *Merseyside UFO Research Group Newsletter no 2* (June 1965), at: magonia.haaan.com/1965/craters-their-origin-and-classification/.

UFO Sightings: Research by Category, NICAP website, at: www.nicap.org/special.htm.

Cattle mutilation

'FBI Files: The Vault' website contains news clippings and correspondence related to cattle mutilations in the USA between 1974 and 1978, at: vault.fbi.gov/Animal%20Mutilation.

Hierophant's Apprentice. 'The *Fortean Times* Random Dictionary of the Damned No 50: Animal Mutilations', Fortean Times no 302 (June 2013), pp46–49.

Redfern, Nicholas. *The FBI Files* (Simon & Schuster, London, 1998).

Crop circles

A *Catalogue of Australian Physical Trace Cases*, compiled by Keith Basterfield and Bill Chalker, 'Project 1947' website, at: www.project1947.com/forum/bctrace2.htm.

The International Crop Circle Database, searchable database up to 2008, at: ccdb.cropcircleresearch.com/index.cgi.

7

Close encounters of the third kind and retrievals

The outbreak of flying saucer sightings in 1947 led to all types of speculation. Some people thought they were caused by secret Soviet aircraft sent to spy on the USA in preparation for World War Three, or that they were revolutionary top secret craft being tested by the USA.

When neither explanation seemed to fit the facts, more fanciful theories filled the void. The most compelling and persistent is that UFOs are spacecraft operated by alien intelligences. This wasn't too much of a leap of the imagination, as in the wake of World War Two we were already building rockets and considering the possibility of making our own first faltering steps beyond the cradle of our home planet.

The dominant extraterrestrial hypothesis (ETH) led scientifically inclined ufologists to think that UFOs were remote-controlled and/or robotically operated craft that were making a detailed survey of our planet. Talk of aliens or entities associated with these craft were mainly dismissed, discouraged and ignored in serious ufology circles until the 1960s. Certainly the USAF took a dim view of such reports. Equally, Dr Hynek was originally reluctant to give much attention to such cases, yet the sheer number and quality of these reports meant that he eventually had to accept that there are 'close encounters of the third kind'.

This reluctance to accept the existence of alien beings was down to the extravagant claims of the contactees of the 1950s, and it was already hard enough to prove the existence of flying saucers to a sceptical scientific community without bringing in bug-eyed aliens. Talk of aliens brought to mind low-budget science fiction movies and the wild stories of sensation-hungry contactees.

Yet, if flying saucers were some type of spacecraft, then it was logical to suppose that they would contain pilots. Therefore when such cases got attention from the serious ufology community in the late 1960s and early 1970s they called aliens 'occupants' or 'humanoids'. Indeed, a special edition of *Flying Saucer Review*, which took a detailed look at worldwide cases of abduction and alien encounters, was entitled *The Humanoids*.

Since the 1980s the 'greys', as they are called, have become the most popular image of alien visitors. They have large heads with big almond-shaped eyes, and short, feeble, spindly bodies. The prevalence of the greys in witness testimony, and of the other types of aliens associated with flying saucers, helps us define whether they are more than just the product of our imagination. Finding patterns in their appearance and behaviour, however, is not as convincing as physical or any other supporting evidence for CEIII and abduction stories.

The term 'alien' can be used to describe anything from a two-foot-tall hairy dwarf with a laser gun to a shambling nine-foot-tall robot with flashing lights. From the very start of the flying saucer craze in the late 1940s, aliens were jokingly referred to as 'Little Green Men'.

When British ufologist Peter Hough examined the various descriptions of aliens, he despairingly observed: 'There is an almost total lack of consistency in reports of alleged contact. Occupants are variously described as tall, small, thin, fat, human-like, grotesque, saintly, covered in fur, hairless, with long arms, short arms, hands, claws, large heads, headless, friendly, indifferent, aggressive, appear "solid", able to pass through walls, levitate', and so on.

Abduction researcher John Mack noted that the United States has the largest number of alleged abductions, followed by the United Kingdom and Brazil. He thought this might be because abduction experiences in other countries are put into a supernatural or religious framework and are not thought to be associated with flying saucers. His research also indicated that abductees in the rest of the world see a wider range of alien beings than US abductees. In the US the so-called greys are most likely to be seen, but even here all manner of different aliens have been reported.

Other ufologists assert that there are hundreds of different types, and that they claim to come from a vast range of different star systems. The Burlington National UFO Center website features 67 different alien descriptions and races, and that is without including various sub-categories. The wide variety of alien descriptions could be because no two witness descriptions of even real objects are the same, let alone aliens encountered under stressful circumstances.

Hilary Evans, the author of *Visions, Apparitions, Alien Visitors*, defined four categories of aliens:

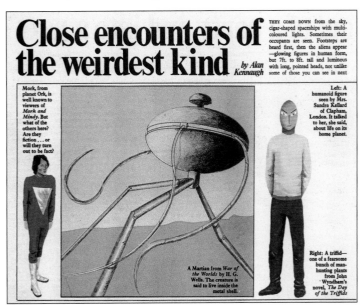

1. Those that look indistinguishable from any Earthly human being.
2. Human-like aliens that have a few differences. They might have less fingers or toes than us, or none at all; they might lack reproductive organs.
3. Humanoids who have large heads and wrap-round eyes, like the 'greys'.
4. Bear- or monkey-like beings that display intelligence but rarely interact with witnesses.

He stated: 'Almost without exception, UFO-related entities are bi-pedal, and have heads, trunks and limbs disposed much as ours are; their faces have much the same features, disposed in much the same configuration – single eyes and no mouths, though occasionally reported, are rare.'

Certainly the majority of reports do not contain as many exotic-looking aliens as you might imagine. To be more specific than Evans' outline of alien types, most aliens would fit one of the following categories:

Humanoid

Contactees like George Adamski have reported meeting fair-skinned aliens who had long blonde hair and seemed androgynous. Other than their long hair, they did not look out of the ordinary in 1950s America.

Besides these spiritual Nordic or Aryan types, human-looking aliens are often described as looking foreign or oriental. In 1952 contactee Truman Bethurum met Aura Rhanes, the lady captain of a flying saucer, whom he described in these glowing terms: 'Her skin was dark olive and her brown eyes, lighting up when she smiled, seemed to make her complexion glow even more ... Her short black hair was brushed into an upward curl at the ends.'

It is noteworthy that during the 1896–97 US phantom airship scare, the pilots of these craft were described as dark-skinned, slant-eyed and Oriental-looking men and women. It has been speculated by sceptics that these 'foreign' attributes have evolved to become the small dark-skinned greys with almond-shaped eyes that slant upwards and wrap round their head in an exaggerated fashion.

Humanoids can also be related to the mysterious Men in Black who force UFO witnesses not to publicise or report their experiences. They have been described, like the pilots of the airships and flying saucers, as dark-skinned and/or slant-eyed.

Humanoids are generally clothed in close-fitting silver suits or uniforms, which appear to be seamless, with no visible buttons or zips.

RIGHT: Contactee George Adamski met this Nordic-type Venusian in the California desert on 20 November 1952. Humanoid aliens can blend in with human society, and are often seen by abductees working with grey-type aliens.
Fortean Picture Library

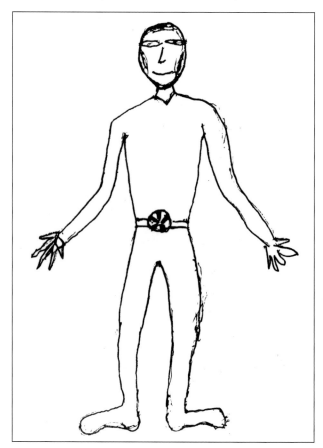

FAR RIGHT: Drawing by witness Elias Seixas de Matos, a truck driver abducted by aliens in Brazil on 25 September 1980.
Fortean Picture Library

SPACE ENCOUNTER TERROR

SUNDAY PEOPLE, November 30, 1980   7

MARIO LUISI has had close encounters of a strange kind — with what he claims are beings from another planet.

Mario, 36, came face-to-face with the strangers while walking his dog on a river bank near his home at Burnside, Kendal, Cumbria. He claims he saw:—

● A CIGAR - SHAPED spacecraft hovering three feet in the air. It was about 16ft. long with smoke-darkened glass along the side.

● TWO beings — a man and a woman — wearing black, skin-tight suits with strange markings.

● A PENCIL - LIKE weapon which shattered his torch.

Mario, a paper worker, said: "I spotted the craft hovering in the air. As I shone my torch I heard slushing footsteps behind. I turned round and came face-to-face with two of the most beautiful people I have ever seen.

"The woman told me I would not come to harm if I did not reveal the strange markings on their badges or crafts.

Mario said that the couple then climbed into their craft which slowly rose into the night, silent and with a bright glow."

Five days later, farmer

Sue Critchley, of Grasmere Road, Kendal, says she saw a similar object in daylight eight miles from where Mario spotted the craft.

She said: "I am used to seeing plenty of military aircraft in the area, but I have never seen anything like that."

MARIO—Met strangers

The spaceman

The spaceship

SUE—Saw craft

LEFT: Newspaper report of an encounter with humanoid aliens by Mario Luisi near Kendal, Cumbria, UK, in November 1980.

N. Watson

LEFT: Carl Higdon UFO encounter case, Medicine Bow National Forest, Wyoming, USA, 25 October 1974: artist's impression of the Devilish-looking entity.

Fortean Picture Library

Greys

The greys have become the 'classic' shape for aliens. They have large, bald heads and large eyes that seem to stare right into the soul of the observer. The eyes are the most prominent and literally hypnotic aspect of the aliens' faces. They have small slit-like nostrils and thin lips, but do not seem to have any ears.

Some aliens have wrinkled skin from below their eyes down to their neck. Some have long necks, whereas others have no neck at all. Their arms and legs are long and spindly and their body is small. Greys can be short or tall.

Although greys became the dominant type of alien in the 1980s, there are several earlier accounts of them. For example, in July 1974 an anonymous witness driving near Warneton, Belgium, saw a UFO land in a nearby field. His car engine and electrics stopped working and he was forced to watch, no doubt with some degree of horror, 'Two entities ... walking slowly and stiffly towards the witness. Both were about 4 feet tall, with greyish skin, round eyes, a rudimentary nose, and a slit-like, lipless mouth. They wore helmets and metallic grey coverall-type uniforms.'

The ever-industrious US ufologist Martin Kottmeyer, in a survey of UFO literature, has found

LEFT: Artist's impression of the classic grey alien, based on witness descriptions.

Fortean Picture Library

descriptions of large-headed small beings with skin colour ranging from black to white and transparent, brown, tan, pink, orange, yellow, green and blue to purple. This variation has been explained as being due to different alien metabolisms and their ability to change colour. Kottmeyer has suggested that we need a better name for the greys, but I think it is too late now. Their name has stuck, whatever they really look like.

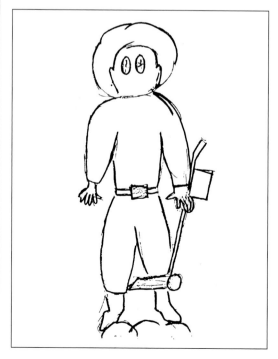

Pencil-necked aliens

Martin Kottmeyer notes that the appearance of pencil-necked aliens in abduction literature from 1987 onwards can be attributed to the influence of Spielberg's *Close Encounters of the Third Kind* film. For artistic reasons, rather than based on any factual reports, the aliens in the film were given long necks and large heads. It seems that abductees have unconsciously absorbed these images and incorporated them into their stories.

Dwarfs

Small, hairy humanoids that act aggressively seem to be most common in South America, but have also been reported elsewhere. Small entities of a general humanoid appearance are not uncommon and are comparable to the creatures of traditional folklore.

Giants

There were several reports of very tall beings been seen with their craft during the US airship wave of 1896–97, and in South America aliens over 1.8m (6ft) tall have been nearly as common as sightings of dwarfs.

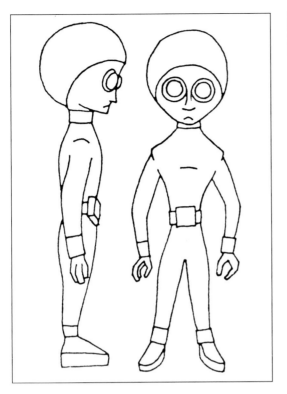

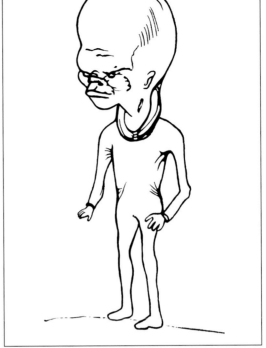

FAR LEFT: Drawings of two entities seen by Prof R. L. Johannis at Raveo near Villa Santina, Italy, on 14 August 1947. The 0.9m (3ft) tall creatures wore helmets and blue translucent overalls with red belts and collars. They appeared from a disc-shaped UFO that landed nearby.
Fortean Picture Library

LEFT: In 1978 British contactee Norman Harrison described 1.2m (4ft) tall, yellow-skinned, hairless aliens. They had disproportionately large heads due to 'evolved brain capacity'.
N. Watson

Brains

Brains or blob-like beings have been seen inside UFOs, but these are fairly rare. Robert Dickhoff many years ago put forward the idea that that flying saucers serve a Super-Brain that was created by biological brain engineering, with 'more or less of an atrophied, limp, and useless body, with hands resembling flippers and feet dangling uselessly, beside the shrivelled remainder of what would substitute for the body of this God-Brain-Head.'

Reptoids

These have hairless, scaly skin and vertical irises. In the minds of abductees, they are regarded as the descendants of the dinosaurs that roamed on Earth millions of years ago. In one case a witness saw a green and red coloured baby dinosaur walking outside a grounded flying saucer.

Insectoids

As early as 1950 Dr Gerald Kuiper, professor of astronomy at the University of Chicago, claimed it was possible that flying saucers contained either intellectual insects or incredible vegetable creatures. Several abductees have reported seeing grasshopper-like entities.

The most common insect type reported since 1986 is the praying mantis. This could be attributed to the influence of Whitley Strieber, who in a hypnotic regression session on 14 March 1986 recalled seeing, in his grandmother's home back in 1967, a 'big bug'. He went on to say, 'It looks exactly like a bug. A praying mantis is what it looks like. Only it's so big. How can it be so big?'

Even if the aliens do not look insect-like, some witnesses report that they seem to act as if they are under instruction or control, like worker ants or bees.

RIGHT: Hobgoblins are legendary, small, hairy creatures, much like the entities seen or associated with UFOs in South America. Both types of entity act in a mischievous fashion.
N. Watson

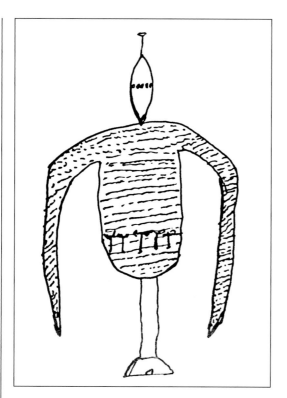

Robots and androids

There are plenty of cases of robots or machine-like beings being seen in conjunction with UFOs. One of the most famous is that of the Flatwoods Monster that appeared to a group of boys who were playing football

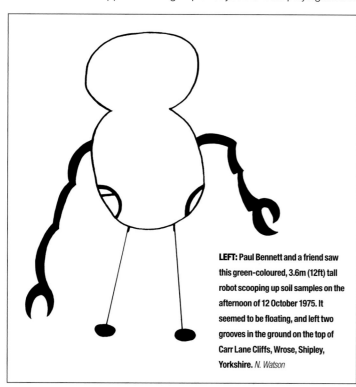

LEFT: Paul Bennett and a friend saw this green-coloured, 3.6m (12ft) tall robot scooping up soil samples on the afternoon of 12 October 1975. It seemed to be floating, and left two grooves in the ground on the top of Carr Lane Cliffs, Wrose, Shipley, Yorkshire. *N. Watson*

in Flatwoods, West Virginia. On the evening of 12 September 1952 they saw a round, red light cross the sky and land behind a nearby hill. Gathering a couple of adults and some other boys, who had also seen the light, they ran up the hill, where they encountered a strange mist and an unpleasant odour in the air that made them feel sick.

As they got to the top of the hill they were shocked to see two glowing eyes. The light from one of the boys' torches showed that they belonged to an 'ace of spades'-shaped head that had a circular window in it. The 3m (10ft) tall creature seemed to have a green skirt-like body, and when it started to glide towards them they ran away in sheer panic.

On the night of 4 September 1964 a young man at Cisco Grove, California, had an even stranger experience. Donald Shrum was bow and arrow hunting with some friends when he lost his way and decided to sleep in a tree. It was then that he saw a domed craft land nearby. Not long afterwards two humanoid beings came into view wearing silvery uniforms with helmets. A dark-coloured robot with large glowing red eyes and a rectangular mouth followed them. A white vapour shot from the robot's mouth and Shrum became unconscious. On awaking he found that the three visitors were still below his tree. Throughout the night, he managed to stop these beings from climbing the tree by throwing lighted matches at them as the robot repeatedly gassed him. At dawn, another robot came on the scene and it exchanged bright flashes of light with the first robot. Finally a large cloud of vapour rendered Shrum unconscious, and on reawakening, everything was back to normal.

In Britain there have been similar robot encounters. On the night of 2 January 1978 four young men were driving through the Simonswood Moss area of Rainford, Lancashire, when they saw a 2m (7ft) tall entity in their car headlights. It had a silver body or suit with matching boots. The head had no facial features and it had short claw-like arms. On its chest was a box with two red flashing lights. As this strange thing started walking towards them the men quickly drove away in panic.

Sightings of robots might really be of alien humanoids inside suits designed to protect them from our atmosphere, or some humanoids might really be androids – ie robots made to look like humans. John Keel noted that Men in Black tend to act in an odd manner – they don't seem to know a lot about normal social interaction and they act in a robotic fashion.

Winged entities

Creatures with wings have often been associated with UFOs or have been regarded as aliens, the most famous example being the Mothman, that was seen in West Virginia from 1966 to 1967. His body was featherless and grey-coloured, and although he had a 3m (10ft) wingspan he never seemed to flap his wings when flying. He was seen taking off vertically and had a penchant for scaring women and chasing cars. He had glowing red eyes.

An angelic being, with piercing blue eyes, told Whitley Strieber that he should not eat sweets. Strieber was also told that in three months' time he would take a journey that would lead to life or death. This prophecy came true four months later when he unexpectedly had to take a long air flight to visit his mother.

Ghostly

Aliens have been seen to glide rather than walk, and have appeared translucent or ghostly. In these cases they do not seem to be solid biological beings. This implies that they are holographic-type projections or beings that are in a different dimension of reality.

LEFT: Sketch by Sally Jensen of a ghostly figure and domed light seen in the Worral district of Sheffield, April 1977.
N. Watson

BELOW: The cover of the Christmas 1995 edition of *Northern UFO News* features the three winged entities that visited the home of Jean Hingley in Rowley Regis, West Midlands, on 4 January 1979. She regarded them as inquisitive robots or animated dolls.
Northern UFO News

FAR LEFT: The dreaded Mothman creature haunted the Point Pleasant region of West Virginia from 1966 to 1967.
Richard Svensson/ Fortean Picture Library

LEFT: Mothman was associated with UFO and Men in Black activity, although some sceptics thought the reports were caused by sightings of large birds and/or hoaxers.
William M. Rebsamen/ Fortean Picture Library

Bigfoot and
out-of-place animals

Sightings of Bigfoot, or creatures like Britain's Surrey
Puma, have been reported during flurries of UFO
activity. Some witnesses have seen such creatures
leave or return to landed UFO craft. In Pennsylvania in
the summer of 1973 a strange creature was seen on
more than 100 separate occasions. It kept to
woodland areas and was associated with local UFO
sightings. The creature or group of creatures was
described as 'hairy, ape-like beings with glowing eyes
and apparent ears, large noses, fang-like teeth, and
the long arms of an ape'.

Charles Bowen, the editor of *Flying Saucer
Review*, interviewed several witnesses of the Surrey
Puma. One reinforced the UFO connection by
reporting that whenever he saw lights moving over
the roofs of his farm buildings, the mysterious puma
would make an appearance.

These could be cases of aliens shape-shifting,
examples of screen memories used by the aliens
to create a psychological smokescreen, or just
wishful thinking.

Shape-shifters

Some witnesses have seen animals change into aliens
or vice versa. Some ufologists say the aliens can take
on any shape or form. The most common form of

shape-shifting alien seems to be the reptoid variety. Not only that, but many witnesses have also claimed that they have actually turned into an alien or seen other people turn into aliens.

John Mack recounted the case of a 34-year-old individual named Joe, who claimed he had weird dreams and alien experiences from childhood onwards. He recalled looking in a mirror as an adolescent and suddenly seeing an alien looking at him. It had green or grey warty and bumpy skin with a small round head on a thin neck. Under hypnosis he told of his struggle between being human and alien. In his abduction memories, he recalled that he had an alien identity, 'Orion'. In this humanoid manifestation he was nearly eight feet tall, but he thought he could shorten himself if he wanted to. In this state he had sexual intercourse with an alien woman called Adriana.

David Icke believes that lizard-like and reptoid aliens are controlling our world. When he visited the United States in 1998 he met several people who said they had seen people turn into reptilian aliens and then return to their usual form. He also quoted from a book by Cathy O'Brien and Mark Phillips, *Trance Formation Of America*, in which Cathy claimed to have seen none other than President George Bush looking at a book about aliens before he transformed into a reptile himself. Icke also suggested that the British Royal Family are really alien reptiles. His views are at the extreme edge of ufology, but most abduction researchers generally accept the possibility of shape-shifting aliens.

Invisibles

When attending a Wicca Circle Sanctuary weekend held near Madison, Wisconsin, in 1987, Whitley Strieber and three other people heard footsteps. They called out a greeting to the person. There was no reply, and the footsteps seemed to walk through underbrush and towards a cliff edge. No sound or sign of anyone falling down the cliff was evident, though there had been sightings of UFOs earlier that evening.

Footsteps created by an invisible walker were commonly heard by sky watchers who visited Warminster in the UK during the height of its UFO flap in the 1960s.

Alien round-up

If we accept that the aliens can change colour, shape-shift and become invisible, any attempt at classifying the appearance of aliens is doomed to considerable confusion and failure!

It is noteworthy that aliens are reported as having cartoon-like aspects. They are not seen to eat or drink; they do not have teeth, stomachs or any variation in weight or body mass. Their skin is smooth, without hair, spots or blemishes. They do not seem to breathe. Their faces do not have unique features to tell them apart. They do not have fingerprints, and often have only three fingers with no opposing thumb. Given the aliens' predilection for sexual intercourse with abductees they do not show any genitalia and are often regarded as androgynous or sexless. Combined with the fact that their behaviour is businesslike, and no living or recreational facilities are ever seen inside their craft, they seem more like blank automated machines than living entities.

ABOVE: Fairies acted much like the aliens of today. They stole human babies and abducted, entranced, healed or hurt people. They could also change their appearance and look like normal human beings.
Fortean Picture Library

LEFT: Fairies lived in caves and in underground homes. If you danced in a fairy ring you could enter fairyland for a few minutes and return to find that years have passed by in the real world.
Fortean Picture Library

RIGHT: The famous face on Mars, in the planet's Cydonia region. Higher resolution images revealed it was an optical illusion.
NASA

Alien bases

If hundreds, if not thousands, of UFOs are regularly filling our skies, where are they coming from? Early on it was thought they operated from bases on the Moon and planets in our solar system, but as our space programmes have gradually probed and even reached some of these places such ideas have taken a beating – though there are still many people who scrutinise every image taken by our exploratory craft in the hope of finding alien signs and artefacts, such as the 'face' and pyramids photographed by NASA's Viking Orbiter 1 on 25 July 1976.

More recently the Mars rover vehicle 'Spirit' has taken pictures of what looks like a Martian mermaid or Yeti, and of machined artefacts. Sceptics think that

most of these pictures are produced by tricks of the light and over-interpretation by imaginative viewers, but believers think the pictures show artificial constructs that were built by an ancient Martian civilisation.

Rather than bases beyond Earth, or huge Earth-orbiting 'mother ships', ufologists have taken to thinking that aliens have a number of bases on our planet. This is not an altogether new concept. There has been a persistent undercurrent of thinking that Adolf Hitler faked his own death and set up an underground base in Antarctica. Flying saucers were then built at this base and sent out to harass the world. There are also claims that aliens from Aldebaran sent information astrally to help and support these endeavours.

The presence of an alien base in Antarctica was reinforced by the writings of Albert K. Bender. In 1952 he set up the International Flying Saucer Bureau (IFSB) in Bridgeport, Connecticut, and it quickly gained branches throughout the USA and the world. As he got nearer to the 'truth' about UFOs, he was told to close down his operations by three menacing Men in Black. Later he recounted being taken on an astral journey to an underground base in Antarctica. Regarding this trip, he wrote: 'How much time this floating consumed I do not know, but it seemed like days.' At the base he saw beautiful female aliens, and aliens in the form of men. The purpose of the base was to extract chemicals from seawater to send back to their

BELOW:
Underground alien bases are claimed to exist throughout the world.
N. Watson

'THERE ARE UFO BASES HIDDEN IN AMERICA'

FIFTEEN secret UFO bases are hidden beneath the earth's surface, claims a Rhode Island woman who says aliens have contacted her by telepathy.

"They've told me they tunnel into the earth through the oceans and lakes, which is where they also land and take off," the woman told *The Globe* this week.

"And I've drawn several sketches, which I received telepathically, of the leaders of the bases."

Three of these amazing sketches are shown here, exclusively for *Globe* readers.

The woman — who calls herself Irena — has requested that her last name be kept secret.

She explained American bases are located beneath Portland, Maine; Barrington, Rhode Island; Norfolk, Virginia; Miami, Florida and Chicago, Illinois.

Other bases are located in South America, Africa and Europe, she said.

"It began in 1975 when I started having dreams of spaceship landings," said Irena, of Barrington, Rhode Island.

"I realized I was really receiving

LEADERS... Irena's sketches of the UFO captains in (from left) Miami, Barrington and Chicago.

By RITA ROSS

telepathic messages in my sleep and I was told my name was 'Goddess Irena.' YAWN!

"The UFO captains told me they have been studying the earth for some time and they say there is a large craft circling the earth right now.

"Most of the UFOs we see on earth are smaller ships, 10-15 ft. in diameter, that are sent here to

observe us.

"They are just waiting until humans agree to accept them.

"Then they will share information with us that will help life on earth to be much happier for all."

Irena said that she has seen several craft near her home over the years.

And other observers have joined Irena to await the UFOs.

Walter Perkins, of Providence radio station WEAN, told *The Globe*: "I did see something in the dis-

tance that wasn't a plane or a helicopter.

"I can't say for sure it was a UFO. But it WAS something you don't usually see."

Paul Crawford, of Rehoboth, Massachusetts, told *The Globe* that Irena told him a UFO would soon be passing his area.

"On November 18 of this year, I saw a red light moving erratically in the distance. I do think it was an extraterrestrial craft because it flew in such a strange manner."

home planet. They told him that they could detonate all of our atomic weapons if we attacked them.

In a similar manner to the rumours surrounding Adolf Hitler, it is claimed that inventor Nikola Tesla's death was faked in 1943, and that he escaped to a secret city run by Guglielmo Marconi in an extinct volcanic crater in the southern jungles of Venezuela, from where a colony of scientists built and operated a fleet of flying saucers.

Underground UFO bases are not new to ufology, but the concept got an enormous boost on 29 December 1987 when John Lear posted a 4,000-word document on the Internet. What is now known as the 'Lear Document' claimed that, in 1979, 66 US Special Forces soldiers were killed in a gunfight with alien forces while trying to rescue human workers in an underground alien base near Dulce, New Mexico.

This document was partly inspired by the conspiratorial ramblings of Paul Bennewitz. These began in 1980, when Bennewitz attended hypnotic regression sessions with abductee Myra Hansen, conducted by Dr Leo Sprinkle. During these sessions Hansen and her son claimed they saw aliens mutilating animals. Furthermore, she recalled being flown by a spacecraft to New Mexico, where she was taken inside an underground base. Here she saw human body parts floating in huge tanks. It was Bennewitz's contention that Hansen had been fitted with an alien implant that they could use to control her thoughts and actions.

A witness even came forward to say that he was one of the survivors of the 'firefight' at Dulce. Philip Schneider said he was involved in extending the underground military base at Dulce when the alien base was accidentally revealed. He managed to shoot two aliens before he was shot in the chest by an alien weapon. This emanated from a box attached to the chest of an alien and it gave him a dose of cancer-inducing cobalt radiation. Schneider was the only 'talking survivor'; two others went under close guard.

Nearly every mysterious or remote region seems to have its own underground alien base, and there are thought to be undersea alien bases as well. Some ufologists believe that these bases are linked by a worldwide network of tunnels.

BELOW: The alleged underground base at Dulce, New Mexico, has numerous levels.
N. Watson

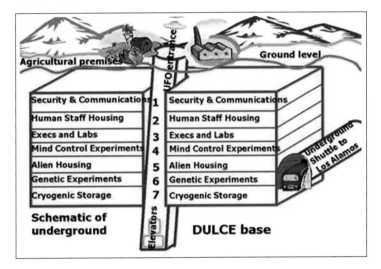

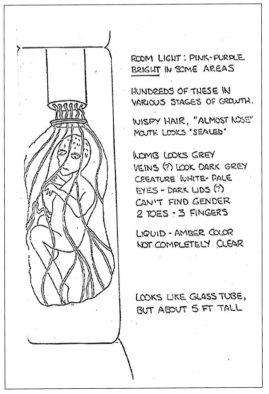

FAR LEFT: The Torments of Hell, from the Hortus Deliciarum, a 12th-century manuscript. The levels of hell are similar to the hell-like levels at Dulce.
Fortean Picture Library

LEFT: Underground bases, such as the one at Dulce, are said to have tanks and containers holding human and alien bodies and body parts.
N. Watson

RIGHT: An artist's depiction of the recovery of alien bodies from a crashed flying saucer.
SUFOI/Fortean Picture Library

Crash retrievals

Despite being able to whizz across our skies at great speed and make stupendous manoeuvres that can run rings around our own aircraft, flying saucers have a bad habit of having to land to make repairs, or simply fall out of the sky and crash. So their technology is not much more infallible than, or superior to, ours.

Of all the crash retrieval cases, that at Roswell, New Mexico, is the most familiar. On 8 July 1947 the Roswell Army Air Base publicly announced that they had recovered the remains of a crashed flying saucer from a nearby ranch. The wreckage was sent to Wright Patterson Air Base and it was quickly announced that it was the remains of a conventional weather balloon. The case was then largely forgotten, or at best dismissed as a footnote in UFO history, until the late 1970s. Since then it has encouraged all manner of 'eyewitnesses' (or friends of friends of eyewitnesses) who claim to have seen the debris, and talk of dead alien bodies being retrieved and held in storage by the USAF. To some this is the ultimate proof that the US government has concrete evidence of alien visits to our planet; to others it is a myth that has been inflated out of all proportion to the facts.

Rather than being a spaceship, some ufologists have claimed that the crash at Roswell was one of the Japanese Fugo balloons launched during World War Two finally coming to earth. Another explanation was that it was a balloon used in Project Mogul, a top secret US project intended to spy on the USSR. Due to public pressure, internal investigations were launched by the General Accounting Office to disclose the truth of the matter. Their first report, in 1995, confirmed that the wreckage was of a Project Mogul balloon. In 1997 their second report looked at the rumours and stories about recovered alien bodies. This concluded that they were a combination of rumours and half-forgotten memories of missions involving the recovery of injured pilots or anthropomorphic dummies used in experimental projects unconnected with UFOs.

These reports did little to dent the public's enthusiasm for speculation about the Roswell crash. Indeed, in 1995 more fuel was added to the flames when Ray Santilli, a British entrepreneur, released film footage which showed a graphic autopsy of a recovered alien from the Roswell crash. Several years later he admitted that this was a reconstruction of the autopsy, as the 'genuine' film footage had been lost.

In 2011 Roswell hit the headlines yet again when journalist Annie Jacobsen's book *Area 51: An Uncensored History of America's Top Secret Military Base* claimed that the aliens recovered from Roswell were actually genetically mutated 12-year-old children.

ABOVE: The 60th anniversary of the Roswell crash was celebrated on the front cover of the July 2007 edition of *UFO Magazine*.
UFO Magazine

BELOW: The confession by Marine Lieutenant Colonel Marion Magruder that he saw debris and aliens recovered from Roswell is the cover story for the June 2006 edition of *UFO Magazine*.
UFO Magazine

RIGHT: In the late 1970s, US ufologist Len Stringfield collected numerous stories about recovered UFOs and alien bodies. He called them 'retrievals of the third kind'.
N. Watson

They were sent to the USA by the Soviet Union in a remotely piloted aircraft to promote hysteria in the American population. Several years earlier a similar theory was put forward by Nick Redfern, who claimed that the Roswell crash was caused by a balloon based on Japanese technology. The balloon was used to launch a glider that had a pilot and crew consisting of handicapped people. The object of this and other missions was to study the effects of radiation and high altitudes on the human body.

Such continued speculation reinforces the concept of the 'Roswellian Syndrome' put forward by Joe Nickell and James McGaha. They note that there are five main stages to this myth-making process:

1. The incident: This is the event that initially triggers the crash-retrieval rumours.
2. Debunking: The recovered wreckage is quickly given a mundane explanation.
3. Submergence: The story lingers in the fading memories and speculation of the local population.
4. Mythologising: As time passes faulty memory, exaggeration and deliberate hoaxing comes into play.
5. Re-emergence and media bandwagon effect: The story resurfaces in the media and takes on a life of its own.

This process also plays out with other crash retrieval cases and UFO incidents. Roswell is only the tip of the iceberg, as there have been nearly 300 alleged flying saucer crashes throughout the world since 1947. Like the Roswell incident, they become more spectacular and mysterious as time passes.

Crash retrieval motifs

British ufologist John Harney has identified the following crash retrieval motifs:

- The precursor – eg something seen in the sky, an explosion heard, or mysterious object tracked by radar.
- Crashed UFO – almost always in a remote place. Aliens, dead or alive, in or near crashed UFO.
- Arrival of military.
- Civilians expelled from crash area.
- Aliens cruelly treated by military.
- Aliens helpless and unarmed, and apparently not very intelligent.
- Military personnel sworn to secrecy.
- Civilian witnesses threatened or bribed to keep silent.
- Authorities give unconvincing cover story to media.
- Authorities remove all wreckage from crash site, usually on a flat truck covered with a tarpaulin.
- Witnesses pick up bits of wreckage but authorities always recover all of it from them.
- US Air Force nearly always get involved, sometimes allegedly by putting pressure on government of country where crash occurs.
- Long after event, persons contact ufologists to claim they were involved in recovery operation.
- Such persons claim to have seen alien bodies or worked on UFO wreckage.
- Official photographs, films or videos of aliens are never made available or are obvious fakes.

LEFT: An artist's impression of the triangular UFO that was claimed to have landed in Rendlesham Forest one night in the last few days of December 1980.

Philippa Foster/Fortean Picture Library

A good example is the British equivalent of Roswell, the crash of a UFO in Rendlesham Forest, Suffolk, during December 1980. This escalated from the sighting of lights in the sky by US personnel from nearby RAF/USAF Woodbridge airbase, to stories of contact with aliens. In 2010, James Penniston – who was part of the team that approached the landed craft – claimed that when he touched the craft it telepathically downloaded binary codes into his brain. Coordinates in the code apparently indicate the position of Hy-Brasil, which is a mythical island off the west coast of Ireland.

Sceptics have come up with all manner of explanations for the Rendlesham incident, but, like the Roswell case, these are largely ignored or dismissed. Considering stories of recovered alien bodies and their craft, British ufologist Peter Rogerson notes that: 'The ultimate problem with any crash-retrieval story is that there is no point in a cover-up. For all anyone knew, within days of Roswell a flying saucer could have landed on the White House lawn to demand the aliens' wreckage back. Conspiracies only work if you are in control of the situation, and if Roswell had been real it would have been the aliens who were in control. Thus it seems that Roswell conspiratorialists are almost forced into the position of arguing that the authorities are actually in collaboration with the aliens.'

To this, it should be added that there is some point to a cover-up if the government/military do know the explanation for a UFO crash incident, and in many cases governments have used or allowed a UFO explanation to come into play to cover up secret missions or projects that have nothing to do with aliens. They know full well that any mention of UFOs will attract ridicule and ufologists, thereby hiding the 'truth' behind a smokescreen of rumour and mythology.

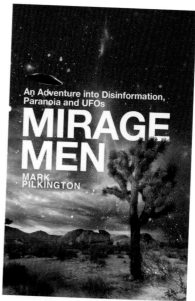

ABOVE: Mark Pilkington's book, *Mirage Men*, reveals how government agencies have used UFO reports and stories to spread disinformation and paranoia.
Mark Pilkington

References

Alien Races and Descriptions, Burlington National UFO Center website, at: www.burlingtonnews.net/secretsufo.html.

Evans, Hilary. *Visions, Apparitions, Alien Visitors* (Aquarian Press, Wellingborough, 1984).

Hough, Peter. 'The Development of UFO Occupants', in *Phenomenon: From Flying Saucers to UFOs – Forty Years of Facts and Research*, ed. Hilary Evans and John Spencer (Macdonald & Co., London, 1988), pp109–20.

Huyghe, Patrick. *The Field Guide to Extraterrestrials* (Avon, New York, 1996).

Kottmeyer, Martin. *Pencil-Neck Aliens*, REALL website, at: www.reall.org/newsletter/v01/n01/pencil-neck-aliens.html.

— 'What Colour are the Greys?', *Magonia* Supplement no 43 (November 2002), pp1–4.

Randle, Kevin. *Faces of the Visitors* (Fireside, New York, 1997).

Steiger, Brad and Steiger, Sherry. *Real Aliens, Space Beings, and Creatures from Other Worlds* (Visible Ink Press, USA, 2011).

Strieber, Whitley. *Transformation: The Breakthrough* (Arrow Books, London, 1989), pp70–77 and 163–174.

Alien bases

Bender, Albert K. *Flying Saucers and the Three Men* (Saucerian Press, Clarksburg, West Virginia, 1962).

Howe, Linda Moulton. *An Alien Harvest* (Linda Moulton Howe Productions, USA, 1993).

Friedrich, Mattern. *UFOs, Nazi Secret Weapon?* (Samisdat, Toronto, Canada, 1975).

Good, Timothy. *Alien Base: The Evidence for Extraterrestrial Colonization of Earth* (Harper Collins, London, 1999).

Pilkington, Mark. *Mirage Men: A Journey into Disinformation, Paranoia and UFOs: The Weird Truth Behind UFOs* (Constable, London, 2010).

Sauder, Richard. *Underground Bases and Tunnels: What is the Government Trying to Hide?* (Adventures Unlimited, Illinois, USA, 1995).

Shriner, Sherry. *Joint Human and Alien Underground Bases*, at: www.orgoneblasters.com/joint-bases.htm.

Tesla and the Pyramids of Mars, at: www.bibliotecapleyades.net/tesla/esp_tesla_35.htm.

Unmasking the Face on Mars, NASA Science website, at: science1.nasa.gov/science-news/science-at-nasa/2001/ast24may_1/.

Crash retrievals

Berlitz, Charles and Moore, William L. *The Roswell Incident* (Granada, London, 1982).

Harney, John. 'UFO Crash Retrievals – A Developing Myth', *Magonia* no 58 (January 1997), at: magonia.haaan.com/2009/crashretrievals/.

Nickell, Joe and McGaha, James. 'The Roswellian Syndrome: How Some UFO Myths Develop', Skeptical Inquirer vol 36.3 (May/June 2012), at: www.csicop.org/si/show/the_roswellian_syndrome_how_some_ufo_myths_develop.

Printy, Timothy. Roswell 4F: *Fabrications, Fumbled Facts, and Fables*, at: home.comcast.net/~tprinty/UFO/Roswell4F.htmLIST OF POSSIBLE .

Randle, Kevin D. *A History of UFO Crashes* (Avon, New York, 1995).

Randles, Jenny. *UFO Retrievals: The Recovery of Alien Spacecraft* (Blandford, London, 1995).

— Roberts, Andy and Clarke, David. *The UFOs That Never Were* (London House, London, 2000).

Redfern, Nick. *Body Snatchers in the Desert: The Horrible Truth at the Heart of the Roswell Story* (Simon & Schuster, London, 2005).

'The Rendlesham Forest Incident official website', at: www.therendleshamforestincident.com/Home.htmlWebsite.

'The Rendlesham Forest UFO Case', a sceptical website authored by Ian Ridpath, at: www.ianridpath.com/ufo/rendlesham.htm.

'UFO Crashes & Retrievals', UFO evidence website, at: www.ufoevidence.org/topics/ufocrashes.htm

'UFO/ET Craft Crashes and Retrievals', CSETI website, at: www.checktheevidence.com/disclosure/Web%20Pages/List%20of%20Possible%20UFO-ET%20Craft%20Crashes%20and%20Retrievals.htm.

A collection of articles about crash retrievals originally published in *Magonia* magazine is available at: magonia.haaan.com/tag/ufo-crashes/.

8

Close encounters of the fourth kind: abductions

The Betty and Barney Hill abduction case was the first to attract worldwide publicity, and resulted in a permanent change in the direction of ufological research. It began on the fateful night of 19 September 1961, as they drove from Canada to their home at Portsmouth, New Hampshire, USA.

They were frightened by a light that followed their car, and, at a place called Indian Head, Barney got out of the car to view a UFO hovering at about tree-top height. Looking through binoculars, he saw six uniformed beings working at a control panel inside the craft.

Overwhelmed with fear Barney drove away from the scene, and he and Betty seemed suddenly to arrive at Ashland, 56km (35 miles) south of the sighting location. The next day they discovered that their journey had taken two hours longer than they had anticipated.

From 29 September to 3 October, Betty had many nightmares about their UFO sighting. She dreamt that some men took them to a landed craft in the nearby woods and conducted medical examinations on them before returning them to the car. These dreams outlined what they later recalled under hypnotic regression. Betty tended to think these dreams were memories of real events, but Barney just thought they were vivid dreams.

In January 1964 the anxiety and stress produced by the event led them to participate in a series of hypnotic regression sessions with psychiatrist and neurologist Dr Benjamin Simon. Under hypnosis they both recalled being taken inside a landed UFO during the missing period of time.

Inside the disc-shaped craft, Betty was taken to an examination room. They looked at her mouth, eyes, ears and throat, and took samples of her skin, nails and hair. She was asked to remove her dress,

ABOVE: An artist's impression of the landed UFO into which the Hills were taken for 'medical' examinations.
Dezsö Sternoczky/SUFOI/ Fortean Picture Library

LEFT: Betty and Barney Hill were the first couple to report a UFO abduction, which had a huge impact on ufology and the popular concept of this phenomenon.
Fortean Picture Library

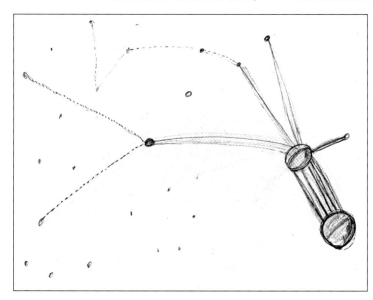

LEFT: Betty remembered what she described as a 'Star Chart', displayed inside the UFO. By using models of star systems, it is believed that it shows the aliens to have originated from Zeti Reticuli.
Fortean Picture Library

ABOVE: When under hypnosis, Barney Hill produced the sketch of the 'leader' alien shown on the right. He produced the other sketch when he listened to a tape recording of his hypnosis session, which helped him recall more details.
Fortean Picture Library

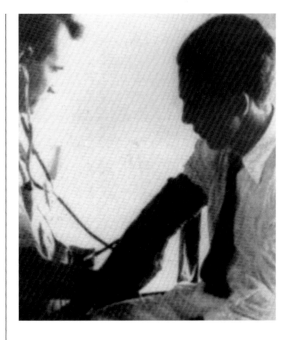

and was prodded all over her body with needles attached to wires. This procedure did not hurt. When asked to roll over they pierced her navel with a long needle. As the needle was withdrawn she felt sore, and on asking why they did it she was told it was a pregnancy test. She replied that it was not like any pregnancy test that she had ever known.

When allowed to put her dress back on, she asked if she could take some proof of this meeting home

with her. Finding a book with strange writing in it, the aliens' leader agreed to let her take it. After asking if she knew anything about the universe, he showed her a map with dots and lines on it.

Just as she was about to leave the UFO, the book was taken away from her. Betty screamed, 'You can take the book but you can never make me forget!' As she walked back to the car the aliens' leader apologised for frightening them at the beginning of the encounter. In just a few moments, her extreme anger with the aliens turned to joy: 'I'm saying to the leader, "This is the most wonderful experience of my life. I hope you'll come back. I got a lot of friends who would love to meet you."'

The most important case in relation to the Hills' experience and to our concept of alien abductions is that reported by Antonio Villas Boas. At 1:00am on the night of 14 October 1957 he was ploughing a field at his family's farm near Sao Francisco de Sales, Minas Gerais, Brazil, when a luminous egg-shaped object landed in front of him. He was forcibly taken into the craft by three beings, and in a small room five aliens took off his clothes. The aliens left, and after a long wait a beautiful, slim, short, naked woman walked into the room. She had long, flowing fair hair, milk white skin, and slanted blue eyes. She had a pointed chin and high cheekbones. They had sexual intercourse twice, in the normal way according to Villas Boas, except that the woman made grunting sounds and did not kiss him.

ABOVE: Aliens are often reported 'invading' bedrooms, and seem intent on interbreeding with humans according to Peter Brookesmith in a cover article for *Fortean Times*.
Fortean Times

ABOVE: Several men and women claim to have had sexual intercourse with aliens. It is debateable whether these were fantasies or real experiences.
Beyond Magazine

LEFT: Budd Hopkins (1931–2011) established the non-profit-making Intruders Foundation to research alien abductions and offer support to abductees. He believed that the aliens are operating a human/alien hybrid breeding programme.
Lisa Richards/Fortean Picture Library

RIGHT: British ufologists were impressed by the evidence Budd Hopkins presented at the Sheffield International Congress in August 1991.
UFO Brigantia

UFO BRIGANTIA

THIS IS BUDD HOPKINS
HE BELIEVES THAT THOUSANDS OF ADULTS AND CHILDREN HAVE BEEN ABDUCTED
BY ALIENS
THE QUESTION IS – DO YOU BELIEVE HIM?

November 1991   *No. 50*

Ufologists were reluctant to investigate or publicise abduction cases until the 1970s, and even then reports of such abductions were relatively uncommon. The abduction phenomenon became firmly established in the 1980s with the publication by New York artist Budd Hopkins of *Missing Time* in 1981 and *Intruders* in 1987, the same year that horror writer Whitley Strieber's best-selling *Communion*, a striking account of his own alien experiences, put the subject firmly in the mainstream of public consciousness. Strieber tells of being floated from outside his cabin in upstate New York by alien visitors on 26 December 1985. He found himself in a smelly, circular room where he was subjected to several medical procedures, including a needle

being jabbed behind his right ear and a probe being inserted into his rectum. For better or for worse, the powerful combination of *Intruders* and *Communion* set the standard for future abduction experiences and research.

The publication in 1992 of UFO researcher and historian David Jacobs' *Secret Life* – a survey of 60 abductees, involving 300 abduction experiences – and Harvard professor of psychiatry John E. Mack's case histories of 12 abductees in his 1994 book *Abduction*, set the seal on the subject. These gave powerful support to Hopkins' view that thousands of US citizens were being abducted, and confirmed that such abductions followed a stereotypical pattern.

FAR LEFT: In his best-selling book *Communion*, Whitley Strieber wrote about his abductions that began on the evening of 26 December 1985 at his cabin in upstate New York. The book and subsequent feature film gained worldwide publicity for the subject.
Lisa Richards/Fortean Picture Library

LEFT: The cover of Whitley Strieber's book *Communion* triggered many people to remember being visited and abducted by similar beings. *N. Watson*

The abduction experience

The trigger to someone remembering that they have been abducted does not have to be an actual UFO or alien encounter. A series of strange nightmares or some other traumatic experience might make someone think that they have been abducted. Reading about the subject, or seeing a film or documentary about UFOs, can also trigger a memory of an encounter. Visual images of aliens seem to be particularly potent.

All these instances indicate that abductees have no control over how and when they are contacted, but there are also cases of people making deliberate contact on their own initiative. This might be done through meditation, trance or even drug-induced states.

Bedroom encounters usually involve the person waking suddenly. They hear a buzzing or whizzing sound, and they are paralysed so that they cannot get out of bed. At this moment they might see a strange figure or figures at the bottom of their bed. They are usually described as being human-like with a large head, wearing one-piece silvery outfits.

In the case of abductees in cars or outdoors, they usually see a light in the sky that comes towards them. Just as in CEII cases, they might then go through a fog or mist that causes their car to stop. Everything in the area might seem to be silent and strange, as if time or space has become distorted.

This change has been termed the 'Oz Factor' by British UFO investigator Jenny Randles, who thinks that witnesses enter an altered state of conscious at this stage. She explains this in relation to a sighting by two fishermen of a large disc-shaped UFO: 'The witnesses said that they were not afraid; indeed, they were strangely calm and subdued. They felt themselves isolated in time and space, as if removed temporarily from the real world and melded with the UFO above them; only they and it existed.'

Minutes or hours later, the person will 'wake' and discover that they cannot remember anything during this period. Motorists who experience this will suddenly find themselves miles down the road without knowing how they got there.

Entering the alien world

The trigger event causes the abductee to seek out the reason why they cannot remember a period of missing time after witnessing a UFO, or they might want to know why they feel traumatised by 'alien'

nightmares. In his 1987 study of 270 abduction cases, folklorist Dr Thomas Bullard identified six major elements of abduction accounts:

- Capture.
- Examination.
- Conference.
- Tour.
- Otherworldly journeys.
- Theophany.

It is worthwhile to use these points to gain an understanding of what might occur during an abduction. First of all, capture involves the abductee either being floated up to a flying saucer or simply walking up a stairway that extends from the craft. Much to the disbelief of more hard-headed ufologists, many abductees have reported being floated through solid walls or windows on their journey to a saucer hovering over their home or car. Often people do not remember how they got inside the flying saucer; this has been labelled 'doorway amnesia'.

Inside, the craft usually has a clean, sterile environment with no windows, and light that emanates from no apparent source. The abductee is taken down a curved, white or grey metallic corridor, which eventually takes them to the centre of the craft, which seems to be a medical chamber. Working in a businesslike manner, with great efficiency the aliens strip the abductee and place them on an examination table where they are medically examined.

Generally, spindly 'grey' aliens are regarded as the main abductors of human beings, but this is not always the case, and the abductors can be seen

ABOVE: From left to right, Louise Smith, Elaine Thomas and Mona Stafford. They claimed that on the night of 6 January 1976 they were abducted when driving towards Hustonville, Kentucky, on Highway 78.

Fortean Picture Library

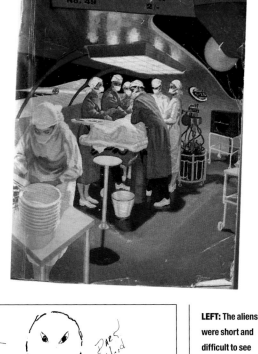

RIGHT: An operating theatre inside a spacecraft illustrated on the cover of a British science fiction magazine, July 1956. Some ufologists and sceptics believe that SF imagery has had an important influence on the perception of UFOs and aliens.

Dennis Stacy/Fortean Picture Library

working with other types of aliens. Humans in military uniforms have also been seen helping the alien examiners. The aliens who conduct the examinations tend to be taller than the ones who bring the abductee to the examination table, and they wear close-fitting outfits, sometimes featuring a cowl or hood. Like surgeons, some wear boots and surgical masks.

The aliens use strange-looking surgical equipment to scan the subject and to probe their body. Needles are inserted in their abdomen. There is usually an intense interest in the person's genitalia, and they might extract blood, sperm, or ovum samples. Parts of the body, such as eyes or whole brains, have been

LEFT: The aliens were short and difficult to see clearly. They had no mouth and communicated using telepathy.

Fortean Picture Library

FAR LEFT: The three women saw a disc-shaped craft that seemed to take control of their car and shot a blinding beam of light into it. When they got home they realised that they could not account for an hour of missing time.

Fortean Picture Library

ABOVE: Under hypnotic regression, the three women all recalled being inside the UFO and being subjected to humiliating and painful examinations.

Dennis Stacy/Fortean Picture Library

allegedly removed and then returned without any damage. Others have reported having a tube placed up their rectum and faecal material sucked out of them.

The aliens are also likely to place small implants into the brain via the nose, or inserted behind the ear, or into other parts of the body. The spine and other areas of the body might be pierced with needles to extract or inject fluids.

There are many reports of people being raped or forcibly seduced by the aliens. To encourage sexual intercourse the aliens have disguised themselves as celebrities, religious figures or even the abductee's dead spouse.

Female abductees who have been raped by the aliens and become pregnant suddenly 'lose' the foetus, and are later abducted again and shown their 'lost' hybrid baby. Other abductees have seen, either on flying saucers or in what they believe to be underground bases on Earth, nurseries containing

such hybrid babies and human bodies in liquid-filled containers. There have been accounts of abductees seeing other humans on the ship being mutilated, flayed, dismembered, drained of blood and stacked in a heap. They are threatened that if they do not cooperate they will end up like these people.

The procedures are conducted on the abductee whilst they are in a conscious yet paralysed or sedated state. More than one type of alien might be present during the examination, and they often induce great fear, pain and humiliation.

Conference with the alien captors is usually limited. The aliens do not ask permission to operate on their victim, and there is usually no explanation for their activities. The aliens tend to communicate telepathically with the abductee. If other human abductees are present, they seem to be in a trance and it is impossible to talk to or have any other form of contact with them. When the aliens communicate with each other it is either in an unknown language or in a manner that is inaudible to the abductee.

Abductees are sometimes given a tour of the ship; they might be shown film or slide shows presented on TV monitors. There is an attempt to train abductees in the use of alien technology, or they are lectured on how this alien technology works. They might also see the ship's control room, which contains maps of star systems showing where the aliens come from. According to David Jacobs, none of the 50 abduction cases he investigated contained any reports of seeing living quarters on the alien craft.

Some abductees are taken on what Bullard calls 'otherworldly journeys', either to the home planet of the aliens, or on a short ride round the solar system. Contactees of the 1950s were most likely to report such trips, usually garnished with detailed descriptions of alien civilisations on Mars and Venus. Since our own space probes have proved that life of this type does not exist in our solar system, defenders of the contactees' accounts contend that they must have travelled in a different dimension or astral plane.

After this the abductee receives important information about the future of our planet and our species. They warn that we will be destroyed, and that only the chosen will be saved and taken to another planet. The aliens are regarded either as our spiritual benefactors or as the minions of the Devil. After an abduction experience the abductee will want to spread the word that the aliens have come to save us or to destroy us. This could be because there are both evil and good aliens carrying out these abductions, or it could be that they do not act in the same way towards everyone. In the latter case, it is how the abductee responds to them that conditions whether they are perceived as good or evil. Ufologists have noted that the biases of the investigator seems to have a bearing here, as some investigators seem to only

see abductees who have negative and painful experiences while others only get abductees that have been spiritually uplifted by their experience.

Finally, the abductee returns to full consciousness several miles from where they were taken if the incident involves a car, or they are dumped several yards away from where they were originally taken. Others wake up in their bed and wonder if the abduction was a dream or not. Jacobs notes that abductees often wake up to find themselves in odd positions, or with their clothing

rearranged, or they find unusual stains in the bed, and feel that they have not had a proper sleep.

Abductees have a screen memory planted in their subconscious mind to hide their abduction experience. The screen memory takes the form of seeing owls, wolves, eagles, raccoons, and mythical birds like the phoenix, or angels or devils. Yet the memory of the abduction is never totally erased and most of it can be retrieved through hypnotic regression.

ABOVE LEFT: A gang of woodcutters, including Travis Walton, saw a UFO in the Sitgreave-Apache National Forest, Arizona, on 5 November 1975.
Fortean Picture Library

RIGHT: Travis was found in a telephone booth in a confused state a few days later. Under hypnotic regression, he recalled being inside a UFO where aliens with large heads examined him.
Fortean Picture Library

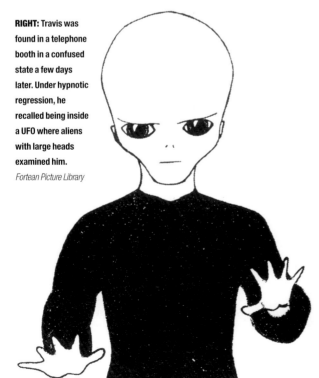

ABOVE: The UFO shot a green/blue light at Walton, sending him flying to the ground. His companions were so scared that they drove off in panic. When they returned Travis could not be found.
Fortean Picture Library

LEFT: Travis wrote about his abduction experiences in a book, *The Walton Experience*, which became the basis for the feature film *Fire in the Sky*.
Fortean Picture Library

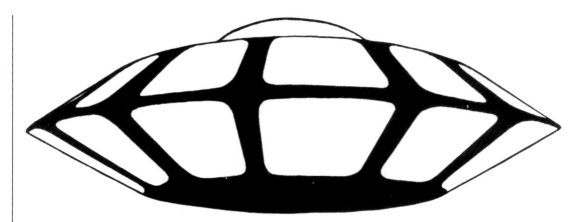

RIGHT: The
domed UFO
made a beeping
sound, followed by
a louder rumbling
noise as it rotated
on its vertical axis.
Travis ran
towards it to
 get a better view.
*Fortean Picture
Library*

Post-abduction experiences

After the trigger event, the person can suffer a multitude of physical and psychological signs that indicate that they have been abducted. These can be listed as follows:

1. Amnesia or 'missing time' after seeing a UFO.
2. Nightmares, insomnia, and fear of the dark and enclosed spaces.
3. Scars, scoop marks, bruises and punctures will be found on the person's body, without any immediate explanation for them. The abductee might have frequent nosebleeds and feel that they have an unusual growth or implant inside them.
4. The health of the person deteriorates. Serious illness – sometimes leading to death – can occur in the months following an abduction. Terminal brain tumours can appear after abductions. Female abductees can develop serious gynaecological problems.
5. Behavioural changes. These can be for good or bad. Abductees might become born again Christians, or become more spiritual and relaxed in general. They might become vegetarian and support animal rights issues and other charitable works.
6. The abductee might become psychic and/or be plagued by paranormal apparitions or poltergeists.
7. Abductees may take to drug, food and alcohol abuse. Their behaviour can become excessive and erratic. They get obsessive about their abduction experience and its implications. They lose any meaningful relationship with their wife or partner, family and friends. They cannot deal with normal life any more and can become suicidal.

One or a combination of these indicators will cause the person to seek help that will uncover their abduction experience. Hypnotic regression is used to recall this information, but sometimes this is not necessary and it is spontaneously recalled.

When recalling their abduction experience the person often remembers that they have been in contact with aliens since childhood; it is only after the trigger event that they realise why they have had certain phobias or strange screen memories.

Ufologists have also come to believe that abductees are chosen, rather than randomly snatched away. This is indicated by the fact that whole generations of families have been plagued or blessed by alien abduction experiences.

Discussion

John Rimmer, editor of the *Magonia* website, agrees that there is strong 'family resemblance' between a great many cases, and 'many uncanny details [are] repeated in case after case'. Bullard's study equally conveys the impression that abductions fit a highly structured format that suggests they are the product of real experiences rather than rumour or fantasy.

Each abduction case seems to gain details from previous cases and other cultural images and sources, which would explain the consistency of abduction details. Wittingly or not, abductees and researchers have picked up on these details and helped feed and sustain the alien abduction mythology.

Ironically, Budd Hopkins, the very person who helped establish the concept of abduction, published ever-more fantastic accounts that even his followers found hard to accept at face value, and eroded the validity of his original concepts.

The doubts set in with the publication of Hopkins'

OPPOSITE: Linda
Napolitano claims
she was floated out
of her Manhattan
apartment to a UFO
hovering nearby.
*Dennis Stacy/Fortean
Picture Library*

book *Witnessed* in 1996. This claims that in the early morning of 30 November 1989, Linda Napolitano (referred to as 'Cortile' in the earliest reports) was floated through her closed Manhattan apartment window. She was taken inside a hovering spaceship, which plunged into the Hudson river. On board the craft she was shown a visual presentation about ecological matters and then returned home.

The Secretary-General of the United Nations, Javier Pérez de Cuéllar, and his two security guards allegedly witnessed the vision of Napolitano floating in a blue-white light. It seems that they were abducted at the same time. One of the guards and Cortile had apparently met as imaginary playmates during previously shared abductions many years earlier.

Napolitano reported her abduction on the same day, and it was under hypnotic regression that the details of it were revealed. Then in February 1991 the two guards, calling themselves Richard and Dan, began writing to Hopkins, revealing that they and their VIP witnessed the event. Next Richard and Dan began visiting Napolitano at her apartment. At first they went on a friendly basis, and then in April 1991 they kidnapped her in a black Mercedes and interrogated her about her abduction for hours as they drove through the streets of New York. A few months later, in October, Dan threatened her with a gun and made sexual advances to her. At Christmas he wrote a long letter saying he hated her and thought she was the spawn of hybrid breeding. His claim that 'the staff here usually keeps me pretty

Millions of abductions?

Several polls of varying reliability and quality have been conducted to try to find out the number of people who have been abducted by aliens. In the 1990s, David Jacobs conducted a poll of students at Temple University which showed that 5.5% of those questioned might have had an abduction experience. Projecting these figures, this indicated that 15 million people in the United States and 60 to 200 million people worldwide are potential abductees. Another poll, by Robert Durant in 1995, revealed that five million Americans had probably been abducted in the past 50 years, which indicated that there are 2,740 abductions per day.

A more organised attempt at assessing the true extent of alien abductions began in 1991, when Robert Bigelow and an anonymous financial backer employed The Roper Organization to poll the US population. When the results from the selection of 5,947 American adults were analysed they found that one in fifty people fitted the abductee profile, which would indicate that there are 3.3 million abductees living in the United States.

Critics like Paul Devereux and Peter Brookesmith noted that the poll had a plus or error margin of 1.4%, which rendered the finding of 0.3% full abductees as statistically meaningless. They concluded that the results 'reveal absolutely nothing about the incidence of abductions by aliens in the US'.

Whatever the validity of these polls, they have been used to prove the prevalence of the abduction phenomenon. David Jacobs, in a lecture at the 1998 MUFON UFO symposium entitled *Thinking Clearly about UFO Abduction*, asserted that since the 1890s (yes, 1890s), about 2% of the US population has each had 200 abductions throughout their lifetimes.

Assuming a more conservative figure of 100 abductions per lifetime, MUFON investigator Craig Lang worked out that in a metropolitan area of two million people there would be 200 abductions every 24 hours, so by projecting these figures to a global basis there would be 600,000 abductions a day. As he rightly noted, if they are 'nuts and bolts' events this would require thousands of aliens to operate and maintain a vast fleet of flying saucers. From this, Lang concluded that we must consider four possibilities:

1. Individual abductees have far fewer than 200 abduction experiences in a lifetime.
2. The number of abductees throughout the population is lower.
3. Alien technology is such that it can operate on this scale without (much) detection.
4. As John Keel suggested, flying saucers and abductions are non-physical 'events'.

Missing foetus syndrome

The association of abduction experiences with 'missing foetus syndrome' is a difficult and sensitive area of abduction research. Mary Rodwell, a trained midwife as well as an abductionist, has produced a useful list of possible medical explanations for this syndrome:

1. Blighted ovum. This occurs when the embryo degenerates, or is not even present in the first place, but hormones are secreted that will give a positive reading in a pregnancy test.
2. Spontaneous abortion or miscarriage.
3. Missed abortion. A non-viable foetus can stay in the uterus for up to five months, but is not rejected by the body as in note 2 above.
4. Hydatidiform mole. A mass of tissue grows from a fertilised egg that has degenerated. Hormone secretions would indicate that the person is pregnant. This can be a dangerous condition that requires urgent medical attention.
5. Secondary amenorrhea. Periods cease or are later than usual due to stress or other physiological factors (eg anorexia).
6. Pseudocyesis. Men and women can experience false or phantom pregnancies. This is a psychological rather than a physiological condition. The same psychosomatic processes as are used to explain UFO stigmata could also trigger phantom pregnancies.

Not included in her list is the process of absorption. This sometimes happens in a person having twins, when one foetus withers away and is absorbed whilst the remaining twin thrives. Rodwell, although aware of all the possible medical explanations, still believed that the missing foetus syndrome in connection with contact experiences is real.

The most damning criticism of the 'missing foetus syndrome' is why would aliens so graphically and callously rape their victims and take away foetuses for their hybrid baby programme? We already use in vitro fertilisation techniques that avoid this sort of trauma and pain, so why wouldn't the aliens?

much sedated' implied that he was safely ensconced in some form of mental institution.

A letter from one Janet Kimble (pseudonym) confirmed that she and other drivers on Brooklyn Bridge saw four people being floated into a brightly lit object on the morning in question. There was screaming and panic, and, oddly, she thought a film was being made of *Snow White and the Seven Dwarfs*. Napolitano also claimed that Pérez de Cuéllar had written to Hopkins telling him to stop looking for the 'third man' (presumably he meant himself) as it would upset world peace.

Ufologist George Hansen made the sensible suggestion that if any of this was true then the activities of Richard and Dan should be reported to the police or other authorities. This brought down a firestorm of criticism from supporters of Hopkins. Hansen and his associates also showed that Hopkins had done little work to confirm Napolitano's assertions. Furthermore, Hopkins only ever met Napolitano face to face; all the other evidence came from correspondents who were reluctant to meet him.

Since Hopkins and Jacobs were convinced of the literal truth that 'nuts and bolts' spacecraft are coming to abduct us, how did they account for stories full of magical happenings? Jacobs acknowledged that when he started hypnotically regressing abductees they recounted wild and impossible events. He regarded these factors as the result of false memories and dreams that filled the vacuum of the 'legitimate memories'. Through continued work he felt he was able to distinguish between the false and truthful memories, and after two and a half years of work he was able to fit them into a three-tiered matrix. His abduction matrix consists of physical, mental and reproductive procedures that the aliens carry out on a regular, less frequent and irregular basis.

Jacobs is selective about the people he regresses and uses in his abduction studies, and he is dismissive of alien contact that involves the use of automatic writing, mediumship and other psychic means that became popularly known as 'channelling'. Jacobs determines whether an abductee is genuine or not by using a set of 25 questions and interviewing them to get a 'feel' for their character.

Like Bullard's narrative structure for abduction accounts, Jacobs' matrix does not distinguish between fact and fiction. A fictitious abduction story would neatly fit into his ever-evolving matrix. The skill of the investigator is the main factor in distinguishing between real and imaginary abduction stories.

The abduction scenario, although worldwide, is heavily influenced by US periodicals, websites and books. This means that they broadly agree with the

US abduction accounts; yet they also introduce their own national and/or cultural biases. In Britain, Jenny Randles notes that when she conducted a study of 19 British abduction cases, between 1979 and 1986, none of them involved the stereotypical grey beings. Instead, British abductees saw monsters, robots or Nordic-type human entities.

When John Mack first looked at cases referred to him in 1990 by Hopkins, Jacobs, Leo Sprinkle and John Carpenter, he could not explain them within terms of psychiatry or the Western scientific framework. Unlike Jacobs, he did not think that we should try to discriminate between real and false abduction memories. His criteria for studying a case were whether the abductee felt that what they experienced was real, and that they were sincerely communicating these experiences.

Hopkins' philosophy was equally open-ended in that he asserted that we should never pre-judge, and that genuine sceptics should accept 'the impossibility of anything'. This contrasts with Charles Fort's philosophy that 'we accept nothing'.

These different approaches to the subject are due to the role of the researcher. Those who are members of UFO organisations are likely to be more interested in collecting evidence about abductees' experiences, whilst counsellors/therapists are more interested in helping people come to terms with the traumas associated with abduction experiences. However, whether UFO researcher or therapist, they should put the interests of the abductee first and foremost, which is often at odds with proving the literal existence of alien contacts. This also means that since abductees are regarded as victims in need of protection, any criticism or questioning of their accounts tends to be met with great hostility.

Alien technology

IMPLANTS

Abductees have reported implants being placed in virtually every part of the body. Mary Rodwell, in her book *Awakening*, carefully noted that implants could be introduced for the following purposes:

1. Confirming to abductees that they have had a real experience.
2. Downloading information into the abductee's brain.
3. Monitoring and tracking the abductee's movements.
4. Monitoring the abductee's feelings and biochemical processes.
5. Controlling the actions of the abductee.
6. Boosting creativity, psychic abilities, telepathic and healing powers.

7. Facilitating the integration of alien bodies with human bodies.
8. As a form of alien shamanistic initiation.

   In addition, we can add:

9. Initiating molecular changes enabling the abductee to be transported to and into UFOs.

Such implants tend to be very small and elusive. Rodwell observed that: 'These anomalies or implants have often strangely disappeared, just as they were due to be removed, or they would dissolve or disappear just after removal from the body.' They also have the ability to elude magnetic resonance imaging (MRI), X-rays and CAT scans, though on occasion the odd inconclusive shadow has been spotted.

David Jacobs stated that the aliens use long instruments to insert round or spiky BB shot-sized balls into abductees' ears, noses or the sinus cavities between eye and cheek. They cause abductees to suffer unexplained nosebleeds and ruptured eardrums.

Implants are less frequently inserted near the ovaries of women or in the penile shaft of men. One abductee reported finding an implant in his penile shaft, which turned out to consist of cotton fibres that had formed around dead human cells. Believers suggest that the aliens deliberately hide their devices in this manner to avoid suspicion.

Jacobs' confidence about these implant procedures is undermined by the fact that of the 62 abductees he interviewed, not one was able to provide proof of their existence. Whitley Strieber described having an implant removed from his ear by a physician, but on analysis it was found to be collagen. Other 'implant' recoveries have been equally disappointing.

INVISIBILITY

In their book *Sight Unseen*, Budd Hopkins and his wife Carol Rainey report the experiences of abductee Katharina Wilson in relation to invisibility. When she arrived at Chicago O'Hare Airport to attend a UFO conference, she was an hour late meeting the organisers who were awaiting her. She was in a confused state before leaving the aircraft, and then in the airport toilets she had trouble operating the washbasin taps. Her hands would not trigger the automatic sensors, and in exasperation she asked a woman, 'Am I invisible or something?' The woman just ignored her. Hopkins speculated that Wilson was abducted, teleported or that her energy field had been changed.

A more sceptical view is that she suffered a mental fugue and had merely 'lost' the hour by wandering around the airport.

Star People

Apparently there are thousands of 'Star People' on our planet, and many of them do not even know it. They are reborn incarnations of aliens, or emissaries of the space people in human form. The belief that we might be so-called Star People gained considerable popularity in the 1970s. When Francie Steiger had a dream about two men who told her 'Now is the time', she regarded this as a message to reveal that she is a Star Person.

According to Steiger, Star People have more sensitivity to sound, light, electricity and electromagnetic fields. They are subject to chronic sinus trouble, subnormal blood pressure, sleeping problems, lower body temperature, and are more likely to have a rare blood group. A Star Person has psychic abilities and an extra vertebra.

All the aspects of the Star People phenomenon seem to have been absorbed into the abduction mythology. The signs of being a Star Person are now the signs that you have been abducted. To be fair this is probably because the terminology has changed, but the experience of discovering or realising you are an alien from outer space has not.

RIGHT: On the evening of 25 January 1967 Betty Andreasson was abducted from her home in South Ashburnham, Massachusetts. Under hypnotic regression she recalled being taken by UFO to a planet where she was taken through tunnels and floated over a city with tall buildings connected by bridges in the air.
Dennis Stacy/Fortean Picture Library

TRANSPORT THROUGH SOLID MATTER

Aliens can move themselves and abductees through solid matter such as windows and doors. Betty Andreasson was floated through her own kitchen door when she stood behind the alien leader. Jacobs confirmed that abductees can be passed through walls or ceilings, although they prefer to transfer people through windows that are not blocked by boxes or similar obstacles. So far I have not read of anyone claiming that they had been passed through blinds or curtains as well as the window, though I assume this is equally possible. What bothers me about such claims is that highly intelligent aliens have not learnt to open doors and windows.

Martin Kottmeyer questioned the physics of two objects being able to occupy the same place at the same time, and shows that passing through walls is an attribute of supernatural beings and fictional characters.

FLOATING AND LEVITATION

Aliens have the ability to float people through the sky like Peter Pan or Superman. This is often achieved by some form of light beam from a flying saucer. In the case of Linda Napolitano, witnesses allegedly saw her and the three UN staff being floated into a UFO over Manhattan, though Jacobs thinks that abductees are often rendered invisible when they are floated to a UFO. This would explain the rarity of sightings by independent witnesses of people flying about in their nightwear.

Elusive evidence

Abductions never take place in public; they tend to occur at night when the abductee is alone. As Jacobs put it: 'The greater the victim's seclusion and the less others will miss her, the longer the experience tends to last.'

If there are other people present during an abduction, they are 'switched off' by the aliens. If it is a bedroom encounter, the person's partner will remain in a deep sleep; or if a UFO is spotted whilst riding in a car, the driver might pull over and go to sleep or become unconscious. The targeted person will then be floated through the windscreen. When outdoors with a group of people, the abductees generally walk away to where a UFO has landed and experience their abduction there. To hide the time they are away, the rest of the group is 'switched off' until the abductee returns.

However, there are some abduction episodes that do involve more than one person, like the Betty and Barney Hill case. Unfortunately, they tend to involve close friends, family or partners; there tends to be a dominant abductee and a passive partner or friend, and often only one of the abductees will consent to be hypnotised. When two or more abductees are taken on board a flying saucer, they are nearly always separated by the aliens, so they cannot corroborate the main details of their abduction. There are few reports of witnesses seeing landed flying saucers taking abductees on board, though several abductions have taken place where UFO activity has been reported by independent witnesses.

Hard-line abductionists dismiss astral journeys and channelling, but by acknowledging the ability of aliens to levitate, use telepathy, move through walls and become invisible they have accepted the encroachment of many paranormal factors into nuts-and-bolts ufology. As John Harney observes, physical beings should not be able to ignore the laws of physics: accepting paranormal theories or happenings means it is not 'necessary for any further thought or investigation. In other words, it is merely a form of intellectual laziness.'

In terms of abductions, we are told that abductees get an inclination to walk or drive to a certain spot before they are walked, half-dragged or floated to a flying saucer. As we have seen, on their return they are left outside their home, several yards from where they were originally abducted, or in their beds, where they wake the next morning to find they are wearing different clothing or wearing them back-to-front. Yet since the aliens possess technology that can float and transfer people through solid matter, why don't they simply take and return people without all this elaborate rigmarole? If these aliens can move through solid matter, why do some abductees report elaborate procedures to find a window to travel through when others claim they have gone straight through walls and ceilings?

Furthermore, the aliens are curiously selective about covering up their activities. They can 'switch off' people, create screen memories and elude video equipment, photography and radar, yet they cannot fully block people's memories or put their clothes back on properly. They also leave scratches and scars all over people's bodies (even though some abductees claim the aliens have fast-acting healing powers), and their sophisticated implants drop out of people's bodies.

Looking at the evidence of UFOs in the early 1970s, John Keel found 'that flying saucers are not stable machines requiring fuel, maintenance, and logistical support. They are not permanent constructions of matter.' In stark contrast, Budd Hopkins believed that abductions are what he calls real, event-level occurrences that have provided a wealth of photographic, medical and physical evidence.

References

Brookesmith, Peter and Devereux, Paul. *UFOs and Ufology: The First 50 Years* (Blandford, London, 1997).

— and Pflock, Karl (eds). *Encounters at Indian Head: The Betty and Barney Hill UFO Abduction Revisited* (Anomalist Books, USA, 2007).

Bryan, C.D. *Close Encounters of the Fourth Kind* (Weidenfeld & Nicolson, London, 1995).

Bullard, Thomas E. *UFO Abductions: The Measure of a Mystery* (Fund for UFO Research, Mount Rainier, 1987).

Clancy, Susan. *Abducted: How People Come to Believe They Were Kidnapped by Aliens* (Harvard University Press, USA, 2005).

Creighton, Gordon. 'The Amazing Case of Antonio Villas Boas', in *The Humanoids*, edited by Charles Bowen (Futura, London, 1977).

Fowler, Raymond E. *The Andreasson Affair* (Bantam, New York, 1980).

Friedman, Stanton T. and Marden, Kathleen. *Captured! The Betty and Barney Hill UFO Experience* (New Page Books, USA, 2007).

Fuller, John G. *The Interrupted Journey: Two Lost Hours Aboard a Flying Saucer* (Souvenir Press, London, 1980).

Goertzel, Ted. 'Measuring The Prevalence of False Memories: A New Interpretation of a "UFO Abduction Survey"', at: crab.rutgers.edu/~goertzel/UFO.htm.

Hopkins, Budd. *Missing Time* (Richard Marek, USA, 1981).

— *Intruders* (Random House, USA, 1987).

— Jacobs, David and Westrum, Ron. *Unusual Personal Experiences: An Analysis of Data from Three National Surveys conducted by the Roper Organization* (Bigelow Holding Corporation, Nevada, 1992).

— *Witnessed* (Pocket Books, New York, 1996).

Jacobs, David M. *Alien Encounters: First-Hand Accounts of UFO Abductions* (Virgin, London, 1994), originally published in 1992 as *Secret Life*.

— 'Thinking Clearly about the Abduction Phenomenon', at: www.ufoabduction.com/thinking1.htm.

Keel, John. *UFOs: Operation Trojan Horse* (Abacus, London, 1973).

Klass, Philip J. *UFO Abductions – A Dangerous Game* (Prometheus, USA, 1988).

Kottmeyer, Martin. 'If that someone's from outer space, they'll just go through the wall anyways', *Magonia Supplement* no 53, November 2004, pp1–5.

Lang, Craig R. 'The Logistics of UFO Abduction', at: craigrlang.coffeecup.com/traffic.html.

Mack, John E. *Abduction: Human Encounters With Aliens* (Pocket Books, London, 1995).

Randles, Jenny. *Abduction* (Robert Hale, London, 1988).

Rimmer, John. *The Evidence for Alien Abductions* (Aquarian Press, Wellingborough, 1984).

— 'Manhattan Transfer', *Magonia* no 45, March 1993.

Rodwell, Mary. *Awakening: How Extraterrestrial Contact Can Transform Your Life* (Beyond Publications, Leeds, 2002).

Rogo, D. Scott (ed). *Alien Abductions* (New American Library, USA, 1980).

Steiger, Brad and Steiger, Francie. *The Star People* (Berkley, USA, 1981).

Strieber, Whitley. *Communion* (Morrow, New York, 1987).

— *Transformation: The Breakthrough* (Morrow, New York, 1988).

Walton, Travis. *The Walton Affair* (Berkley, USA, 1978).

9

Contactees and Space People

Contactees are different from abductees because they enter into communication with alien entities on an equal and friendly basis and are invited, rather than forced, to go for a flight on board a flying saucer. They thrived in the 1950s.

The UFO occupants met by contactees were tall, humanoid, long-haired and elegant Nordic-types. They looked like perfectly formed and attractive examples of the male or female gender. However, in a period when men did not grow their hair long some contactees found their aliens to be disconcertingly androgynous in appearance. The aliens would show the contactees around their flying saucer, discuss religion and philosophy, and even take them on rides to planets in our solar system. Mars and Venus, as we now know, are inhospitable – indeed, downright deadly – to us, yet in those heady days the contactees were always visiting them without the need for a space suit or even so much as a flu jab.

Compared to the encounters reported by abductees, who are physically and mentally subdued by their captors, the contactees met their visitors in a normal fashion. Indeed, the Space People looked so similar to us that they even met contactees in diners or coffee bars without raising suspicion. The contactees often kept in contact with the aliens through ham radio messages, telephone conversations, séances, automatic writing, trances, dreams and telepathy. Abductees sometimes use these techniques, but the more stringent abduction researchers frown on them.

Contactees were the charismatic, self-promoting and self-proclaimed heroes of a new era for humanity. They were riding shoulder-to-shoulder with the beautiful Space People into the starlit future, where there will be harmony, peace and love. For them there were no anal probes or painful implants. They were equals with these highly evolved beings who promised a heaven on Earth.

If we believed the contactees and their friends from outer space, we would no longer need to worry about atomic warfare, pollution, over-population, natural disasters, famine, disease, pain or even death itself.

ABOVE: Worldwide fame came to Adamski in 1953 with the publication of his book *Flying Saucers Have Landed*, which he co-authored with Desmond Leslie.
Fortean Picture Library

FAR LEFT: George Adamski became the best-known contactee of the 1950s, and he still casts a shadow over the subject to this day.
Fortean Picture Library

LEFT: Adamski was a self-declared professor who gave the impression that he was an astronomer at Mount Palomar observatory. In reality he worked at a nearby hamburger stand.
Fortean Picture Library

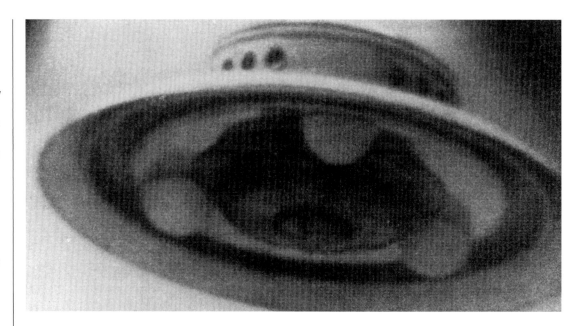

So, were (and are) contactees exploiting our personal and universal anxieties for their own private gain? Many UFO researchers and organisations would not even consider them. As Jacques Vallée put it in *UFOs: The Psychic Solution*, 'No serious investigator has ever been worried by the claims of the "contactees".' Later in the same book Vallée condemned the contactees for their childish stories that are just 'little space operas'. Such language did not upset the contactees, as they did not seek others to investigate or examine their claims. They preferred to appear on radio shows, give lectures and pass on the knowledge of the Space People through newspapers, magazines and books. Some would establish their own cults or cult-like organisations with fanatical followers ready to do the bidding of the contactee.

For the sake of clarity, it makes life simple to say that there was a great divide between the believers of the contactees and the 'scientific' ufologists. Yet there have been many credible and scientific ufologists who have

believed the contactees. We can point to the fact that what became the world's most respected UFO magazine, *Flying Saucer Review* (FSR), began in 1954 by publishing articles by contactees and was willing to consider evidence of their claims. This led to a small argument between Jacques Vallée and FSR's editor, Waveney Girvan. The latter thought that Vallée should have included the Venusian aliens as reported by contactees in his classification of Type 1 events. In response, Vallée argued that his survey of Type 1 events only included reports of UFO landings that are consistent and 'are simple and very clear'.

Belief in contactees took a battering when space missions conducted by the USA and USSR in the 1960s showed that planets such as Venus and Mars were nothing like the planets described by the contactees. This should have totally demolished any interest in contactees, but by the late 1960s there was renewed interest in the possibility that UFOs were from other dimensions or were some form of psychic or elemental force. John Keel spoke of his own network of 'silent contactees' who did not publicise or brag about their dealings with the Space People. In the 1970s Jacques Vallée also amended his views on contactees, and began to see them and their attendant cults as part of a social phenomenon that could have important consequences for all of us.

Vallée made the distinction between direct and indirect contactees. The former have a physical encounter with a UFO and have a special relationship with the alien intelligence. Indirect contactees have communications with an alien intelligence (eg via automatic writing or trance mediumship) and have a special relationship with it, but they do not have a physical encounter.

The airship wave of 1896–97 contains many newspaper reports that sound like the contactee stories of the 1950s. Most of these are what Vallée would categorise as involving direct contactees. Whilst the phantom airships were whizzing about in the skies, there was considerable interest in contacting the dead through séances, automatic writing and other forms of mediumship.

All the contactees seem to think peace will come to Earth if we win the right to join some fancifully titled galactic federation. We can only do this if we give up our warlike behaviour and stop polluting our planet. Many of the contactees of the 1950s emerged from or were associated with right-wing groups, and the coming of the flying saucers gave them the chance to re-brand their views in an extraterrestrial package. Contactee messages sometimes had anti-Semitic elements. They wanted to do away with international monetary systems, because they distrusted the elite groups and 'Jewish' bankers that they believed secretly ruled the world. And the good Space People themselves tended to be Aryan-types who were

ABOVE: The captain of the flying saucer was a beautiful, olive-skinned woman called Aura Rhanes.
Fortean Picture Library

BELOW: Truman Bethurum enjoyed at least 11 trips in Aura Rhanes' flying saucer.
Fortean Picture Library

ABOVE: Aura Rhanes said she and her fellow humanoid aliens (who dress like Greyhound bus drivers) live on the planet Clarion, which is permanently hidden from us by the Moon.
Fortean Picture Library

RIGHT: Daniel Fry
was invited on
board a flying
saucer and taken
for a ride to New
York and back.
Fortean Picture Library

THE
WHITE SANDS
INCIDENT
Actual photograph from color movies
by
DR. DANIEL FRY
Internationally-known scientist, author and lecturer

A true and exciting account of Dr. Fry's ride in a "flying saucer" from the rocket-testing ground near White Sands, New Mexico to New York and return at 8,000 miles per hour.
Also his discussions with "the pilot" and the answers to the questions millions of people have asked.

ABOVE: Daniel Fry
came across a
remote-controlled
flying saucer at
White Sands
Proving Grounds,
New Mexico, on 4
July 1950.
Fortean Picture Library

From a cynical perspective, contactees blatantly exploited the belief in space visitors for their own purposes. They were simply conmen, hoaxers, tricksters and opportunists. By spinning a few yarns they could easily achieve fame and fortune. In some cases they might have started by reporting a simple UFO sighting, and were then inspired to report past experiences and encounters that are more complex and far harder to explain. Their stories thereby took on a life of their own, and the contactee might even have come to believe their own fantasies.

Conspiracy theorists regard contactees as being the victims of trickery or duplicity by the CIA or other groups for their own nefarious purposes. Ufologists have suggested that contactees like Adamski were set up by the US government. According to Leon Davidson, the testing of secret US aircraft caused many UFO sightings from 1947 onwards, and to deflect the USSR from gaining knowledge of these experimental flights the CIA sponsored NICAP and contactee clubs to spread confusion and disinformation. Ufologist Leonard Stringfield, in a similar vein, thought that contactees were government plants to discredit serious UFO research. However, the flaw with this argument is that Adamski's and most other contactees' aliens extolled ideologies that challenged Western democracy.

Contactees have also been subject to covert studies by academics. The most famous case involved Marian Keech (pseudonym). The messages to Keech from the planet Clarion obtained via automatic writing contained the usual mixture of cosmic philosophy and warnings of imminent doom.

intellectually, spiritually and physically superior, whilst the evil aliens tended to be small, ugly and deformed.

Most contactee encounters are with beings who spout the same religious or mystical philosophies with which the contactee already agrees. The contactees often met Biblical figures, especially Jesus, and they usually put forward warnings of apocalyptic doom. Old-hat religion, just like old-hat fascism was re-branded by the contactees for the Space Age.

RIGHT: Howard
Menger married
Connie Weber in
1958. They both
thought they were
citizens of Saturn in
their past lives.
Fortean Picture Library

RIGHT: From childhood, Howard Menger met beautiful space women in the woods near his home in New Jersey. They visited him regularly from 1946 onwards.
Fortean Picture Library

My Contact with
FLYING SAUCERS

DINO KRASPEDON

FROM
OUTER SPACE
TO YOU
by HOWARD MENGER

*An account of visitors from space
... documented by actual photographs*

LEFT: Aladino Felix (aka Dino Kraspedon) saw a UFO land near Parana, Sao Paulo, Brazil, in 1952. He was invited inside and he spoke to its human-looking Venusian crew. In the 1960s he was arrested for being the leader of a terrorist gang.
Fortean Picture Library

LEFT: In the 1950s Orfeo Angelucci met humanoid aliens who were very spiritual in nature. He said that on one occasion he was taken into Earth orbit by an unmanned flying saucer.
Fortean Picture Library

ABOVE: George Van Tassel had several telepathic communications from and contacts with Venusians. Under their direction he built a four-storey 'Integration' building in the Yucca Valley, California.
Fortean Picture Library

One of her contacts was called Sananda, who was a reincarnation of Jesus, and for up to 14 hours a day she would receive messages from 'The Guardians', as she called these Space People.

In 1954 her warnings of devastating floods and geological changes throughout the United States were published in her local newspapers, and she held out the promise that her followers would be saved by the flying saucers. Sociologists at the University of Minnesota monitored and joined her group to see how the group acted and responded to the anticipated day of doom.

When the predicted floods did not come the sociologists were surprised to find that the group was not despondent; instead, they were encouraged by the fact that their efforts had saved the world. Besides the dodgy ethics, we can see how easy it would be to infiltrate or even manipulate such groups. Fears of infiltration of all types made contactee groups suspicious of newcomers, and some had 'inner circles' that had higher levels of knowledge than the normal membership.

Another possibility is that contactees are duped by their own subconscious mind. Most of us only know Uri Geller for his ability to bend spoons with his mind, and as a friend of Michael Jackson, but back in the early 1970s he had numerous communications with a cosmic intelligence called SPECTRA. Under hypnotic regression, he recalled seeing a light in the sky above his garden in Tel Aviv when he was three years old. A faceless, shining figure appeared before him, which sent a ray of light at him that made him pass out.

Significantly this took place on Christmas Day, 25 December 1949. The implication is that he was 'born' like Jesus on this day to serve humanity. SPECTRA admitted that on this day they had programmed Uri, so that we could be prepared for a mass landing of flying saucers. Geller and Dr Andrija Puharich continued to receive communications from SPECTRA through automatic writing and messages left on a

RIGHT: Raymond Palmer, editor of *Amazing Stories* magazine, promoted the incredible stories by Richard Shaver as fact. They began being published four years before flying saucers became all the rage.
Fortean Picture Library

LEFT: The Deros own ray machines that can influence people's minds and cause all types of accidents and disasters to humanity. They can also abduct people, according to Shaver. Palmer was convinced that the so-called 'Shaver Mystery' was linked to the flying saucer phenomenon.
Fortean Picture Library

LEFT: Norman Harrison began having telepathic messages from aliens after he saw a massive UFO hovering over the Beeston area of Leeds, Yorkshire, some time during 1973.

Norman Harrison

RIGHT: According to Harrison there are evil alien forces that seek to destroy us, and good aliens that try to protect us from them.

Norman Harrison

RIGHT: French sports journalist Raël (Claude Vorilhon) met a visitor from outer space in December 1973. Since then he has been on a mission to prepare humanity for their imminent arrival.

Raëlian Movement

FAR RIGHT: Raël claims that thousands of years ago the Elohim aliens manipulated DNA to create humans in their own image. One of Raël's aims is to build an embassy for the Elohim.

Raëlian Movement

tape recorder. Jacques Vallée was surprised that they took the rambling pseudoscientific messages seriously, and he noted that they reflected many of the ideas held by Geller and Dr Puharich. Indeed, they even confused astronomical units of time with units of space in just the same way Uri Geller did.

Cases involving contact using automatic writing or telepathic communications are often full of philosophical musings and statements that are virtually indistinguishable from those of the contactee. The messages relate as much to their own personal experiences as they do to the universal themes of love

and peace or warnings of planetary doom. Norman Harrison (pseudonym), for example, was a very depressed person who had premonitions of disasters and a coming Judgement Day. He started writing a stream of consciousness novel with a guerrilla leader as the hero. The main drive of the story, which begins with an atomic explosion, is about this man being threatened and sadistically tortured by technocratic police authorities. He admitted that the hero represented his own feelings of being an outsider from established authority and society.

There is also the possibility that contactees intuitively tell their followers and readers what they want to hear. In this manner, the communications reflect the ideology and interests of a group rather than an individual. Messages received through mental impressions, automatic writing and séances can be neatly explained as the outpourings of the unconscious mind of the contactee. This does not easily explain encounters where the contactee says he has actually met the Space People and ridden in their spaceships. In some cases these could be attributable to hallucinations or other visionary experiences. George Adamski admitted that he was an expert at hypnotising himself and other people, and that he could easily put himself into a trance. He added that he did not use these methods to contact the Space People, though even some of his supporters suspected he might have resorted to such techniques.

Another possibility is that the contactees really are in contact with alien beings or intelligences. The simplest thing is to say they have actually ridden in 'nuts and bolts' spacecraft and that their superior technology seems like occult magic to us. Since there is little physical evidence for their literal reality, ufologists have resorted to more sophisticated theories to explain these contacts. In John Keel's

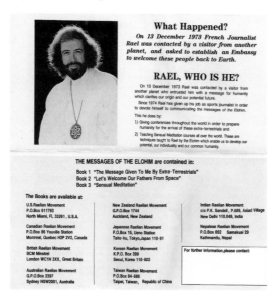

view contactees have minds that are open to manipulation from 'super-high-frequency radiations'. This would explain why certain people are targeted by strange visions and communications from childhood onwards. Their paranormal experiences and perception of streams of telepathic communications can literally send them insane, if they cannot understand where they are coming from.

These dark forces use MIB and hallucinations to totally devastate the minds of contactees. Keel acknowledged that Dr Meade Layne knew about this 'contactee syndrome' as early as 1955, when he considered that: 'It is possible that some persons may be less affected by supersonic frequencies than others; this may account for the selection of certain persons by the Etherians [his name for Space People – NW]. It is also possible that some such persons are now showing signs of amnesia and other physical and mental deterioration.' Such attributes could be applied to today's abductees, who have certainly suffered from amnesia and much psychological torment.

The main characteristics of direct contactees can be summarised as follows:

1. The contactee is usually male.
2. The contactee meets space beings and rides in their flying saucers to other planets.
3. Their meetings with the aliens are voluntary. The contactee might be compelled to seek or initiate alien contact.
4. Meetings and contact are frequent.
5. Descriptions of the aliens, flying saucers and alien planets are nonsensical and pseudoscientific.
6. The contactee is chosen (often in childhood) and is regarded as special.
7. The contactee might have an alien origin, or believe they were an alien in a previous life.
8. Followers spread the messages received by the contactee.
9. The messages from the aliens tend to reflect the ideas of the contactee.
10. The messages contain predictions of doom and the aliens offer salvation.
11. The messages can be inherently totalitarian and/ or anti-democratic.
12. Belief in the contactees' messages is usually based on faith rather than on evidence.

Indirect contactees are more likely to be women, like Hélène Smith and Marian Keech – they do not satisfy points one and two above, but the other points all still apply.

In summary, contactees can be fraudsters, victims of manipulation by terrestrial groups or extraterrestrial intelligences, deluded fantasy-prone individuals, or in extreme cases sufferers of schizophrenia or a similar psychological condition.

References

Adamski, George. *Inside the Space Ships* (Abelard-Schuman Inc, New York, 1955).

Angelucci, Orfeo. *The Secret of the Saucers* (Amherst Press, Amherst, 1955).

Bethurum, Truman. *Aboard a Flying Saucer* (De Vorss and Company, Los Angeles, 1954).

Evans, Hilary. *Gods, Spirits, Cosmic Guardians: A Comparative Study of the Encounter Experience* (Aquarian Press, Wellingborough, 1987).

— (ed). *Frontiers of Reality* (Guild Publishing, London, 1989).

Festinger, Leon; Riecken, Henry; and Schachter, Stanley. *When Prophecy Fails* (Harper and Row, New York, 1966).

Fry, Daniel. *The White Sands Incident* (New Age Publishing Company, Los Angeles, 1954).

Good, Timothy and Zinsstag, Lou. *George Adamski – The Untold Story* (Ceti Publications, Beckenham, 1983).

Keel, John. *UFOs: Operation Trojan Horse* (Abacus, London, 1973).

Kraspedon, Dino. *My Contact with Flying Saucers* (Neville Spearman, London, 1959).

Lewis, James R. (ed). *The Encyclopedic Sourcebook of UFO Religions* (Prometheus Books, USA, 2004).

Menger, Howard. *From Outer Space to You* (Saucerian Press, Clarksberg, 1959).

Nadis, Fred. *The Man from Mars: Ray Palmer's Amazing Pulp Journey* (Tarcher Penguin, USA, 2013).

Palmer, Susan J. *Aliens Adored: Raël's UFO Religion* (Rutgers University Press, London, 2004).

Partridge, Christopher (ed). *UFO Religions* (Routledge, London, 2003).

Redfern, Nick. *Contactees* (Career Press, New Jersey, 2010).

Toronto, Richard. *War over Lemuria: Richard Shaver, Ray Palmer and the Strangest Chapter of 1940s Science Fiction* (McFarland, USA, 2013).

Vallée, Jacques. *UFOs: The Psychic Solution* (Panther, London, 1977).

Van Tassel, George. *I Rode a Flying Saucer* (New Age, USA, 1952).

Watson, Nigel. *Portraits of Alien Encounters* (Valis Books, London, 1990).

10

The search for theories and explanations

O ver the years, many explanations have been put forward to try to 'solve' the UFO enigma. Some sound very convincing, and others sound like a science fiction novel gone wrong. Not surprisingly, there never seems to be an answer that satisfies everyone.

At the dawn of ufology the USAF used experts to consider all manner of natural and man-made phenomena that might cause witnesses to think they had seen a UFO. The cases that remained unexplained were (a) regarded as the result of insufficient information being available for an adequate explanation, (b) ignored as implausible, or (c) were the work of hoaxers. The motives for hoaxers can be fame and fortune, social experimentation or simply the enjoyment of baffling people.

Another theory, which conditioned much of the thinking surrounding the US airship wave of 1896–97 and the early years of ufology, was that the UFOs were the product of human inventors working and experimenting in secret. Variations of this idea are that human inventors have been inspired by alien contacts and communications to build UFOs and develop related technology. In recent years ufology has embraced the concept that UFOs allegedly retrieved by the US government have been back-engineered and tested at Area 51.

Sceptics like Tim Printy, the editor of the US online SUNlite UFO newsletter, think that 'the majority of UFO sightings are misperceptions of man-made and natural events. The remainder that cannot be readily explained are possibly hoaxes, hallucinations, observations of rare natural phenomena, or misperceptions that have been so distorted in the reporting that identification is extremely difficult.'

Nevertheless, most ufologists believe that there remains a kernel of 'true' UFOs, and therefore turn to more exotic or complex concepts to explain them. The default and most dominant idea – especially in the USA – is that UFOs come from outer space.

The ETH

The extraterrestrial hypothesis (ETH) is far from being a new idea. The idea that life exists beyond our home planet has entertained and intrigued our minds for a long time.

The planet Mars has long been seriously considered as the most likely home of intelligent beings. This idea was given scientific credibility by Italian astronomer Giovanni Schiaparelli, who intensively studied the planet in 1877, 1879 and 1881, and produced detailed charts that revealed networks of lines and 'seas' across its surface. He termed the long dark lines *canali*, meaning channels, but when translated into English they were erroneously called 'canals'. He abandoned his observations in 1890 due to failing eyesight, but other astronomers confirmed the existence of Mars' distinctive surface features.

In 1893, after studying occult phenomena in Japan, Percival Lowell returned to the USA to set up an observatory at Flagstaff, Arizona. In his book *Mars*, published two years later, he claimed that the planet is inhabited by intelligent beings, three times larger than we are. Considering that Mars is older than Earth, he postulated that Martian life was superior to our own, and that the canals were evidence that they were still in existence.

Today, of course, we know that his ideas are wrong. Psychoanalyst Charles Hofling asserted that Lowell's observations were illusory; however, his rigorous use of logic to interpret his data was due to an *idée fixe* rather than delusions. When determining which came first, the *idée fixe* or the illusory

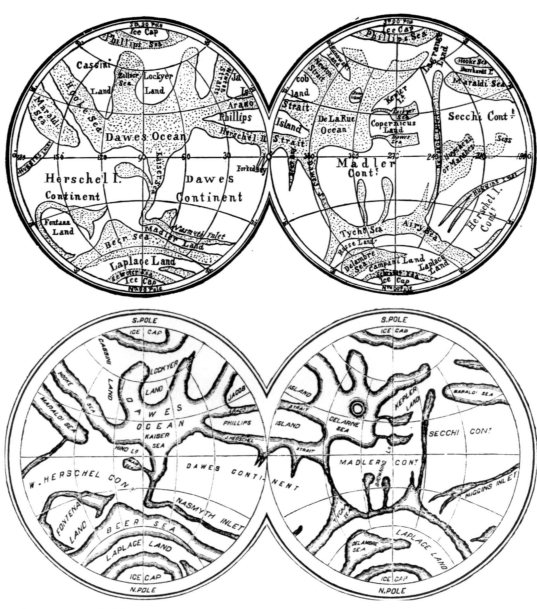

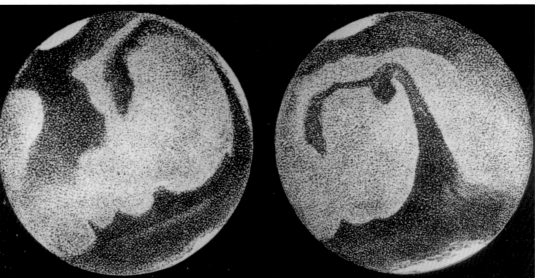

UFO contactees and abductees, but at least it does show that the ETH is a scientifically valid concept.

Ancient Astronaut theories are a logical extension of the ETH. The stories of miraculous events and visions in the Christian Bible and other religious books have been eagerly reinterpreted as being accounts of alien visitations. Ancient structures like the Pyramids and Stonehenge are regarded as being inspired or even created by these Ancient Astronauts, and, as in Stanley Kubrick's movie *2001: A Space Odyssey*, it is thought that they might have boosted our evolution, or even brought us to Earth in the first place. The evidence for this is patchy, and has been plundered from many different historical eras. As Roger Sandell wrote way back in 1973, when the books of Erich von Däniken were extremely popular (especially his *Chariots of the Gods?*), none of these theories 'seems capable of producing evidence that at one particular time and place a unique interference with human history took place. Instead we are merely given a jumble of mysteries.'

observations, Hofling favoured the former, as he thinks Lowell already knew what he would see. Significantly, when Lowell used more powerful telescopes the canals were less visible.

Nonetheless, Mars was regarded as a viable habitat for alien life forms until, in the 1960s, these hopes were dashed when NASA's Mariner space probes detected high levels of carbon dioxide (CO_2) in its atmosphere. There is evidence that there was free-flowing water on Mars millions of years ago, which may well have supported living organisms at some point, but so far we have yet to find even the slightest hint of life on Mars, past or present.

In contrast to Mars, and the rest of the universe, Earth is teeming with life. Given that there are about 400 billion stars in our Milky Way galaxy alone, it would be incredible if we were the only pocket of life in this infinitely small sector of the Universe.

Scientists have used radio telescopes to try to detect any signals that might reveal the existence of alien civilisations lurking within our part of the galaxy, but so far there has been a big fat silence. Despite this, SETI (search for extraterrestrial intelligence) research has had a big boost from the discovery in October 1995 of a Hot Jupiter extrasolar planet in the Pegasus constellation, 50 light years away. Since then about 1,000 more extrasolar planets (or exoplanets) have been found, of which a quarter are in the habitable zone of their parent sun. Signs of any chemical signatures or the existence of oxygen in the atmosphere of these planets is currently being investigated to see if they might support any type of life, as we know it. This is a far cry from the aliens and visitors reported by

The PSH

The psycho-sociological hypothesis (PSH) doesn't have such a ring of authority to it as the ETH, and it is far more complex. It is more highly regarded by European ufologists, and considers UFOs to be created by a combination of psychological and sociological factors.

Psychoanalyst Carl Jung was the first to seriously consider UFO experiences as something more than sightings of spaceships or weather balloons. He regarded them as having a spiritual character that fulfilled the needs of the individual. Yet he also thought they could be solid, material craft from other planets. He hinted that our collective desire for salvation from the skies could bring about the physical manifestation of UFOs and aliens.

Ironically, it was US writer and UFO researcher John Keel who, through his influential book *UFOs: Operation Trojan Horse* and his many articles in *Flying Saucer Review*, helped wean a generation of British ufologists away from the ETH. He argued that UFO sightings are shaped and manipulated by the intelligences that control the phenomena. He called these entities ultraterrestrials, who are believed to be able to move up and down the electromagnetic spectrum. By these means they can appear and disappear from our limited human perception of the world.

Jacques Vallée and even J. Allen Hynek came to think that there was more to the subject than solid, physical spacecraft visiting us. In *Passport to Magonia*, Vallée agreed with Keel that the aliens have been visiting us for thousands of years in different forms, according to our beliefs and expectations. The 'aliens' have appeared as demons, fairies, goblins and dragons, as recorded in folklore, and they have travelled in phantom airships (as seen in the 1890s to 1920s), foo fighters (World War Two period) and ghost rockets (post-WW2), before they finally showed off their flying saucers. They seem to anticipate our own technological developments and challenge our notions of reality. According to this concept of 'cultural tracking' they seem to have been controlling and goading us throughout history.

In his excellent article *Jules Verne and the Great Airship Scare*, Ron Miller notes that the descriptions of phantom airships are very similar to the real and fictional aerial inventions of the period. He sums up the situation by stating that all the phantom airship sightings in the USA during 1896 to 1897 'could be either anomalous and amorphous phenomena, simple "bandwaggoning", or even outright hoaxes. In other words, nothing that we haven't seen taking place in so many modern UFO reports. Those of a century ago

ABOVE: John Keel (1930–2009) disputed the extraterrestrial hypothesis (ETH) and regarded alien visitors as ultraterrestrials who are 'temporary intrusions into our reality or space-time continuum, momentary manipulations of electromagnetic energy'.

Fortean Picture Library

All in the mind?

These are just some of the psychological processes that can produce or encourage the sighting of UFOs:

- Sleep paralysis
- Fantasy proneness
- Hallucination
- Hypnotic regression
- Auto hypnosis
- False memory syndrome
- Subliminal peripheral vision psychosis
- Fabrication and exaggeration
- Temporal lobe epilepsy
- Psychoanalytical factors
- Mental illness
- Psychological trauma
- Boundary theory
- Dissociative tendencies
- Abuse
- Masochism
- Fantasy proneness
- Birth trauma
- Misperception and misinterpretation
- Sensory deprivation
- Mass hysteria

are different only in using 19th century visual references.'

From a sociological perspective, UFOs can highlight and represent wider social concerns. In the Cold War period, for example, they represented the fear of invasion by (literally) an alien army. Abductions in recent years represent our fears of being taken over by cold, anonymous forces that can control every element of our lives.

On a personal, psychological level UFO experiences can help people to articulate deeper subconscious fears or desires.

According to this hypothesis, Hollywood films, TV series, websites, books, magazines and other mass media have a big impact on our perception of UFOs. Peter Rogerson, Britain's leading thinker on this subject, noted that the UFO mythology was 'nurtured, not primarily by the absurd UFO cults, but by the professional myth-makers, the comics, films, science fiction writers, even advertisers. The first great contactee came ... from Hollywood; in the form of the allegorical science-fiction drama *The Day the Earth Stood Still*.'

UFO research and investigation itself goes through a number of filters, conditioned by 'authorised myths'. British researcher Hilary Evans notes that these are 'a belief or set of beliefs which, despite inadequate scientific evidence for its existence, obtains the sanction of widespread acceptance within the prevailing culture.' For example, in the case of UFOs the authorised myth is that they are of extraterrestrial origin. This causes UFO witnesses to shape their sightings and experiences in terms of this myth. In turn, ufologists come along and add more evidence to support such claims, by correlating them with similar sightings and by 'finding' all types of supporting evidence to back them up.

In this way what starts off as a report of a simple CEI light in the sky can escalate into a full-blown CEIII or CEIV abduction report because the authorised myth triggers unconscious dreams and fantasies related to the expectations of the extraterrestrial hypothesis (ETH).

The main problem with these types of explanation for UFO experiences is that we have to consider a complex interaction between our mental processes – which are subject to illness, misperception, genetic predisposition, intoxication and trauma – and our culture, society, myths, beliefs, peer pressures and preconceptions.

Even the methods by which we use psychology to examine these processes in the pursuit of UFO investigations are conditioned by our culture. In the US there has been far more recourse to using polygraph tests, hypnotic regression and psychiatric or therapeutic counselling than in other countries.

In the British *Magonia* magazine, which has

Birth trauma theory

In the late 1970s, when claims of alien abduction were becoming more common, Dr Alvin Lawson and William McCall put forward the theory that such abductions are caused by birth trauma. To prove this, they hypnotically regressed a group of people who had no intimate knowledge of UFO phenomena and found that their accounts matched those of 'real' abductees.

To explain these similarities they argued that we all share the common experience of birth. As a validation of this view, they found that people who had normal births recalled UFO encounters that involved tubes and tunnels, which are symbolic of, or memories of, the birth canal. Those who were born by Caesarean section do not seem to report UFO encounters with these elements.

promoted the PSH since the early 1970s, Anthony Brown lambasted this type of approach to the subject. He claims: 'The attitude of some sceptics in degrading and impugning the character of the average witness in ufology is a disgrace to the subject and of civilised behaviour to one's fellow man. The essence of the Psychosocial Hypothesis is of cheapening the witness's puzzling experience, and questioning their basic honesty as a human being.'

LEFT: Writers for the *Merseyside UFO Bulletin* (MUFOB) – latter renamed *Magonia* – have promoted the psycho-sociological hypothesis (PSH) since the 1970s.

John Rimmer

Exotic explanations

No single explanation has satisfied everyone, so perhaps a combination of explanations needs to be considered. You can take your pick'n'mix from this selection:

LIVING UFOS

Ufologist Trevor Constable pioneered the photography of UFOs using infrared film during the 1960s. He considered UFOs to be biological beings, which live in the sky. As they come closer to Earth they become more visible, and they can fire bolts of lightning to defend themselves. They are invisible to our eyes, but infrared film can capture images of them as they fly above us. Today some ufologists have adapted video cameras to capture infrared images of UFOs.

THE THIRD REALM

Rather than conjuring up UFOs, the third realm hypothesis suggests that they exist independently in a realm that has only been accessible to shamans through mystical means. Harvard professor John Mack claimed that modern science blinkers us from the third realm because it only accepts the reality of the first realm (the mind) and the second realm (the material world). People who experience UFO events glimpse the third realm.

VIRTUAL REALITY

UFOs could be holographic or quasi-solid projections from extraterrestrial or extradimensional aliens. Alternatively, our universe is a virtual reality created by aliens. UFOs come from beyond our simulated reality and indicate the falseness of our existence.

TIME TRAVELLERS

UFOs might be visiting us from our future, when time travel has become possible. Alternatively they are time machines created by aliens from other planets or dimensions who are coming from the future or even the past.

PARANORMAL AND OCCULT

Psychic phenomena, ghosts, invisible entities and poltergeists have all been associated with UFO and alien activity. Aliens have been contacted through Ouija boards, séances, mental telepathy and automatic writing. This suggests that the aliens live on the same astral planes as ghosts and other entities, or that they are created by similar psychological factors. Using meditation or even magic, some have tried to bring such mental projections into the real world.

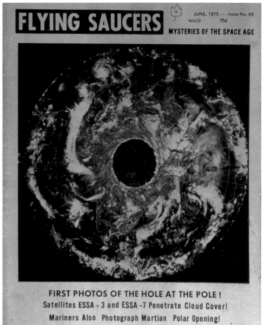

FIRST PHOTOS OF THE HOLE AT THE POLE !
Satellites ESSA - 3 and ESSA -7 Penetrate Cloud Cover!
Mariners Also Photograph Martian Polar Opening!

LEFT: When conducting atmospheric electrical experiments in Colorado Springs, USA, pioneering electrical engineer Nikola Tesla (1856–1943) received a series of signals that repeated the numbers 1, 2, 3 and 4. In 1901 he claimed that they came from Mars.
Fortean Picture Library

LEFT: It is claimed that the North and South Poles contain entrances to the Hollow Earth, which contains its own sun and has cities populated by beings who build and fly the UFOs that we see in our skies.
Fortean Picture Library

ELECTRONIC POLLUTION

Albert Budden put forward the theory that electronic and electrical pollution could affect 20% of the population. This pollution upsets our biochemistry and causes UFO and abduction hallucinations that warn us that our bodies are in danger.

EARTH LIGHTS

Lights in the sky are caused by strains in the earth's crust, according to this theory. These lights and related electromagnetic activity have an influence on the temporal lobes of our brains. People sensitive to these influences can experience mood changes, memory loss, rich fantasies and abduction-like experiences.

PLASMA BALLS

The British Ministry of Defence's Project Condign claimed that rare, short-lived plasma balls in the upper atmosphere could cause pilots to see 'classic' flying saucers. They could also create electromagnetic disruption to vehicles and elude radar detection. The report suggested that meteors are involved in their creation by an as yet unknown process.

CONSPIRACY

It is claimed that the US and other governments know all about the real origin of the aliens, and are in league with them to keep humanity in ignorance of the real situation. This information is suppressed because it could cause mass panics and completely disrupt our existence on this planet.

Certainly government agencies have used the UFO mythology to spread disinformation and to hide the testing of aircraft and other highly secret activities.

On a similarly sinister note, in the 1950s agencies like the FBI were worried that Communist supporters were using UFO and alien contact stories to undermine democratic values. For this reason they monitored the activities of ufologists and contactees who appeared to be spreading subversive ideas.

LEFT: The public road that leads to the entrance to the restricted area known as Area 51, which is about 12 miles beyond the hills in the distance.
Mark Pilkington

LEFT: The outer perimeter of Area 51. Crossing beyond this point, even by accident, will result in certain arrest.
Mark Pilkington

Sleep paralysis

The work of Dr Jorge Conesa Sevilla, a neurocognitive and biosemiotic researcher, confirms that sleep paralysis (SP) can involve vividly experiencing floating, going through tunnels, seeing lights and hearing noises. Furthermore, these types of experience can be triggered by anxiety, tiredness and sleep deprivation, making them common in shift workers, truck drivers, hospital workers and other people who work long and odd hours. Conesa also suggests that geomagnetic activity might trigger SP experiences, and that birth trauma memories might shape the imagery of those who interpret their SP experience in terms of an alien abduction. He also indicates that these experiences run through families, and that people can learn to use SP to have out of the body experiences, lucid dreams and shamanic journeys.

Professor Christopher French, head of the Anomalistic Psychology Research Unit, Goldsmiths, University of London, is a bit more circumspect about applying such all-embracing theories. In his considered opinion: 'I think that most claims of alien abduction involve an initial bizarre experience, such as an episode of sleep paralysis or highway hypnosis, that leads the individual concerned to postulate that perhaps they have experienced alien contact. That expectation may subsequently lead to the formation of a false memory for such an alien encounter. However, we should be wary of proposing 'one-size-fits-all' explanations for this complex and fascinating phenomenon. It is undoubtedly true that some cases will require different explanations – including occasional deliberate hoaxes.

LEFT: Sleep paralysis occurs at the point of going into or coming out of sleep. The former type of sleep paralysis is associated with hypnagogic hallucinations, and the latter with hypnopompic hallucinations.
Carla MacKinnon, The Sleep Paralysis Project

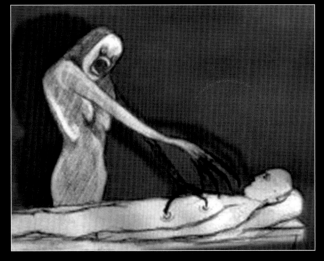

LEFT: Sleep paralysis can induce intense feelings of terror. It sometimes also causes the perception of an intruder lying on your chest, who is trying to suffocate you.
Carla MacKinnon, The Sleep Paralysis Project

LEFT: In the past, witches and demons were often regarded as being responsible for sleep paralysis experiences. Today they may manifest as alien bedroom intruders.
Carla MacKinnon, The Sleep Paralysis Project

Summary

The psycho-sociological hypothesis covers a broad range of phenomena that governs our perceptions. At one end of the scale it can be used to speculate that our own minds can create or perceive 'real' aliens and their spacecraft; at the other end the PSH has inclined some ufologists to consider the subject as modern-day folklore. In the light of this, UFOs and the theories surrounding them constitute a UFO mythology, and it is in the realms of psychology and sociology that we should therefore concentrate our research.

Such research is important, because, as John Spencer notes in his book *Perspectives*: 'The phenomenon has affected much of our modern society, our culture, our fiction, areas of our religion and much more. It has done this without proof of reality, people's perception of the world has changed because of the existence of the literature, whether or not there is a basis in reality. This will continue into the future whether there is a foundation in reality or not, so long as people believe something.'

The extraterrestrial hypothesis is more clear-cut and simple. The problem for ETH proponents is finding scientifically valid evidence to back up their claims. The exopolitics movement that has arisen since 2000 assumes the fact that aliens from outer space are visiting us and are in regular contact with our governments. Their evidence relies heavily on rumours and stories from whistleblowers.

As 'The Pelican' perceptively notes in *Magonia* magazine: 'The notion that the true explanations for sightings that remain unidentified after being investigated by Serious Ufologists is that they are alien craft, [and] is what makes ufology a pseudoscience. It is not just the nuts-and-bolts ETH Serious Ufologists who are rather flaky, but also those who seek more subtle explanations ... all but a very few ufologists do not have a purely objective approach to the subject. And, of course, they usually get away with their dodgy hypotheses and tall stories.'

Certainly, ufologists, whether at the sceptical or believer ends of the spectrum, can easily have a tendency to have 'dodgy hypotheses'. What is paramount is to look at the evidence itself and to consider the pros and cons of its validity. Unfortunately, many cases are invested with a power that transcends any rational arguments or logical explanations, and they become an established part of the UFO mythology.

What is really needed to confirm the ETH is incontrovertible proof, like an actual flying saucer parked on the White House lawn.

References

Brown, Anthony R. 'The Decline and Fall of the Psychosocial Empire' *Magonia* no 72, October 2000.

Evans, Hilary. 'The Myth of the Authorised Myth' *Magonia* no 16, July 1984, at: magonia.haaan.com/2009/myth/.

Haines, Richard (ed). *UFO Phenomena and the Behavioral Scientist* (Scarecrow, USA, 1979).

Hendry, Allan. *The UFO Handbook* (Doubleday, New York, 1979).

Hofling, Charles K. 'Percival Lowell and the Canals of Mars' *British Journal of Medical Psychology* vol 37, part 1, 1964.

Hufford, David J. *The Terror That Comes in the Night: An Experience-centered Study of Supernatural Assault Traditions* (University of Pennsylvania Press, Philadelphia, 1982).

Jung, Carl. *Flying Saucers: A Modern Myth of Things Seen in the Skies* (Routledge and Kegan Paul, London, 1959).

Keel, John. *UFOs: Operation Trojan Horse* (Abacus, London, 1973).

Klass, Philip J. *UFOs Explained* (Random House, New York, 1974).

Miller, Ron. 'Jules Verne and the Great Airship Scare' *International UFO Reporter* vol 12, no 3, May–June 1987.

Moravec, Mark. 'UFOs as Psychological and Parapsychological Phenomena' in *UFOs 1947–1987*, compiled and edited by Hilary Evans and John Spencer (Fortean Tomes, London, 1987).

Pelican, The. '*Declassing the Classics Magonia No 98*, September 2008', at: magonia.haaan.com/2011/declassing-the-classics-the-pelican/.

'Prehistoric Proof' website, at: pinterest.com/frankjanice/prehistoric-proof/.

Randles, Jenny; Roberts, Andy; and Clarke, David. *The UFOs that Never Were* (London House, London, 2000).

Rogerson, Peter. 'The Mythology of UFO Events and Interpretations' *Merseyside UFO Bulletin* vol 5, no 3, Summer 1972, at: magonia.haaan.com/2008/the-mythology-of-ufo-events-and-interpretations-a-new-examination-peter-rogerson/.

Sandell, Roger. 'Archaeologists and Astronauts' *Merseyside UFO Bulletin* vol 6, no 1, July 1973, at: magonia.haaan.com/tag/ancient-astronauts/.

Sevilla, Jorge Conesa, PhD. *Wrestling with Ghosts: A Personal And Scientific Account Of Sleep Paralysis* (Xlibris, 2004).

'The Sleep Paralysis Project' website, at: www.thesleepparalysisproject.org/.

Spencer, John. *Perspectives: A Radical Examination of the Alien Abduction Phenomenon* (Futura, London, 1989).

SUNlite UFO newsletter, at: home.comcast.net/~tprinty/UFO/SUNlite.htm.

Vallée, Jacques. *Passport to Magonia: From Folklore to Flying Saucers* (Tandem, London, 1975).

Von Däniken, Erich. *Chariots of the Gods?* (G.P. Putnam's Sons, New York, 1970).

Appendices

1 Producing a UFO investigation report

First of all it is helpful to get the witness to give some information about themselves and their interests, and to get them to describe what they saw in their own words. One thing to remember is not to ask leading questions, or to discuss your theories or other cases with the witness before the interview. It is not a good idea to show pictures or diagrams of UFOs before the interview either. You can then ask them about what they saw in more detail by means of a sighting report form or a list of questions like the ones below. With the permission of the witness, it is a good idea to record the interview as well as to write down their answers.

DETAILS ABOUT THE WITNESS
1　Name, address and contact details.
2　Age and occupation.
3　Does the witness wear glasses?
4　Is the witness colour blind or colour deficient?
5　Has the witness any professional or amateur experience related to viewing the sky?
6　Names, addresses and contact details of other witnesses.

ABOUT THE SIGHTING
1　Date and time of sighting.
2　Location of sighting. Obtain GPS or map reference.
3　Weather conditions, including temperature and strength of the wind.
4　If it was a daylight sighting, where was the sun in relation to the UFO?
5　If a night-time sighting, where were the moon and stars in relation to the UFO?
6　Was the UFO viewed through a telescope or binoculars at any time?
7　Did anything obscure their view of the UFO, such as trees or buildings?
8　Duration of sighting.
9　Compass direction in which the UFO was first and last seen.
10　At what elevation in the sky was it?
11　What sort of manoeuvres did the UFO make?
12　How would you describe its movement compared to an aircraft, balloon or rocket?

13　What did the UFO look like? What colour, shape and size was it?
14　Did it look like a solid craft or was it a light or groups of lights?
15　Did the UFO change its appearance during the sighting?
16　Did the UFO make any sound?
17　Did it make any impact on the environment, such as radiating heat, burning or damaging nearby objects or plants?
18　Were any animals nearby? Did they respond in any way to the UFO?
19　How did the witness feel during and after the sighting?
20　Did the UFO cause any physiological effects, such as tiredness, nausea, burn marks or any other type of injury?
21　Has the UFO witness had any dreams or nightmares since the encounter?
22　What did they think the UFO was during the sighting?
23　What makes them unable to identify what they saw?
24　Did they discuss the sighting with other people?
25　What made them report this sighting?
26　Have they experienced any other UFO sightings or had any paranormal experiences?
27　In retrospect, what do they think they saw?

It is useful if you can get the witness to draw a picture of what they saw and its movement through the sky – this can often clarify information given verbally. If possible, it is useful to go to the actual location where the UFO was spotted, and to go through the sequence of events experienced during the encounter.

If several people saw the same UFO it is best to interview them separately. After the interview, or after receiving a sighting report form, you should check out any information that might possibly identify what was seen.

In the case of complex sightings more details should be obtained regarding any equipment that might have been affected by the encounter, or used to record images or other data during the sighting. For cases

other than CEI it is best to have a fellow ufologist or helper with you, especially for abduction cases or cases involving children. An assistant can also be useful for taking pictures of the location, collecting any potential evidence and offering a second opinion.

The Code of Practice for UFO Investigators, developed by UK ufologists in the early 1980s, is worth adhering to, as it covers most of the ethical issues that the ufologist will encounter. It is available at: www.deltapro.co.uk/cop.html.

The US Computer UFO Network (CUFON) has also produced a very useful Code of Conduct at: www.cufon.org/standards/draftcode.htm#top

The US Mutual UFO Network (MUFON) has the best and most detailed report forms that have been created for virtually every type of UFO encounter, from CEIs and animal mutilation cases to entity sightings and abductions. They can be viewed at: www.mufon.com/InvestigatorCorner.html.

The online Alien Sight Investigation Manual takes you through all the phases of a UFO investigation. Available at: thedisbeliever.wikidot.com/manual

NARCAP
The National Aviation Reporting Center on Anomalous Phenomena website has detailed report forms for pilots to download and submit, at: narcap.org/files/pilotrptprintver.htm. For air traffic controllers or radar operators there is a form at: narcap.org/files/Radar.htm.

BUFORA
The British UFO Research Association has an online sighting report form at: www.bufora.org.uk/content/index.php?option=com_fabrik&view=form&fabrik=2&random=0&Itemid=74.

NUFORC
The US National UFO Reporting Center has a UFO sighting report form at: nationalufocenter.com/reportingform2.htm.

CUFOS
The J. Allen Hynek Center for UFO Studies has a UFO report questionnaire at: www.cufos.org/sighting.html.

2 UFO investigation kit essentials

A useful UFO investigation kit doesn't have to be very elaborate. For interviewing witnesses, it is handy to have the following:

- Notepad.
- Pens and pencils.
- Blank paper that witnesses can use to sketch the appearance and movements of the UFO.
- Sighting report forms, and/or a list of questions specific to the case under investigation.
- Digital audio recorder.
- Camera (still or video).

For examining landing sites and physical traces you should have the following:

- Compass.
- Maps of locality.
- Tape measure.

- Ruler.
- Magnifying glass.
- Tweezers.
- Trowel.
- Sample container bags.
- Plaster of Paris.
- Binoculars.

A very extensive range of UFO-hunting equipment, and useful advice, is available on the 'UFO Stop. com' website, at: www.ufostop.com/articles.asp?id=144.

RIGHT: Skywatching equipment.
Darren Ashmore

3 Skywatching

These events are a good opportunity to meet fellow ufologists, learn more about astronomy, and perhaps get a glimpse of a UFO in the bargain. In most climates, warm clothing and flasks of tea or coffee are essential for any skywatch.

For best results try to find a site that has an unobstructed view of the sky that is as free from light pollution as possible. Skywatches are most often held at UFO hot spots where the chances of seeing a UFO are higher, these but are not always ideal for a perfect view of celestial events.

Binoculars and telescopes are obviously essential pieces of equipment, along with still and video cameras. These should all be mounted on tripods to obtain stable images of anything worth viewing and recording. Such equipment is becoming more sophisticated, allowing you to easily track and record any UFOs that come into view.

Sighting report forms, notepad and pen should be used to record any unusual events. A digital audio recorder can also be used to record a commentary of anything spotted in the sky that might be a UFO.

It is also a good idea to have two or more teams of skywatchers at different locations, to triangulate the position of any possible UFOs. Lots of information about how to film and video UFOs and conduct skywatches is available on the 'UFO Skywatch' website, at: ufonv.com/.

'UFOs – Exposed', a website by Darren Ashmore, shows how to modify video cameras to obtain infrared (IR) images of UFOs, at: infrared-aerial-phenomena-research.blogspot.co.uk/. Darren notes: 'The reason I use infrared to skywatch is not only to hopefully capture unconventional aerial objects, but also objects that have the ability not

to reflect visible light. Obviously, if UFOs do possess technologies to travel to our planet, it's not unreasonable to assume they have the ability to manipulate the visible light spectrum. The Mexican UFO hunter Pedro Avilia uses two camcorders side by side, one filming in IR and the other in the visible spectrum. And with so many skywatchers now using IR night vision and Sony's IR night shot along with IR pass filters to control exposure, more and more strange anomalies are coming to light.'

The 'Project 1947' website has an excellent page entitled Investigation of Unidentified Flying Objects. This offers advice on the type of information that should be collected from witnesses and gives links to report forms and questionnaires related to short-lived phenomena (such as ball lightning and fireballs, as well as UFOs), at: www.project1947.com/howto/.

4 Web references

There are literally hundreds of websites about UFOs and abductions that vary greatly in quality and validity. Use your favourite search engine to find more information, or use the links below as a good starting point for further research. As with all web links these are subject to temporary or even permanent disappearance from virtual reality.

'About.com', at:
    ufos.about.com/od/aliensabductions/.

'Alien Abduction Case Files', at:
    www.ufocasebook.com/alienabductions.html.

'The Alien Jigsaw - True Experiences of Alien Abduction', at:
    www.alienjigsaw.com/.

'The Center For UFO Studies' (CUFOS), at:
    cufos.org/.

'Flying Saucer Review', at:
    www.fsr.org.uk.

'Fortean Times', at:
    www.forteantimes.com.

'International Center for UFO Research'
    (David Jacobs' website), at:
    www.ufoabduction.com.

'John E. Mack Institute', at:
    www.johnemackinstitute.org/.

'Magonia' website, at:
    magonia.haaan.com/.

'Magonia blog', at:
    pelicanist.blogspot.co.uk/.

'Magonia Supplement', at:
    www.users.waitrose.com/~magonia/index.htm.

'Mutual UFO Network' (MUFON), at:
    www.mufon.com.

'National Investigations Committee on
    Aerial Phenomena' (NICAP), at:
    www.nicap.org/.

'National UFO Reporting Center', at:
    http://www.nuforc.org/.

'Project 1947', at:
    www.project1947.com/index.html.

'Spirit Writings.com' provides full texts of famous and obscure contactee literature and psychic-related writings, at:
    www.spiritwritings.com.

'SUNlite UFO' newsletter, at:
    home.comcast.net/~tprinty/UFO/SUNlite.htm.

'UFO Database',
    at: www.larryhatch.net/.

'UFO Evidence',
    at: www.ufoevidence.org.

'UFOInfo', at:
    www.ufoinfo.com/contents.shtml.

'UFO Magazine', at:
    www.ufomag.com/.

'UFOseek.com', at:
    www.ufoseek.com.

'The UFO Skeptic's Page', hosted by Robert Sheaffer, at:
    debunker.com/ufo.html.

'UFO Warminster', at:
    http://www.ufo-warminster.co.uk/.

'UFOs at Close Sight', at:
    ufologie.patrickgross.org/indexe.htm.

'UFOs: You've Been Hoodwinked', at:
    midimagic.sgc-hosting.com/ufopage.htm.

OTHER USEFUL RESOURCES
A Worldwide Catalogue of University Theses and Dissertations about UFOs, by Paolo Toselli, CISU (Italy), at: www.euroufo.net/wp-content/uploads/2012/01/UfoTheses2010.xls.
    List of online UFO magazines/journals, compiled by Isaac Koi, at: ufoupdateslist.com/2012/may/m08-006.shtml.

Glossary

Abductee – Person who is involuntarily abducted by aliens.

Abductionist – Person who investigates or believes in alien abductions.

AFOSI – Air Force Office of Special Intelligence.

AISS – Air Intelligence Service Squadron.

APRO – Aerial Phenomena Research Organization.

AR – Army Regulation.

ASC – Altered state of consciousness.

Astral travel – A non-physical form of travel unlimited by time and space.

ATC – Air traffic control.

Bracewell probe – Theoretical unmanned interplanetary spacecraft.

BSRA – Borderland Sciences Research Association.

BUFORA – British UFO Research Association.

CAS – Classic abduction syndrome (or scenario).

CAUS – Citizens Against UFO Secrecy.

CDR – Constant data recording.

CEI, CEII, CEIII (etc) – Close encounter of the first, second, third (etc) kind.

CE4K – Close encounter of the fourth kind: an addition to Dr Allen Hynek's classification system to denote an abduction case.

Cereology – The study of crop circles.

Channeller – Person who uses paranormal means to contact aliens.

CIA – Central Intelligence Agency.

CME – Coronal mass ejection.

CNES – Centre National d'Études Spatiales (National Centre for Space Studies).

Colorado Project – Edward Condon headed this investigation to determine the scientific value of UFO reports. His Condon Report justified the cancellation of Project Blue Book.

Contactee – Person who voluntarily meets aliens.

CSICOP – Committee for the Scientific Investigation of the Paranormal.

CUFON – Computer UFO Network.

CUFOS – The J. Allen Hynek Center for UFO Studies.

Cultural tracking – The suggestion that UFOs mimic our social and cultural expectations.

DIA – Defense Intelligence Agency.

Direct contactee – Contactee who has had face-to-face encounters with aliens.

DIS – MoD Intelligence Staff.

Doorway amnesia – Term used to describe abductees often having no recollection of how they arrived inside a UFO.

EAT – Experienced anomalous trauma.

EBE – Extraterrestrial biological entity.

EL – Earth lights.

ELF – Electronic low frequency.

EM – Electromagnetic.

EMP – Electromagnetic radiation pulses.

ERIT – En-route intelligence tool.

ESP – Extra sensory perception.

ET – Extraterrestrial.

ETH – Extraterrestrial hypothesis.

Etherian – A being that lives in the invisible world of Etheria.

FAA – US Federal Aviation Administration.

FBI – Federal Bureau of Investigation.

Flap – An intense period of UFO activity.

Flying saucer – An aerial craft presumably operated by aliens.

FOIA – Freedom of Information Act.

Fortean – A person interested in the philosophy of, and curiosities collected by, Charles Fort.

FSR – *Flying Saucer Review*.

FTE – Flux transfer event.

GAO – General Accounting Office.

GEIPAN – Groupe d'Études et d'Informations sur les Phénomènes Aérospatiaux Non-identifiés.

GPS – Global positioning system.

Grey – Large-headed, small-bodied alien.

GSW – Ground Saucer Watch.

IFO – Identified flying object.

IFSB – International Flying Saucer Bureau.

Implant – Object inserted into the body of an abductee.

Incubatorium – Room on a flying saucer that contains foetuses that are being incubated.

Indirect contactee – Person who does not meet aliens face to face but via astral travel, etc.

ISS – International Space Station.

IUR – *International UFO Reporter*, journal published by CUFOS.

Ley lines or leys – Lines linking ancient sites and buildings. Claimed to be conduits of magical or electromagnetic energy along their pathways or at strategic points.

LITS – Lights in the sky.

Magonia – Alleged historical home of alien beings, and name of British UFO magazine/website.

Majestic 12 – See MJ-12.

MIB – Man in Black.

MJ-12 – Operation Majestic Twelve. Alleged secret US government agency that deals with UFOs and aliens.

MoD – Ministry of Defence.

Mother ship – Large alien spaceship that does not land on Earth itself, but dispatches scout craft.

MUFON – Mutual UFO Network.

NARCAP – National Aviation Reporting Center on Anomalous Phenomena.

NASA – National Aeronautics and Space Administration.

NDE – Near-death experience.

NICAP – National Investigations Committee on Aerial Phenomena.

NMCC – National Military Command Center.

NUFORC – National UFO Reporting Center, Seattle.

Nuts and bolts – Physically and literally real spacecraft or aliens.

Oz factor – The impression that time and reality are frozen when a UFO is encountered.

Pelicanist – Usually a derogatory term for a UFO sceptic.

PPI – Plan position indicator.

PRO – Public Record Office.

Project Blue Book – United States Air Force project to investigate UFO reports. It ran from 1953 to 1969.

PSH – Psycho-sociological hypothesis.

RAF – Royal Air Force.

SDI – Strategic Defense Initiative.

Scout craft – Small flying saucer that is dispatched from a mother ship.

Screen memory – Phenomenon in which aliens distort our perceptions to present themselves as animals or people.

SETI – Search for extra-terrestrial intelligence.

Silent contactee – Person who does not make public their voluntary contact with aliens.

SP – Sleep paralysis.

Spooklights – Apparently intelligent or intelligently controlled balls of light.

Switched off – Term used to describe how, whilst an abductee encounters aliens, the people around them seem to enter some form of trance state.

Telepathy – Mental communication between people and/or aliens.

TNA – The National Archives.

Trigger event – Something that causes a person to believe they have had a UFO close encounter.

TST – Tectonic strain theory.

UAP – Unidentified aerial phenomenon.

UAV – Unmanned aerial vehicle.

UFO – Unidentified flying object.

UFOCAT – Database of evidence for UFO sightings and encounters.

UFOIN – UFO Investigators Network.

Ufologist – Person who studies the subject of UFOs.

Ufology – The study of UFOs.

Ufonaut – Alien associated with a UFO encounter.

Ultraterrestrials – Intelligent alien beings who secretly seek to control human society.

USAF – United States Air Force.

Wave – An intense period of UFO activity over a period of days, weeks or months.

Window area – A location where UFOs and other phenomena are seen on a regular basis.

Wise Baby – Human/alien hybrid baby.

Index

Where page numbers are given in *italics*, there is a relevant photograph/illustration and/or caption on that page. If a page number is in **bold type**, there is also relevant text on that page. Where page numbers are followed by the letter 'g', this indicates that the entry will be found in the glossary.

A

abductions 109, **125–37**, 151, 154
Adamski, George 110, *126*, *139–40*, 142, 144
Air Force Office of Special Intelligence (AFOSI) 36–7
aircraft **73–4**
airship wave *see* phantom airships
Alexander, Reginald 103
alien abductions 109, **125–37**, 151, 154
alien bases **118–19**
alien bodies 120–1
alien technology 135–6
aliens, types of **109–17**
in different countries 135
Allen, Mr C.W. 16
Alpert, Shell *32*
Alton Barnes pictogram *105*
Amazing Stories magazine 11, *143*
Ancient Astronaut theories 8, 49, 149
Andreasson, Betty **136**
android aliens 114–15
Angel Hair 101
Angelucci, Orfeo *143*
animal mutilation 99, 119
Anthony, Gary 38
Area 51 45, 147, *153*
Arnold, Kenneth 11, **25**, 26
explanations for UFO sighting 79–81, 88
Ashmore, Darren 159
Aubeck, Chris *70*
Aura Rhanes 110, *141*
Australia, early sightings in 20
automatic writing 134, 141–4, 152
Avilia, Pedro 159

B

ball lightning **81**, 101
balloons **76–8**
Bartholemew, Robert E. 15
Bartoll, Karl-Gosta *22*
Battelle Memorial Institute 30, 43
Battle of Los Angeles 92
Bender, Albert K. 118–19
Bennewitz, Paul 36–7, 119
Bethurum, Truman 110, *140–1*
Biela's Comet 84
Bigelow, Robert 133
Bigfoot **116**
birds **80**
birth trauma theory 151
black helicopters 74–5
animal mutilation 99
Blanchard, Roy 103
Blériot, Louis 13
blimps **78**
Blue Book, Project 32–5, 40, 43, 86–7, 159g
blue jets 81
Bowen, Charles 116
Bower, Doug 106
Bracewell space probes 57, 159g
brain aliens **113**
Brancker, Lieutenant Colonel W.S. 19
British UFO Research Association (BUFORA) 7
UFO sighting forms 158
Brookesmith, Peter 133
Brown, Anthony 151
Brown, Lieutenant Frank M. 26
Budden, Albert 101, 153
BUFORA (British UFO Research Association) 7
UFO sighting forms 158
Bullard, Dr Thomas **128**, 130, 132
burn marks *102*
Byrne, Judge Lawrence A. 13

C

Campbell, Steuart 80
Canada, early sightings in 19
Cathie, Bruce 50
cattle mutilation 99, 119
Center for UFO Studies (CUFOS) 38, 74
UFO report forms 158
Central Intelligence Agency (CIA) *see* CIA (Central Intelligence Agency)
Centre National d'Etudes Spatiales (CNES) 39–40
channelling 68, 134, 137
Charlton crater 103–4
China, early sightings in 20
Chinese lanterns **76**
Chorley, Dave 106
CIA (Central Intelligence Agency) 27, 38
conspiracy theories 142
Robertson Panel 31
Clark, Jerome 8
Clarke, Dr David 38, **39**, 40, 55–6, 58
classification systems for identifying UFOs 65–71
close encounters classification system 67–69, 159g
clouds 79
CNES (Centre National d'Etudes Spatiales) 39–40
Code of Practice for UFO Investigators 158
Collins, George D. *14*
Colorado Project 159g
COMETA Report 40
comets 83, **84**
Computer UFO Network (CUFON) 69
Condign, Project 38–9, 153
Condon, Professor Edward U. **34**
Condon Committee/Report 7, 34–5, 80, 100, 106
photographic evidence 93
Conesa Sevilla, Dr Jorge 154
conspiracy theories 8, 35, 153
contactees 142
helicopters 75
Constable, Trevor **152**
contactees 130, **139–45**
coronal mass ejections 56, **57**
Cradle Hill *43*, **51**, *52*
crash retrievals 120–2
craters 103–4
Creighton, Gordon 52
Crisman, Fred 26
crop circles 53, **105–6**
Crowe, Dennis *70*
CUFON (Computer UFO Network) 69
CUFOS (Centre for UFO Studies) 38, 74
cultural tracking 150, 159g

D

Dahl, Harold A. 26
Davidson, Captain William 26
Davidson, Leon 142
daylight discs 66, 73
Denmark, early sightings in 16
Devereux, Paul **54**, 55, 133
Dewey, Steve **53**
Dickhoff, Robert 113
digital ufology 8
direct contactees 141, 145
doorway amnesia 159g
Doty, Richard 37
drones 75
Dulce alien base **119**
Durant, Robert 133
dwarf aliens 112

E

Earth lights *54*, 55–6, 101, 153
Eckstein, Henry 97–9
Edwards Air Force Base *98*
electromagnetic effects 100–1
electronic pollution theory 153
Elohim aliens *144*
elves 81
Estimate of the Situation (Project Sign report) 29
Etherians/Space People 139–45, 159g
Euronet 38
Evans, Hilary 109–10, 151
examinations by aliens 125–31
Exopolitics movement 8
explanations (of UFO sightings) **73–88**
extrasolar planets 149
extraterrestrial hypothesis (ETH) 147–51, 155

F

face on Mars *118*
fairies *117*
Faulkner, Gordon 53
FBI (Federal Bureau of Investigation) 153
Maury Island case 26–7
film evidence of UFOs **97–8**, 99
Finch, Dr Bernard E. 46
fireballs 85
flaps 43, 159g
flares 75
Flatwoods Monster 114
floating 136
flux transfer events 57
Flying Saucer Review 141, 150
Flying Saucer Working Party 38
foo fighters **21**, 82, 150
Fort, Charles Hoy **11**
Fortean Times 31, 126
Fortune, Ella Louise *34*
Free, Mr Egerton S. 16
French, Professor Christopher 154
Fry, Daniel *142*

G

gateways 46–9
Geller, Uri 143–4
ghost fliers 20
ghost rockets *23*, 25, 150

ghostly aliens 115
giant aliens 112
Giffard, Henri 13
Girvan, Waveney 141
Glastonbury *48*, **49**
Good, Timothy 36, *37*
Goodman, Kevin *53*
Grahame-White, Claude 18
Grasso, Giuseppe *95*
Great California Airship **12**
grey aliens (greys) 109,
   111–12, 160g
ground traces of UFO activity
   102–6
Grudge, Project 30–1, 33

H

Haines, Gerald K. 74
Hale-Bopp Comet 84
Hall, Richard *68*
Halley's Comet 84
Halt, Lieutenant Colonel
   Charles I. *122*
Hamilton, Alexander 15
Hansen, George 134
Hansen, Myra 119
Harney, John 106, 137
Harris, Paola 97–8
Harrison, Norman **144**
Hassan II, King of Morocco 87
Heaven's Gate cult 84
helicopters 74–5
   animal mutilation 99
Hendry, Allan 74
Hennessy, Julian 38
Herschel, Frederick *149*
Hessdalen valley 57
Hibbard, Robert 13, 15
Hill, Barney and Betty
   125, 126
Hitler, Adolf 118–19
hoaxes 15
   Bigfoot **116**
   contactees 142
   crop circles 106
   moving images **97–8**, 99
   photographs **94–6**
Hofling, Charles 147, 149
Holiday, F.W. 49
Holloman Air Force Base
   29, *34*
Hollow Earth theory *153*
Holton, David 51–2
Hopkins, Budd **127**, 132,
   134–5, 137
Hopkins, W.H. 13
Horton brothers 28
hot air balloons **13**
hot spots 46–9, 58, 159
   Tectonic Strain Theory 54
Hough, Peter 109
Hucks, Lieutenant B.C. 18

Hughes, Stephen 81
humanoid/Nordic aliens
   110, 139
Hynek, J. Allen 38, **66**, 71,
   109, 150
   close encounters
   classification system
   67–69, 159g
   swamp gas 80
hypnotic regression 7, 132, 151
   Andreasson, Betty *136*
   Hansen, Myra 119
   Hill, Barney and Betty **125**
   Napolitano, Linda **133**
   Walton, Travis *131*

I

Icke, David 117
ignis fatuus *56*, 80
implants 36–7, 119, 130,
   135, 160g
indirect contactees 141,
   145, 163g
inferior mirages 79
insectoid aliens 113
Intelligence Circulars 19
International Flying Saucer
   Bureau 118
International Space Station 86
investigating UFO activity
   158–9
Investigation Levels rating
   system 70
invisibility 135
invisible aliens 117
iridium flares 86
Italian UFO film footage 97–9

J

Jacobs, David 127, 130–1,
   133–6
Jacobsen, Annie 120–1
Jamaludin, Ahmad 46, 49
Jaroslaw brothers *94–5*
Jones, Staff Sergeant Harold
   T. *32*
Jung, Carl 150

K

Keech, Marian 142–3, 145
Keel, John 45–6, 65, 115, 137,
   141, 144–5, **150**
Keffel, Ed *31*
Kell, Lieutenant Colonel
   Vernon 19
Kettle, Police Constable 16
kites 78
Klass, Philip 93
Kölmjärv (Lake) *22–3*
Kottmeyer, Martin 111–12, 136
Kuiper, Dr Gerald 113
Kulik, Leonid 15

L

La Pez, Dr Lincoln 29
Lafreniere, Gyslaine 54, 58
Lake Kölmjärv *22–3*
Lang, Craig 133
lasers 78
Lawson, Dr Alvin 151
Layne, Dr Meade 145
Lear, John 99
   Lear Document 119
lenticular clouds **79**
Lethbridge, Mr 16–17
Levine, Norman 34–5
levitation 136
ley lines 49, **50**, 53, 55, 59,
   163g
lightning **81**
Lindback, Ludvig *23*
living UFOs theory 152
Low, Robert 34
Lowell, Percival 147, 149
Lubbock Lights *28*
Luftwaffe 20
Lundie, Captain 18

M

Maarup, Evald 100
McCall, William 151
McCampbell, James 100–1
McGaha, James 121
McGonagle, Joe 38
Mack, John 109, 117, 127,
   135, **152**
McMinnville photos *27*
Magnet, Project 38
*Magonia/Merseyside UFO
   Bulletin* 101, 106, **150**, 155
Magruder, Marine Lieutenant
   Colonel Marion *120*
Majestic Twelve 36–7, 160g
Mantle, Philip 98
Marano, Second Lieutenant
   Carmon *32*
Mariana, Nicolas *29*
Mars **118**, **147**, *148*, 149
   correlation with UFO
   waves 45
Martinez, Victor 37
mass media impact 151
Mauge, Claude 59
Maury Island case 26–7
medical examinations 125–31
Men in Black 16, **26**, 110,
   115, 118
Menger, Howard *142*
Menzel, Donald 45
*Merseyside UFO Bulletin/
   Magonia* 101, 106,
   150, 155
meteors **84–5**
Michel, Aime 50, 58
Michell, John 49

military balloons **77**
Miller, Ron 150–1
Ministry of Defence (Britain)
   38–40, 64, 84
mirages 79–80
missing foetus syndrome 134
MJ-12 36–7, 160g
model aircraft 74
Mogul, Project 120
Montgolfier brothers **13**
Moon, the **83**
Moore, Patrick 103
Moore, William **36**, 37
Mothman **115**
Moulton Howe, Linda 37
moving image evidence of
   UFOs **97–8**, 99
Mutual UFO Network
   (MUFON) 62, 133
   investigation report
   forms 158

N

Napolitano, Linda **133**, 134
National Archives (Britain)
   39–40
National UFO Reporting
   Center (NUFORC) 61
   UFO sighting forms 158
New Zealand, early sightings
   in 17
Nickell, Joe 121
Niotti, Captain Hugo F. *35*
noctilucent clouds **79**
nocturnal lights 66, 73
Nordic/humanoid aliens
   110, 139
Northern UFO News 115
NUFORC (National UFO
   Reporting Center) 61
   UFO sighting forms 158

O

Oberg, James 87
O'Brien, Cathy 117
Odgers, George 105
Official UFO magazine *64*
Old Sarum ley *50*
Operation Animal
   Mutilation 99
Operation Majestic Twelve
   36–7
Oram, Mike *53*
Orthon/Orthoteny 50, 58, *140*
Ouija boards 152
Oxcart, Project 74
Oz Factor 128, 160g

P

Palmer, Raymond 11, **26**, *143*
paranormal alien theory 152
paranormal triangles 57

pelicanists 8, 160g
pencil-necked aliens 112
Penniston, James 122
Pérez de Cuéllar, Javier 133–4
Persinger, Michael 54–5, 58
Petrozavodsk Jellyfish 87
phantom airships 12–23,
    147, 150
    pilots 110
phone apps **96**
photographic evidence of
    UFOs **93–6**
planets 82–3
plasma balls 57, 81–2,
    100, 153
Poland, early sightings in 12
Pope, Nick **39**, 40, 98–9
portals 46–9
Portugal, early sightings in 19
post-abduction
    experiences 132
Pratt, Stephen *94*
Printy, Tim **147**
Pritchard, David E. 106
Probability Ratings 69
Project Blue Book 32–5, 40,
    43, 86–7, 160g
Project Condign 38–9, 153
Project Grudge 30–1, 33
Project Hessdalen 57
Project Magnet 38
Project Mogul 120
Project Oxcart 74
Project Second Story 38
Project Serpo 37
Project Sign 28–30
Project Twinkle 29
psycho-sociological
    hypothesis (PSH)
    150–1, 155
Puharich, Dr Andrijia
    143–4
Pyramids 8, 49–50, 149

Q

Quintanilla, Lieutenant
    Colonel Hector *32*

R

radar evidence of UFOs 91–3
radar-visual UFOs 67
Rael *144*
Rainey, Carol 135
Randall, Dr Robert J. 103
Randles, Jenny 70, 128, 135
Redfern, Nick 121
reflections 81
Rendlesham Forest incident
    121, **122**
report forms 62, 64–5, 158
reptoid aliens 113, 116
Rhanes, Aura 110, *141*

Ries, John 53
Rimmer, John 132
Roberts, Andy 38
Robertson, Howard P. 31
Robertson Panel 31
robot aliens **114**, 115
rockets **86–7**
Rodwell, Mary 134–5
Rogerson, Peter 122, 151
Rommel Jnr, District Attorney
    Kenneth M. 99
Roper Organization 133
Roswell incident 36–7, 57, 77,
    120–2
Ruppelt, Lieutenent Edward J.
    29, **30**, 32–3
Ryan, Bill 37

S

Saintbury ley *50*
Sananda 143
Sandell, Roger 101, 149
Santilli, Ray 120
Santorinis, Paul 25
satellites **86–7**
Saunders, Dr David 34–5, 45
Schiaparelli, Giovanni 147
Schulgen, Brigadier General
    George 27–8
screen memories 116, 131,
    160g
séances 141, 144, *152*
searchlights **78**
Second Story, Project 38
Serpo 37
sexual encounters 126, 130
shape-shifting aliens 116–17
Sharp, Alan 104
Shaver, Richard *143*
Shrum, Donald 114–15
Shuttlewood, Arthur 52–3
Sibeck, David 57
sighting classification
    systems 65–71
sighting report forms 62,
    64–5, 158
Sign, Project 28–30
Simon, Dr Benjamin 125
skywatching 159
sleep paralysis **154**
Smith, Louise *129*
Sneider, Captain
    Robert R. 28–9
solar activity 56, **57**
solar balloons **77–8**
Source X theory 46, 49
South Africa, sightings in 18
Southern, John 104
Space People/Etherians
    139–45, 159g
SPECTRA 143–4
Spencer, John 155

sprites 81
Stafford, Mona *129*
Stanscomb, Marilyn *32*
Star GateSG7 *see*
    Eckstein, Henry
Star People 136
stars **82**
Steiger, Francie 136
Stock, George *33*
Stonehenge 46–7, 49–50, 149
Stony Tunguska River 15
Strangeness Ratings 69
Strieber, Whitley 113,
    115, 117, **127**, 135
Stringfield, Leonard 142
Sun, the **83**
sunlight 81
sunspots 56
super bolts 81
superior mirages 79
Surrey Puma 116
Svahn, Clas 25
swamp gas *56*, 80
Sweden, early sightings
    in 20, **22–3**

T

Tassel, George Van *143*
technology 135–6
Tectonic Strain Theory 54
telepathy 130, 137, *140*, *143*,
    144, *152*, 160g
temperature inversions 79–80
Tesla, Nikola 119, *153*
Thing of Warminster 51–3
third realm theory 152
Thomas, Elaine *129*
Tillinghast, Wallace Elmer 17
time travellers theory 152
traces of UFO activity **102–6**
transport through solid matter
    136
Trent, Mrs Evelyn *27*
triangles 57
Troncoso, Domingo *31*
Truman, President Harry 36
Twining, Lieutenant General
    Nathan F. 27
Twinkle, Project 29

U

U2 spy planes 74, 91
UFO bases **118–19**
UFO desk 39–40
UFO investigating 158–9
UFO Magazine 69, *71*, *120*
UFO over a river in Italy
    (YouTube footage) 97–9
UFO sighting forms 62,
    64–5, 158
UFO Sightings website 62
ufology 7–8, 160g

UFOs – Exposed
    website 159
ultraterrestrials 150, 160g
underground alien bases
    118–19
United Kingdom, early
    sightings in 16, 18
United States Air Force
    (USAF) 7, 39–40, 43, 45,
    74, 147
    Majestic Twelve 36
    military balloons 77
    Project Grudge 30
    Roswell incident 120
unmarked helicopters
    see helicopters
USA, early sightings in
    12–15, 17, 19

V

Valdez, State Patrol Officer
    Gabe *99*
Vallée, Jacques **65**, **140**,
    141, 144, 150
    classification system
    65–6, 70–1
Van Tassel, George *143*
Vandenberg, General Hoyt 29
video evidence of UFOs
    97–8, 99
Villas Boas, Antonio 126–7
virtual reality theory 152
virtual ufology 8
Vorilhon, Claude (Rael) *144*

W

Walton, Travis *131*
Warminster 51–3
Warrington, Peter 70
Watkins, Alfred **49**
waves 43–9, 163g
    Warminster 51–3
weather balloons **76**
Weber, Connie *142*
Wedd, Tony 50
will-o'-the-wisps *56*, 80
willy willies 105
Wilson, Katharina 135
window areas 46–9, 160g
    Tectonic Strain Theory 54
winged aliens **115**
wise babies 160g
wreckage (from UFOs) 106
Wright brothers 13
Wright Patterson Air Force
    Base 29, 120

Z

Zeppelin, Count Ferdinand
    von 13
Zeta Reticuli solar system 37
Zond IV lunar spacecraft 86–7